# More Than a Score

Edited by Jesse Hagopian

# More Than a Score

## The New Uprising Against High-Stakes Testing

Haymarket Books
Chicago, Illinois

Published in 2014 by Haymarket Books
PO Box 180165
Chicago, IL 60618
www.haymarketbooks.org
773-583-7884
info@haymarketbooks.org

ISBN: 978-1-60846-392-3

Trade distribution:
In the US, Consortium Book Sales and Distribution, www.cbsd.com
In Canada, Publishers Group Canada, www.pgcbooks.ca
In the UK, Turnaround Publisher Services, www.turnaround-uk.com
All other countries, Publishers Group Worldwide, www.pgw.com

Cover design by Rachel Cohen. Cover art by Kris Trappeniers.

Published with the generous support of Lannan Foundation
and the Wallace Action Fund.

Printed in Canada by union labor.

Library of Congress cataloging-in-publication data is available.

10  9  8  7  6  5  4  3  2  1

## About the photos appearing on section start pages

Teachers (p. 29): Chicago Teachers Union president Karen Lewis speaking to thousands of protesters gathered on March 27, 2013, against the planned closure of more than fifty public schools.

Students (p.133): Garfield High School senior Falmata Seid performs his poem "Modern-Day Slavery" at a January 2014 event commemorating the one-year anniversary of the MAP test boycott.

Parents (p. 193): Kirstin Roberts addresses the media at the "play-in" in the lobby of the Chicago Board of Education in spring 2013, sponsored by the Chicago-based parent group More Than a Score. Photo by Sarah Jane Rhee, loveandstrugglephotos.com.

Administrators and Advocates (p. 243): Professor Wayne Au addresses the crowd at the Educating the Gates Foundation rally in Seattle on June 26, 2014.

*To the Garfield High School Bulldogs who boycotted the MAP test, changed my life, and ignited a movement*

*And to the test-defiers of tomorrow who don't yet know the might of their courage but will one day soon rise up to make education more than a score*

# CONTENTS

# Students

# Parents

# Administrators and Advocates

# FOREWORD

This is a dark and puzzling time in American education. As the essays in this book make clear, public education is under attack. So is the teaching profession. People who call themselves "reformers" seek to transfer public funds to privately managed schools and even to religious schools. These "reformers" want to abolish any job protections for teachers so that teachers may be fired at will or fired because they cost too much or fired because their students got low test scores. With few exceptions, those leading this movement to privatize public schools, to eliminate collective bargaining, and to change the nature of the teaching profession are not educators. Those who are leading the charge are very wealthy individuals, hedge fund managers, corporate executives, and venture philanthropists.

The attack on public schools and the teaching profession is fueled by a zealous belief in test scores. The narrative of the so-called reform movement claims that public schools are failing because test scores are low, or because there is a test score gap between children who are advantaged and children who live in poverty, or because the average test scores of American students are not as high as students in other nations. The reformers then insist that public schools must be closed and replaced by privately managed charters. The reformers place the blame for low test scores on teachers; their solutions: weaken or eliminate unions, offer higher pay for higher test scores, fire teachers whose students do not get higher scores.

Reformers treat standardized tests as both a measure of quality and the goal of schooling. They don't care that their fetishizing of tests has perverse consequences, that it leads to narrowing of the curriculum, cheating, teaching to the test, and gaming the system. Reformers don't care that their focus on scores as the be-all and end-all of schooling has warped education, particularly in districts where children have the highest needs and the lowest scores. Test-prep is all-important; it leaves no time for projects, activities, and deep learning.

The reform narrative is reflected in federal policy, in George W. Bush's No Child Left Behind and in Barack Obama's Race to the Top. Teachers are demoralized by the deskilling caused by federal policy. They are expected to comply, not to create or innovate. They are judged by their students' test scores.

Standardized tests are not good enough to serve as the arbiter of the fate of schools, teachers, or students. They do not capture all that matters in education. They are subject to many kinds of error. Sometimes the questions are confusing. Sometimes there is more than one right answer. Sometimes they are incorrectly scored, whether by humans or machines. Standardized tests are normed on a bell curve, and they distribute privilege. On every such test, the results reflect family income and family education. Those who have the most end up on top; those with the greatest needs cluster at the bottom. Standardized tests don't close gaps; they don't produce equity. They reinforce existing inequities. Elite private schools, where many reformers send their own children, seldom, if ever, rely on standardized tests; instead, the teachers write their own tests.

The forces arrayed against public schools and teachers are formidable because of their wealth and political power. Yet this collection of essays demonstrates that there is cause for hope. Teachers, parents, students, and scholars are speaking out. The test boycott at Garfield High School in Seattle in 2013 was a dramatic act of conscience and consciousness-raising. The creative resistance of the Providence Student Union showed that high school students were thinking more clearly about the meaning of their education than the state board of education or the state commissioner of education. The critique of high-stakes testing by parents in Texas managed to persuade the state legislature to roll back its excessive testing mandates.

Hardly a week goes by without a new act of resistance by parents, teachers, administrators, or local school boards. More and more groups are forming to spread the word about the importance of saying no to high-stakes testing. The movement to stop the testing behemoth is growing, and it is not going to be assuaged by a moratorium of a year or two. When the moratorium on high-stakes testing ends, the problems with the tests and the punishments attached to them will resume.

Those who support public education and a respected teaching profession can find hope in the stories of resistance in this book. They can take solace in the fact that none of the "reforms" promoted by this punitive movement have improved schools or the lives of children and that no other nation—at least none that we admire—is attacking its public schools and its teaching profession. What is happening today is so bizarre and anomalous that it cannot prevail. Everything the "reformers" advocate has failed and failed again. As the American public awakens to the threat posed by this fraudulent "reform" movement, the resistance will grow stronger, becoming an unstoppable force.

Jesse Hagopian, Karen Lewis, John Kuhn, Nancy Carlsson-Paige, and the many other contributors to this book have proven their commitment to children and to real education. They are on the front lines. Long after the "reformers" have lost interest in controlling the nation's schools, these dedicated educators will still be there. They will not quit, nor will they tire. For them, education is not a pastime or a hobby; it is their life's work. They will still be teaching and leading and caring for children long after the "reformers" have found something else to do.

Diane Ravitch
July 2014
Brooklyn, New York

# INTRODUCTION
## Alfie Kohn

In early March of 1999, on a chilly Sunday morning in San Francisco, more than a thousand educators packed into a huge convention center space during the annual ASCD (Association for Supervision and Curriculum Development) conference. They were there for an event I was hosting called "The Deadly Effects of 'Tougher Standards,'" which I'd promised would be not just a presentation but "an organizing session, an attempt to form a national network of educators who have had enough and are ready to become politically active."

I should mention that I had (and have) no formal affiliation with any institution, no foundation support, no administrative assistant. At the time I didn't even own a copy machine. Nevertheless, I felt compelled to do something ambitious. I wanted to pull together folks from across the country who were as fed up as I was about prescriptive, one-size-fits-all curriculum standards; high-stakes testing; and the widespread tendency to classify these things as examples of "school reform." A gratifying number of people with families and full-time jobs—and, like me, no expectation of compensation or even an operating budget—signed up to be state coordinators in this new, loose confederation.

The network had no official name, although I briefly considered Standardized Testing Undermines the Process of Intellectual Development just because I liked the acronym. I sent out periodic missives to urge the creation of listservs, phone trees, and rallies. I supported and exhorted, shared background materials, and begged for news. At some point the challenge of finding time to coordinate all these coordinators—and to keep recruiting new volunteers to replace those who dropped out—came to be overwhelming. I eventually folded what was left of the network into a similar initiative being undertaken by FairTest, which at least had a copy machine.

The important point is that all of us were sufficiently outraged to invest a considerable amount of time in this effort. We promoted actions that ranged from polite letters to the editor to civil disobedience. And this, remember, was more than fifteen years ago—before NCLB (No Child Left Behind), Race to the Top, or Common Core, before most states had *annual* tests and high school exit exams, before the push for privatization had really gathered momentum. Back then, we thought things were really bad. And we were right. We just had no idea how much worse they could get.

In the early 2000s there were scattered examples of disciplined noncooperation. Teachers such as Don Perl in Colorado and Jim Bougas in Massachusetts stood up by themselves and refused to participate in the testing. High school students in Northern California, Chicago, and Massachusetts boycotted their states' exams. Parents opted their kids out of testing at, among other places, an inner-city elementary school in Tucson, Arizona, and a middle school in wealthy Scarsdale, New York (where two-thirds of the town's eighth graders were shuttled to the public library on test day so they might spend those hours actually learning something).

The *standardistos*, as Susan Ohanian calls them, were not pleased. When people in poor communities and communities of color resisted having their schools turned into test-prep factories, their objections were dismissed as sour grapes: Well, sure, *they* don't like testing because their scores are so low. But when people in affluent, high-scoring communities spoke out, they were accused of being too selfish to realize that test-based instruction is necessary for poor kids. An ad hoc—and ad hominem—reason was created to deflect each constituency's concerns so no one's had to be taken seriously.

The standards-and-testing apparatus was constructed by politicians and corporate executives—not by educators, a fact that explains a great deal about how things have played out. At some point these authorities appeared to realize that even if they lacked logic or research to justify all the testing—or the numbingly specific standards that the tests were being used to enforce—

they did have one thing going for them. They had the power. They could insert a provision in NCLB to punish any school in which more than 5 percent of the students declined to take the tests. They could pressure superintendents and principals into becoming their accomplices. On the basis of a single test score, they could force a child to repeat third grade or refuse to issue a diploma to a high school student irrespective of his or her broader academic record. They could say what powerful people always say when they can't defend a dictate on its merits: "Like it or not, this is reality now, and we will hurt you if you don't comply." That's what's known as "holding students or teachers accountable."

And most people did comply, all along the food chain of American education, from state school boards down to classroom teachers. Almost all the wildfires of resistance were snuffed out for a time as the heavy-handed authority of state governments—and, under both George Bush and Barack Obama, the federal government—ratcheted up the specificity and uniformity of the standards, the pervasiveness and impact of the testing. People followed orders—even people who knew those orders made no sense and were doing considerable harm.

Back in the early 1960s, Yale psychologist Stanley Milgram began a series of studies "intended to measure the willingness of a participant to obey an authority" whose instructions "may conflict with the participant's personal conscience." Fascinated by the possibility that ordinary people who just did what they were told could commit heinous crimes Milgram convinced volunteers to deliver what they believed were painful electric shocks to anonymous individuals. In 2007, the ABC news-magazine show *Primetime Live* broadcast a replication of the study. One subject they recruited was a seventh-grade teacher. After the experiment, when the setup had been explained to her, she was asked about her willingness to inflict pain on a stranger, even after she heard that stranger crying out, "My heart hurts!"

> Reporter: Just having the guy in the lab coat say, "Keep going; it's fine; I'm telling you it's fine" somewhat divorced you from your own decision-making power?
>
> Teacher: Oh sure. It's just like when I'm told to administer the state tests for hours on end.
>
> Reporter: You're doing your job?
>
> Teacher: I'm doing my job.

My point here isn't that teachers who administer these tests, or who sacrifice meaningful learning opportunities in order to raise scores on those tests, are comparable to Nazis. My point is that, even if one has grave doubts about what one has been told to do, it can take courage to refuse to do it, particularly if there are risks to disobeying orders, as there often are. Yet we are now witnessing another such wave of disobedience, as evidenced by the heartening accounts contained in this book.

The examples you'll find are varied and often inventive: administering student tests to successful adults in Providence and asking them to share their impressions, creating a clever (musical) holiday-themed protest in Portland, putting up lawn signs and bumper stickers in New York, staging a "play-in" at the Chicago Board of Education, holding a rally in Texas. You'll read about individual acts of conscience and organized mass actions.

One recurrent theme is that many people who already oppose the standards-and-testing juggernaut seem to be waiting for someone else to take the lead and give them permission (or the necessary courage) to stand up. When South Minneapolis teachers merely informed parents they had the right not to have their children tested, 40 percent of those parents promptly took advantage of that reminder. Garfield High School teachers in Seattle, with their dramatic and widely publicized test boycott, had a similar experience: The expressions of support and solidarity they received make it clear that many others shared their frustrations, and what these teachers did helped to transform widespread potential energy into kinetic energy. An awful lot of people have felt alone. It can be liberating to learn otherwise, to see that countless others share that anger about what is being done to our children and our schools, and they may be persuaded to do something about it at last.

In contrast, if we persist in following orders, in teaching the inappropriate and generic standards devised by distant authorities, in ignoring our students' interests so as to ready them for bad tests, then we become part of the "they" that others invoke to justify the impossibility of making change. As Carol Burris says, by way of explaining her decision to mobilize opposition among New York principals, "There comes a point where you just have to stand up for what's right." Likewise Texas educator John Kuhn: "What may not have been the best thing . . . for my career" may nevertheless have been the best thing he could have done for his students. In 1846, when Thoreau was imprisoned for refusing to pay war taxes, the jail in Concord, Massachusetts, faced the street. One day, the story goes, his friend Ralph Waldo Emerson was walking by and said, "Henry! What are you doing in there?" To which Thoreau was said to have replied, "The question is what are you doing out there?"

For anyone who accepts the arguments and insights of the contributors to this volume, the challenge is to explain why he or she is helping to perpetuate pernicious policies by taking part in the testing. The challenge is not just to applaud the eloquence and courage of the educators, parents, and students who have taken a stand but to summon one's gumption and join them.

# PREFACE

## The Testocracy versus the Education Spring

*"High schools may opt out of MAP in 2013–14."* These words were buried deep within a meandering all-district communication blast, sent at 2:06 p.m. on Monday, May 13, 2013, by Seattle Public Schools superintendent Jose Banda. I read the words out loud, maybe just so I would believe them. "What did you say, Mr. H?" a student sitting near my desk asked. I didn't respond directly and instead leaped to my feet and blurted out the news to the entire class: "We won! We scrapped the MAP! I told you they should not have threatened teachers!" The cheer let out by the students would have convinced someone passing by that they were hearing a last-play-of-the-game touchdown at the homecoming game and not a world history class. Elation gave way to pandemonium. This was a kind of giddiness that is probably only experienced by people who have suffered though fear, found deep meaning in a common struggle, and won something very precious.

It was the culmination of a standoff launched the previous January, when some twenty teachers at Garfield High School called a press conference to announce their refusal to ever again administer the Measures of Academic Progress (MAP) test, declaring it an irreparably flawed exam that was degrading the quality of their students' education. Our superintendent soon threatened the offending teachers with a ten-day suspension without pay, but for the next several months they held to their convictions and forced the district to abandon the test at the high school level.

Yet this was not only a victory for Garfield and educators at several other schools—Orca, Chief Sealth High School, Ballard High School, Center School, Thornton Creek Elementary—that actively joined in the testing boycott. Ours was also a victory for Joey Furlong. Joey, a fourth-grader in the Bethlehem Central School District in Albany County, New York, who was diagnosed with epilepsy and a life-threatening seizure that hospitalized him in spring of 2013. As doctors studied tests and debated whether or not to perform brain surgery, Joey lay in his hospital bed with an IV dripping into the back of his hand, connected to an EEG machine that measured his heartbeat, while a pulse oximeter measured his oxygen level. But one test was missing. The state education department decided the most important measurement at that very moment was not of Joey's vital signs but rather of his academic test-taking abilities. Fearing the consequences of allowing even one child to escape being reduced to a data point, they sent a teacher-courier to deliver a state-mandated exam to bedridden Joey. In a noble act of test resistance, Joey's father prevented the teacher from administering the test. "It just floored me that somebody is sending teachers to sick kids and expecting them to take a New York State test," Joey's mother Tami said in a subsequent interview.[1]

Our test boycott in Seattle was also a victory for Rigoberto Ruelas. In a particularly vicious attempt to transform living, breathing teachers into lifeless bits of data, the *Los Angeles Times* published a 2010 article titled, "Who's Teaching L.A.'s Kids?" The report ranked some six thousand teachers according to student test data and sorted them into the categories of "most effective, more effective, average, less effective, or least effective." One Los Angeles public school teacher described the brutality of the paper publishing her test scores, saying it made her feel "like I was on public display, like a human being on the auction block or something." Ruelas was rated "less effective" and committed suicide after the publication of his rating. It is unlikely that suicide has a single cause, but friends reported that Ruelas had been distraught specifically because of his public shaming over the test scores of his students.

Ours was also a victory for the many parents who have struggled to cope with the stress of raising children in the age of what we could call the "testocracy"—the test-and-punish corporate education reform tsars whose interests are served by the proliferation of high-stakes standardized bubble tests. The testocracy has long been manipulating our society but rose to supremacy with the bipartisan No Child Left Behind Act that was signed into law by president George W. Bush and completed its coup d'état of the education system with president Barack Obama's Race to the Top and Common Core State Standards (CCSS) initiatives—programs designed to use standardized testing to make high-stakes decisions in education.

NCLB made school funding dependent on state tests, demanding that schools make "adequate yearly progress" (AYP) in raising test scores, so as to reach a stated goal of 100 percent of students being proficient in grade-level math and reading by 2014. That the federal government did not increase resources to the schools—and in reality cut funds to schools that did not achieve AYP—reveals the organized effort to ensure this stated goal would never be reached, and, in fact, not a single state achieved it.

Race to the Top (RttT) provided $4.35 billion for a US Department of Education contest created to pit states and school districts against one another in a desperate struggle for scarce funds. States were awarded points, in a *Hunger Games*–like strategy, for tying teacher evaluations to test scores, implementing merit pay schemes based on test results, adopting the CCSS, and lifting caps on charter schools. While the amount of time diverted from learning and squandered on high-stakes testing varies among school districts, there can be no doubt that these federal education policies have turned schoolhouses into test-prep centers across the county. The American Federation of Teachers (AFT, the second largest teacher's union in the nation) conducted a 2013 study based on an analysis of two mid-size urban school districts that found the time students spent taking standardized tests claimed up to 50 hours per year. In addition, the study found that students spent from 60 to more than 110 hours per year directly engaged in test preparation activities.[2] When I was in Chicago in the spring of 2013 speaking about the MAP test boycott, a parent corroborated these findings, reporting her kindergartener had taken fourteen standardized tests that year.

Who are these testocrats who would replace teaching with testing? The testocracy, in my view, does not only refer to the testing conglomerates—most notably the multibillion-dollar Pearson testing and textbook corporation—that directly profit from the sale of standardized exams. The testocracy is also the elite stratum of society that finances and promotes competition and privatization in public education rather than collaboration, critical thinking, and the public good. Not dissimilar to a theocracy, under our current testocracy, a deity—in this case the exulted norm-referenced bubble exam—is officially recognized as the civil ruler of education whose policy is governed by officials that regard test results as divine. The testocratic elite are committed to reducing the intellectual and emotional process of teaching and learning to a single number—a score they subsequently use to sacrifice education on the altar devoted to high-stakes testing by denying students promotion or graduation, firing teachers, converting schools into privatized charters, or closing schools altogether. You've heard of this program; the testocracy refers to it as "education reform."

Among the most prominent members of the testocracy are some of the wealthiest people the world has ever known. Its tsars include billionaires Bill Gates, Eli Broad, and members of the Walton family (the owners of Walmart), who have used their wealth to circumvent democratic processes and impose test-and-punish policies in public education. They fund a myriad of organizations—such as Michelle Rhee's StudentsFirst,[3] Teach for America, and Stand for Children—that serve as shock troops to enforce the implantation of high-stakes testing and corporate education reform in states and cities across the nation. Secretary of Education Arne Duncan serves to help coordinate and funnel government money to the various initiatives of the testocracy. The plan to profit from public schools was expressed by billionaire media executive Rupert Murdoch, when he said in a November 2010 press release: "When it comes to K through 12 education, we see a $500 billion sector in the U.S. alone that is waiting desperately to be transformed by big breakthroughs that extend the reach of great teaching."[4]

Testing companies got the memo and are working diligently to define great teaching as preparing students for norm-referenced exams—available to districts across the country if the price is right. The textbook and testing industry generates between $20 billion and $30 billion dollars per year. Pearson, a multinational corporation based in Britain, brings in more than $9 billion annually, and is the world's largest education company and book publisher.[5] But it's not the only big testing company poised to profit from the testocracy. Former president George W. Bush's brother Neil and his parents founded a company called Ignite! Learning to sell test products after the passage of No Child Left Behind.[6]

The movement to liberate education from the testocracy has been gaining momentum for some time. Numerous teachers over the years have refused to administer a standardized test, including Carl Chew in Seattle, who was suspended for two weeks in 2008 for his act of civil disobedience. In 2011 hundreds of New York State principals signed a letter protesting the use of students' test scores to evaluate teachers and principals. That same year the Occupy Wall Street movement and its offshoot, Occupy Education, erupted and helped thousands of educators in cities around the country find their voice and chant, "We teach the 99 percent." In 2012, the Texas education commissioner Robert Scott called high-stakes exams a "perversion," inspiring 875 Texas school boards to pass resolutions declaring these tests were "strangling education." The victorious Chicago Teachers Union strike in 2012 slowed standardized testing in the Windy City and fanned the embers of resistance to corporate education reform around the nation. Also in 2012, Maryland's Montgomery County superintendent Joshua Starr announced a three-year moratorium on standardized testing in his district, implying secession from the testocracy was possible at the district level. All of these flashpoints and others signaled an increasing willingness by public school advocates to redefine education so it meets the needs of students instead of enriching the testocracy. But some of biggest acts of collective struggle against standardized, high-stakes testing were yet to come.

In 2000, Alfie Kohn wrote *The Case Against Standardized Testing*, in which he presciently invited readers to

> imagine, for example, that a teacher at any given school in your area—you for example—quietly approached each person on the staff in turn and asked: "If __ percent of the teachers at this school pledged to boycott the next round of testing, would you join them?" (The specific percentage would depend on what seemed realistic and yet signified sufficient participation to offer some protection for those involved.) Then, if the designated number was reached, each teacher would be invited to take part in what would be a powerful act of civil disobedience. Press coverage would likely be substantial, and despairing-but-cowed teachers in other schools might be encouraged to follow suit.[7]

As my colleague Mallory Clarke and I describe in the next two chapters, this is an uncanny description of what happened when Garfield High School teachers launched the MAP test boycott in the winter of 2013, garnered international support, and signaled a new phase in the movement. In the ensuing months, increasing numbers of parents opted their children out of tests, students led walkouts of high-stakes exams, and teachers held protests around the nation in an uprising that commentators dubbed the "Education Spring."

There were many inspired moments of resistance during this first spring of the national education uprising that created a self-conscious movement of what we can call *test-defiers*—those who bear witness, make public declarations, and organize resistance to high-stakes, standardized bubble testing. As student test-defier Alexia Garcia relates in chapter 14 of this book, students in Portland, Oregon, organized a successful walkout of the Oregon Assessment of Knowledge and Skills (OAKS) test only days after the MAP boycott began. As superintendent John Kuhn describes in chapter 23, nearly ten thousand students, parents, and educators in Texas in February 2013 marched on the capital against the fifteen standardized tests then required for high school graduation. In chapter 12, student organizers Cauldierre McKay, Aaron Regunberg, and Tim Shea reveal their supernatural organizing power in Providence, Rhode Island, where they led high school students in a "zombie protest" against high-stakes testing, marching to the state department of education and chanting "No education, no life." As parent activist Jeannette Deutermann of Long Island explains in her essay for this book (chapter 18), she created a test resistance Facebook page for New York parents and attracted four thousand friends pledging to opt out their children from tests during those first weeks of the Education Spring.

As thousands of students, parents, and teachers around the country signed petitions supporting Seattle's MAP test boycott, staff at Garfield realized that what had started as our boycott of a single standardized test had begun to crystallize national resistance to massive indiscriminate and punitive testing in general. As messages of solidarity from Austin to Boston and from Japan to England flooded our school mailboxes and email inboxes at Garfield, we came to appreciate that our resistance was not an isolated action by a local faculty but a signal for others across the globe who believed education cannot be reduced to data points in need of high-stakes punishments.

The 2013–14 school year saw a continuation of the Education Spring that began the previous year. High-stakes testing boycotts by teachers, while still understandably infrequent because of the potential for disciplinary action or even termination, had nonetheless spread across the country. As Sarah Chambers vividly relates in chapter 10, teachers at Chicago's Saucedo Academy and Drummond elementary schools propelled the Education Spring forward when they launched a boycott of the Illinois Standards Achievement Test (ISAT) in the spring of 2014. Not long after, as Jia Lee describes in chapter 9, teachers at the Earth School in New York City announced their intention to never administer a Common Core test. Next, teachers at International High School, as retold by Rosie Frascella and Emily Giles in chapter 11, refused to administer a linguistically and culturally inappropriate test to their English language learners. In May 2014, educators in the Chicago Teachers Union passed a resolution in opposition to the CCSS saying, in part, that "instructional and curricular decisions should be in the hands of classroom professionals who understand the context and interest of their students," and "the assessment practices that accompany Common Core State Standards—including the political manipulation of test scores—are used as justification to label and close schools, fail students and evaluate educators."[8]

And it is the parent movement to opt their children out of testing that has truly reached new heights. The Pennsylvania Department of Education reported a 52 percent increase in opt-outs from the Pennsylvania System of School Assessment, totaling at least 498 students, as of April 2014. More than one thousand opted out in Chicago, across Colorado more than fourteen hundred boycotted, and in New York State more than sixty thousand students opted out of state tests that same spring. According to a 2014 PDK/Gallup Poll, 61 percent of Americans reject using student test scores to evaluate teachers and 54 percent say, in general, standardized tests are not helpful. In fact, as I write, we are experiencing the largest ongoing revolt against high-stakes standardized testing in US history. While this movement is still in its early stages, and certainly has a long way to go before it has a decisive effect on federal education policy, it is important to recognize that never have there been so many test-defiers actively participating in collective efforts to reclaim public education from the testocracy.[9]

During the MAP boycott, I was asked many times why I thought Garfield's unprecedented resistance to a standardized test began when it did. I usually pointed to the experienced, dedicated staff, willing to risk their jobs by refusing to administer this flawed exam, and there can be no doubt that the MAP boycott was the result of the courage and dedication to the highest level of pedagogy in the hearts of educators who took up the boycott. However, I believe the explanation of why the MAP boycott and so many other inspiring actions of resistance to these tests erupted when they did requires more analysis. We need to examine the conditions of public education and the effects of education reform that would drive hundreds of educators in Seattle—and then across the country—to risk their jobs to oppose a flawed test. Why would thousands of parents throughout the nation refuse to allow their children to take these tests even when it could mean that their schools are labeled failures? What would possess students in cities around the country, whose graduation may depend on a passing score, to walk out of their schools in defiance of these tests? In short, what are the roots of this new civil rights movement to demand that students and teachers are more than a score?

# "An Invalid Measure": The Fundamental Flaws of Standardized Testing

The swelling number of test-defiers is rooted in the increase of profoundly flawed standardized exams. Often, these tests don't reflect the concepts emphasized in the students' classes and, just as often, the results are not available until after the student has already left the teacher's classroom, rendering the test score useless as a tool for informing instruction. Yet the problem of standardized bubble tests' usefulness for educators extends well beyond the lag time (which can be addressed by computerized tests that immediately calculate results). A standardized bubble test does not help teachers understand how a student arrived at answer choice "C." The student may have selected the right answer but not known why it was right, or conversely, may have chosen the wrong answer but had sophisticated reasoning that shows a deeper understanding of the concept than someone else who randomly guessed correctly. Beyond the lack of utility of standardized testing in facilitating learning there is a more fundamental flaw. A norm-referenced, standardized test compares each individual student to everyone else taking the test, and the score is then usually reported as a percentile. Alfie Kohn describes the inherent treachery of the norm-referenced test:

> No matter how many students take an NRT [norm-referenced test], no matter how well or poorly they were taught, no matter how difficult the questions are, the pattern of results is guaranteed to be the same: Exactly 10 percent of those who take the test will score in the top 10 percent. And half will always fall below the median. That's not because our schools are failing; that's because of what the word *median* means.[10]

And as professor of education Wayne Au explained in 2011, when he was handed a bullhorn at the Occupy Education protest outside the headquarters of Gates Foundation, "If all the students passed the test you advocate, that test would immediately be judged an invalid metric, and any measure of students which mandates the failure of students is an invalid measure."

Unsurprisingly, the Gates Foundation was not swayed by the logic of Au's argument. That is because standardized testing serves to reinforce the mythology of a meritocracy in which those on the top have achieved their position rightfully—because of their hard work, their dedication to hitting the books, and their superior intelligence as proven by their scores. But what researchers have long known is that what standardized tests measure above all else is a student's access to resources. The most damning truth about standardized tests is that they are a better indicator of a student's zip code than a student's aptitude. Wealthier, and predominately whiter, districts score better on tests. Their scores do not reflect the intelligence of wealthier, mostly white students when compared to those of lower-income students and students of color, but do reflect the advantages that wealthier children have—books in the home, parents with more time to read with them, private tutoring, access to test-prep agencies, high-quality health care, and access to good food, to name a few. This is why attaching high stakes to these exams only serves to exacerbate racial and class inequality. As Boston University economics professors Olesya Baker and Kevin Lang's 2013 study, "The School to Prison Pipeline Exposed," reveals, the increases in the use of high-stakes standardized high school exit exams are linked to higher incarceration rates. Arne Duncan's refusal to address the concerns raised by this study exposes the bankruptcy of testocratic policy.

Perhaps the testocracy's most cherished standardized test concept is "value-added modeling" (VAM), which attempts to gauge the contribution of a teacher toward student learning by complicated formulas involving multiple test scores. The absurdity of using VAM scores to evaluate pedagogy was on full display in Tampa, Florida, when Jefferson High social studies teacher Patrick Boyko was named the 2014 Hillsborough County Teacher of the Year. Despite being recognized by his school community as a stellar teacher, Boyko's VAM score for the 2012–13 school year was -10.23 percent (meaning his students scored 10 percent worse on the Florida Comprehensive Assessment Test (FCAT), supposedly due to his teaching, than comparable students across Florida). In 2011–12, Boyko attained an even lower VAM score of

-19.44 percent. That score "would never reflect on what I do," Boyko said.[11] The American Statistical Association (ASA, the largest organization of statisticians in the world) agreed. The ASA released an April 2014 study stating, "VAMs are generally based on standardized test scores and do not directly measure potential teacher contributions toward other student outcomes." The study continues, "VAMs typically measure correlation, not causation: Effects—positive or negative—attributed to a teacher may actually be caused by other factors that are not captured in the model."[12] As Dr. Audrey Amrein-Beardsley, associate professor at Arizona State University, explained in her invaluable book *Rethinking Value-Added Models in Education*, VAMs are unreliable because "a teacher classified as adding value has approximately a 25–50% chance of being classified as subtracting value the following year."

# Authentic Assessment

Let's make this much clear: Educators are not against the assessment of students. Teachers rely on various forms of assessment every day to help understand the thought processes, progress, and conceptual obstacles faced by their students—all in the service of informing instruction for the next steps in a student's development. In the next chapter I describe how, in the wake of the MAP boycott in Seattle, educators came together to form the Teacher Work Group on Assessment and created guidelines called "Markers of Quality Assessment," which defined authentic assessments as those that reflect actual student knowledge and learning, not just test-taking skills; are educational in and of themselves; are free of gender, class, and racial bias; are differentiated to meet students' needs; allow students opportunities to go back and improve; and undergo regular evaluation and revision by educators. Authentic forms of assessment, used for helpful diagnostic purposes instead of doling out punishment, are prerequisites to an education designed to promote creativity and critical thinking. As Phyllis Tashlik explains in chapter 27,

> The general public gleans what the media throw at them and the tendency is for people to think, "Oh, if you're against standardized testing, then you're against assessments," which is not the case at all. What we're against is an assessment that has the consequence of narrowing curriculum and teaching and learning. It's important to realize that as soon as you institute these standardized tests, you're also affecting curriculum, and you're affecting how teachers

teach, and you're affecting how time is used. And it's that connection between assessment, curriculum, and instruction that just doesn't get explained enough in the public conversation about testing. Performance assessments offer such a greater opportunity to develop interesting curriculum and structure more opportunities for the teacher to relate to the kids in front of them.

Much has been written describing alternative forms of assessment to standardized testing (for a more comprehensive discussion on this topic, read the Rethinking Schools book *Pencils Down*, edited by Wayne Au and Melissa Temple). One straightforward way to visualize a superior substitute to bubble testing is to picture the process of getting a PhD. When PhD candidates prepare to graduate, their committees do not judge their knowledge by having them eliminate wrong answer choices on a standardized test. Candidates engage in the much more meaningful process of defending a dissertation. Doctoral students develop a thesis, conduct research over time, collaborate with an advisor, revise the thesis as needed, and finally defend the thesis before a panel of experts. Innovative classrooms around the nation (and around the world) have adapted just this model, tailoring it to every subject and age. This form of performance-based assessment, often coupled with a portfolio of the student's work over a period of time, has many advantages over standardized bubble testing, but, perhaps most important, it challenges each student to explain her or his ideas around issues actually being taught in the classroom. The drawback to this form of assessment, from the testocracy's vantage point, is that it empowers the teachers and students in the classroom, fosters critical thinking, and, without a standardized exam to sell to every district, makes it harder to turn a profit.

## Rotten to the Common Core

The jewels in the crown of the testocracy are the high-stakes exams encrusted in the Common Core State Standards. As of June 2014, forty-three states had adopted these standards "to ensure all students are ready for success after high school," as the CCSS website explains, and to "establish clear, consistent guidelines for what every student should know and be able to do in math and English language arts from kindergarten through 12th grade."[13] The CCSS were described by Lyndsey Layton in the *Washington Post* as "one of the swiftest and most remarkable shifts in education policy in U.S. history," made possible because of the massive investment by Bill Gates. Layton points out, "The Bill and Melinda Gates Foundation didn't just bankroll the development of what became known as the Common Core State Standards. With more than $200 million, the foundation also built political support across the county, persuading state governments to make systemic and costly changes."[14] And with the testocrats in charge of the development of the standards, the primary stakeholders in education were excluded from providing any meaningful input. As *Rethinking Schools*, a leading journal of social justice education, editorialized:

> Written mostly by academics and assessment experts—many with ties to testing companies—the Common Core standards have never been fully implemented and tested in real schools anywhere. Of the 135 members on the official Common Core review panels convened by Achieve Inc., the consulting firm that has directed the Common Core project for the NGA, few were classroom teachers or current administrators. Parents were entirely missing. K–12 educators were mostly brought in after the fact to tweak and endorse the standards—and lend legitimacy to the results.[15]

In some instances the CCSS have replaced deeply flawed standards or scripted curricular regimes that require teachers to read lessons from a script. In these instances, the CCSS's claim of not prescribing to teachers how to meet the standards and of being "based on application of knowledge through higher-order thinking skills" can appear emancipating. Yet because of the lack of educator and parent input to the standards, there are serious limitations. As Diane E. Levin and Dr. Nancy Carlsson-Paige (the latter a contributor to this book) have explained about the negative impact of CCSS on early childhood development,

> The proposed common core national education standards for K–12—which will impose higher academic standards on younger children—contradict decades of early education theory and research about how young children learn best and how to close the achievement gap. The imposition of one-size-fits-all standards on young children can't solve the problems of an education system that is fundamentally unequal.[16]

Chicago Public Schools preschool teacher and parent Kirstin Roberts elaborates on the research about how children best learn when she writes in chapter 19 that NCLB, RttT, and the CCSS have been responsible for "the dramatic increase in testing of the very young over the last decade," and "[have] pushed out developmentally appropriate curriculum, including play-based learning, from early childhood classrooms."

The pitfalls of the CCSS are best illustrated by what its supporters have to say. Bill Gates said of the Common Core in 2009, "When the tests are aligned to the common standards, the curriculum will line up as well—and that will *unleash powerful market forces* in the service of better teaching. For the first time, there will be a *large base of customers eager to buy products* that can help every kid learn and every teacher get better" (my emphasis).[17] The Thomas B. Fordham Institute, a conservative think tank, estimates implementing the new standards will cost the nation between $1 billion and $8 billion. Nearly all the profits will go to book publishers and test creators like Pearson and CTB/McGraw-Hill.[18] Prominently displayed on one sidebar of the official Common Core website is a pull quote from Edward B. Rust, Jr., Chairman and CEO of State Farm Insurance Companies, who proclaims: "State-by-state adoption of these standards is an important step toward maintaining our country's competitive edge. With a skilled and prepared workforce the business community will be better prepared to face the challenges of the international marketplace."[19]

Here the true purpose of the CCSS is revealed: It has very little to do with helping students develop their capacities and much more to do with empowering US businesses to dominate global markets and stuff additional cash in the already bulging bespoke-suit pockets of testing executives. One of the most glaring examples of how the standards are designed to accomplish this goal is in their approach to literacy. The CCSS emphasize informational texts at the expense of literature, fundamentally impeding students' understanding of a central element of human expression. As award-winning children's author Alma Flor Ada argues in chapter 25, literature "not only gives an example of the power of language, but becomes a model of living consciously, of paying attention to what happens around us, of discovering a deeper meaning in life." But if global competition is the purpose of education, then Ada's contention that education be about investigating the meaning of life should be deemed frivolous and pushed from our classrooms.

In addition to shunning literature, the CCSS also misuse nonfiction in an effort to turn writing into reading passages—and reading passages into test questions. The CCSS emphasize what is called "close reading" and call for students "to be able to answer a range of text-dependent questions, whose answers require inference based on careful attention to the text."[20] The idea is to emphasize "what lies within the four corners of the text" and deemphasize the student's own perspective in order to uncover the author's meaning in the text.

One of the chief architects of the CCSS, David Coleman, even went as far as saying in an address to New York State educators, "As you grow up in this world, you realize people really don't give a shit about what you feel or what you think."[21] As New York–based educator Daniel E. Ferguson has written, "Text-dependent questions, for Coleman, hold everyone accountable to what's within the four corners of the text. What he does not say, however, is that they also make for better standardized test questions."[22]

Whatever you think of the standards themselves, the most detrimental aspect of the CCSS are the standardized tests—and the high stakes—that are attached to the standards. The new generation of CCSS tests, most prominently the Partnership for Assessment of Readiness for College and Careers (PARCC) and Smarter Balanced Assessment Consortium (SBAC) exams, are designed to permanently enshrine high-stakes standardized bubble filling as the arbiter of success in education. Already there are numerous examples of the detrimental results of these CCSS tests. New York State was one of the first to mandate that students take the PARCC exams in the spring of 2013, and only 31 percent of students passed the tests in English and math.[23] The testocracy celebrated this decline in test scores as proof that the new standards were ushering in an era of rigor and accountability, with then New York City mayor Michael Bloomberg calling the results "very good news."[24]

Amber Kudla, a high school student from North Tonawanda, New York, gave a speech at her graduation (the text of which appears in chapter 13) that contains an important analogy exposing the absurdity of Bloomberg's thinking: "As for the argument that the assessments are challenging our students more, sure that's true. It's a challenge to fit the same amount of material into one year with more exams. It's a challenge to memorize loads of facts in time for the next test. It's also a challenge to eat a teaspoon of cinnamon in one bite without choking, but what are you really accomplishing?"

## Hypocrisy of the Testocracy

At first glance it would be easy to conclude that the testocracy's strategy for public schools is the result of profound ignorance. After all, members of the testocracy have never smelled a free or reduced-price lunch yet throw a tantrum when public school advocates suggest poverty is a substantial factor in educational outcomes. The testocracy has never had to puzzle over the conundrum of having more students than available chairs in the classroom, yet they are the very same people who claim class size doesn't matter in educational outcomes. The bubble of luxury surrounding the testocracy has convinced many that most testocrats are too far removed from the realities facing the majority of US residents to ever understand the damage caused by the high-stakes bubble tests they peddle. While it is true that the corporate reform moguls are completely out of touch with the vast majority of people, their strategy for remaking our schools on a business model is not the result of ignorance but of arrogance, not of misunderstanding but of the profit motive, not of silliness but rather of a desire for supremacy.

In fact, you could argue that the MAP test boycott did not actually begin at Garfield High School. A keen observer might recognize that the boycott of the MAP test—and so many other standardized tests—began in earnest at schools like Seattle's elite private Lakeside High School, alma mater of Bill Gates, where he sends his children, because, of course, Lakeside, like one-percenter schools elsewhere, would never inundate its students with standardized tests. These academies, predominately serving the children of the financially fortunate, shield students from standardized tests because they want their children to be allowed to think outside the bubble test, to develop critical thinking skills and prioritize time to explore art, music, drama, athletics, and debate. Gates values Lakeside because of its lovely campus, where the average class size is sixteen, the library contains some twenty thousand volumes, and the new sports facility offers cryotherapy and hydrotherapy spas. Moreover, while Gates, President Obama, and Secretary of Education Duncan are all parents of school-age children, none of those children attend schools that use the CCSS or take Common Core exams. As Dao X. Tran, then PTA co-chair at Castle Bridge Elementary School, put it (in chapter 20): "These officials don't even send their children to public schools. *They* are failing our children, yet they push for our children's teachers to be accountable based on children's test data. All while they opt for their own children to go to schools that don't take these tests, that have small class sizes and project-based, hands-on, arts-infused learning—that's what we want for our children!" The superrich are not failing to understand the basics of how to provide a nurturing education for the whole child. The problem is that they believe this type of education should be reserved only for their own children.

# A Brief History of *Test-defying*

The United States has a long history of using standardized testing for the purposes of ranking and sorting youth into different strata of society. In fact, standardized tests originally entered the public schools with the eugenics movement, a white-supremacist ideology cloaked in the shabby garments of fraudulent science that became fashionable in the late nineteenth and early twentieth centuries. As *Rethinking Schools* editorialized,

> The United States has a long history of using intelligence tests to support white supremacy and class stratification. Standardized tests first entered the public schools in the 1920s, pushed by eugenicists whose pseudoscience promoted the "natural superiority" of wealthy, white, U.S.-born males. High-stakes standardized tests have disguised class and race privilege as merit ever since. The consistent use of test scores to demonstrate first a "mental ability" gap and now an "achievement" gap exposes the intrinsic nature of these tests: They are built to maintain inequality, not to serve as an antidote to educational disparities.[25]

When the first "common schools" began in the late 1800s, industrialists quickly recognized an opportunity to shape the schools in the image of their factories. These early "education reformers" recognized the value of using standardized tests—first developed in the form of IQ tests used to sort military recruits for World War I—to evaluate the efficiency of the teacher workforce in producing the "student-product." Proud eugenicist and Princeton University professor Carl Brigham left his school during World War I to implement IQ testing as an army psychologist. Upon returning to Princeton, Brigham developed the SAT exam as the admissions gatekeeper to Princeton, and the test confirmed in his mind that whites born in the United States were the most intelligent of all peoples.[26] As Alan Stoskopf wrote, "By the early 1920s, more than 2 million American school children were being tested primarily for academic tracking purposes. At least some of the decisions to allocate resources and select students for academic or vocational courses were influenced by eugenic notions of student worth."[27]

Resistance to these exams surely began the first time a student bubbled in every "A" on the page in defiance of the entire testing process. Yet, beyond these individual forms of protest, an active minority of educators, journalists, labor groups, and parents resisted these early notions of using testing to rank intelligence. Some of the most important early voices in opposition to intelligence testing—especially in service of ranking the races—came from leading African American scholars such as W. E. B. Du Bois, Horace Mann Bond, and Howard Long. Du Bois recalled in 1940, "It was not until I was long out of school and indeed after the [First] World War that there came the hurried use of the new technique of psychological tests, which were quickly adjusted so as to put black folk absolutely beyond the possibility of civilization."[28] In a statement that is quite apparently lost on today's testocracy, Horace Mann Bond, in his work "Intelligence Tests and Propaganda," wrote:

> But so long as any group of men attempts to use these tests as funds of information for the approximation of crude and inaccurate generalizations, so long must we continue to cry, "Hold!" To compare the crowded millions of New York's East Side with the children of Morningside Heights [an upper-class neighborhood at the time] indeed involves a great contradiction; and to claim that the results of the tests given to such diverse groups, drawn from such varying strata of the social complex, are in any wise accurate, is to expose a fatuous sense of unfairness and lack of appreciation of the great environmental factors of modern urban life.[29]

This history of test-defiers was largely buried until the mass uprisings of the civil rights and Black Power movements of the 1950s, '60s, and '70s transformed public education. In the course of these broad mass movements, parents, students, teachers, and activists fought to integrate the schools, budget for equitable funding, institute ethnic studies programs, and even to redefine the purpose of school.

In the Jim Crow–segregated South, literacy was inherently political and employed as a barrier to prevent African Americans from exercising their right to vote. The great activist and educator Myles Horton was a founder of the Highlander Folk School in Tennessee that would go on to help organize the Citizenship Schools of the mid-1950s and 1960s. The Citizenship Schools' mission was to create literacy programs to help disenfranchised Southern blacks achieve access to the voting booth. Hundreds of thousands of African Americans attended the Citizenship Schools, which launched one of the most important educational programs of the civil rights movement, redefining the purpose of education and the assessment of educational outcomes. Horton described one of the Citizenship Schools he helped to organize, saying, "It was not a literacy class. It was a community organization. . . . They were talking about using their citizenship to do something, and they named it a Citizenship School, not a literacy school. That helped with the motivation." By the end of the class more than 80 percent of those students passed the final examination, which was to go down to the courthouse and register to vote![30]

## *Testucation* and the End of Assessment

The great civil rights movements of the past have reimagined education as a means to creating a more just society. The testocracy, too, has a vision for reimagining the education system and it is flat-out chilling. The testocracy is relentlessly working on new methods to reduce students to data points that can be used to rank, punish, and manipulate. Like something out of a dystopian sci-fi film, the Bill and Melinda Gates Foundation spent $1.4 million to develop biometric bracelets designed to send a small current across the skin to measure changes in electrical charges as the sympathetic nervous system responds to stimuli. These "Q Sensors" would then be used to monitor a student's "excitement, stress, fear, engagement, boredom and relaxation through the skin."[31] Presumably, then, VAM assessments could be extended to evaluate teachers based on this biometric data. As Diane Ravitch explained to Reuters when the story broke in the spring of 2012, "They should devote more time to improving the substance of what is being taught . . . and give up all this measurement mania."[32]

But the testocracy remains relentless in its quest to give up on teaching and devote itself to data collection. In a 2011 *TIME* magazine feature on the future of education, readers are asked to "imagine walking into a classroom and seeing no one in the front of the classroom. Instead you're led to a computer terminal at a desk and told this will be your teacher for the course. The only adults around are a facilitator to make sure that you stay on task and to fix any tech problems that may arise." *TIME* goes on to point out, "For some Florida students, computer-led instruction is a reality. Within the Miami-Dade County Public School district alone, 7,000 students are receiving this form of education, including six middle and K–8 schools, according to the *New York Times*."[33] This approach to schooling is known as "e-learning labs," and from the perspective of the testocracy, if education is about getting a high score, then one hardly needs nurturing, mentorship, or human contact to succeed. Computers can be used to add value—the value of rote memorization, discipline, and basic literacy skills—to otherwise relatively worthless students. Here, then, is a primary objective of an education system run by the testocracy: replace the compassionate hand of the educator with the cold, invisible, all-thumbs hand of the free market.

Perhaps the most menacing aspect of high-stakes testing is the way it disfigures our society by training people to live in fear of making mistakes. Misunderstandings should be great opportunities for breakthroughs in comprehension. Yet American education policy treats miscalculations as perverse transgressions. The great playwright Oscar Wilde made a magnificent observation in his novel *The Picture of Dorian Gray* when he wrote, in words he ascribed to the fictional character of Lord Henry, "Most people die of a sort of creeping common sense, and discover when it is too late that the only things one never regrets are one's mistakes." Oscar Wilde understood that without mistakes there is no creativity, and that without creativity life lacks meaning.

The central contradiction of high-stakes testing—an incongruity propelling the revolt against these tests forward today—is that knowledge is fundamentally a social phenomenon, yet high-stakes testing attempts to organize our society to deny this fact by individualizing scores and attaching punishments to them. Lev Vygotsky, known as the "Mozart of psychology" for his influential work in child and adolescent psychology and cognition, described mental development in his book *Mind in Society* as a "sociohistorical" process both for the human species and for individuals as they develop. His approach to education understood that ideas have histories and are produced in the context of the society in which they arise. Moreover, human beings learn in concert with one another, and the social conditions of people's lives play a central role in shaping their development.

While Vygotsky understood the social dimension of knowledge, this did not mean he was opposed to assessing an individual student's learning. To explain the interplay between the social and individual aspects of knowledge, Vygotsky developed the concept of the "zone of proximal development," the difference between what a learner can do without help and what he or she can do with assistance. In other words, the zone of proximal development describes the area where the child cannot solve a problem alone but can solve it successfully in collaboration with a more advanced peer or with guidance from an adult. Thus, for Vygotsky, social interaction is vital in developing the cognitive ability of the student.

High-stakes, standardized testing, by focusing solely on what a student can do as an individual (absent the peers and educators who have made the learning process possible), completely rejects the importance of assessing a student's zone of proximal development. High-stakes testing structures our education system and our society so as to deny the collective nature of learning—the ways in which ideas and understanding are developed in cooperation with others—by separating students out and labeling them with individual scores, subsequently punishing students who had the greatest barriers (such as poverty, racism, higher class sizes) to the social acquisition of learning.

In its insatiable quest to quantify intellect, the testocracy has created a profound absurdity: by inundating the schools with standardized testing they are actually doing away with assessment altogether. Instead of a tool to assist teachers in assessing the thought processes of students, so as to help them expand their comprehension and zone of proximal development, high-stakes, standardized tests have become an end in and of themselves. When a test becomes the goal of education, rather than one tool in service of it, meaningful learning ceases to exist, and education is replaced by what we could call a "testucation."

A testucation has many advantages over an education from the perspective of the testocracy. An education invites students to question and critique, which can lead to a populace that asks dangerous questions, such as, "Why is the testocracy is in control of education?" A testucation allows politicians, rather than educators, to set the exam "cut score"—the arbitrary number that determines who passes and who fails. A testucation polices what is acceptable knowledge, leaving elites to determine the available answer choices. Systematically training children to believe that wisdom is the ability to choose a right answer from a prescribed list of options allows the testocracy to set the parameters for what are acceptable choices and what the right answer should be. Whether it is a question posed by a testing company about a reading passage (think of the now famous nonsensical "Hare and Pineapple" question from a New York State test), or a question posed by a politician about which is the correct war to start next, often the question being asked is not the most important question, the list of possible questions is incomplete, and so the "correct" answer is necessarily flawed.[34]

## Education Reform or Revolution?

We face major crises in our world today. The Great Recession of 2008 has ushered in a new era of massive wealth inequality; the disastrous "war on drugs" has propelled mass incarceration, especially of African Americans and other people of color, making the United States the biggest jailer in world history; the United States remains in a seemingly perpetual state of war in the Middle East; and perhaps most frightening of all, scientists agree that continuing the current trajectory of carbon emissions into the earth's atmosphere will result in horrific climate disasters and ultimately make life for human beings impossible on our planet.

None of these social, economic, political, and ecological disasters can be solved with A, B, C, or D thinking. Our nation has sunk hundreds of millions of dollars into organizing education around the idea that the highest form of knowledge is the ability to eliminate wrong answer choices. Yet the major societal problems we face require reorganizing education so that, above all else, it encourages problem-solving, critical thinking, collaboration, leadership, imagination, creativity, empathy, and civic courage. As Richard Shaull explains in the foreword to Paulo Freire's masterwork, *Pedagogy of the Oppressed*, "Education either functions as an instrument which is used to facilitate integration of the younger generation into the logic of the present system and bring about conformity or it becomes the practice of freedom, the means by which men and women deal critically and creatively with reality and discover how to participate in the transformation of their world."[35]

Parents, students, educators, labor leaders, and activists will need to inspire an education revolution if we are going to defeat corporate education reform. We will need to "dream bigger," as Saint Paul Federation of Teachers president Mary Cathryn Ricker explains in chapter 8. I hope the insightful—at times breathtaking—stories of the ongoing resistance contained in this volume inspire you to join this movement or persist in your efforts.

So sign the opt-out form and accompany your kid's class on a field trip. Walk out of the test and tell the adults to take it instead. Invite legislators and school board members to come take the tests and publish their scores. Teach your students about the civil rights movement and scrap the preparation for the test. As the Education Spring blooms, so too will the testocracy wither.

Jesse Hagopian
Seattle
August 2014

# TEACHERS

# 1.
# OUR DESTINATION IS NOT ON THE MAP

## Jesse Hagopian

*This test isn't right for students, so Garfield refuses to give it.*
—Kris McBride, testing coordinator and academic dean,
Garfield High School

*The students aren't going to take it. Not in the literal sense. Not in the figurative sense.*
—Obadiah Terry, Garfield High School student body president

*We want people to know that parents stand firm with the teachers on this issue. We really don't believe the time of the kids and the teachers should be wasted on a test that really isn't helping anyone.*
—Phil Sherburne, Garfield High School PTSA president

I cannot remember ever feeling so nervous.

On January 10, 2013, the teachers at Garfield High School called a press conference in Adam Gish's second-floor language arts classroom to make our announcement. We knew there were several possible outcomes of our efforts that day: the press might not show up. They could show up, but we would fail to convey our message. Or our announcement could help gather our community to stand at the barricades of the nation's school reform debate.

My advocacy up until then for research-based policies to improve our public schools had been a slow but steady effort. Over the last couple of years, there have been times when I felt lonely in my debates with some of the most prominent of the corporate education reformers. I had debated secretary of education Arne Duncan on charter schools in a closed-door session with a few other educators when he came to the Seattle area in 2010. I had risen from the audience to debate *Waiting for Superman* film director Davis Guggenheim at the conclusion of a special showing in Seattle of his union-bashing film. I had been arrested at the Washington State Capitol when I attempted a citizen's arrest of the legislature for failing their constitutional duty to fully fund education. Now my colleagues at Garfield High School and I were preparing to engage in a collective act of resistance that had the potential to transcend these more symbolic acts—but also had the potential to end in calamity.

Nathan Simoneaux (then a student teacher) was correcting papers in the back corner of the classroom. A few of us were setting up chairs and putting finishing touches on the press packets. Slowly, reporters began filing in. One TV camera crew, then another. My initial fear that the press would ignore our story gave way to a new terror: Was I about to aid an effort that would result in my colleagues losing their jobs?

As a history teacher, I was not in one of the MAP-tested subjects of math or language arts in which we were required to administer the test. My greatest agony was not that I would be reprimanded, but rather that my agitation could contribute to the dismissal of one of my coworkers. I knew of cases where the Seattle School District acted punitively toward people who prominently expressed disagreement with their policy, but more than that I feared if we failed in our endeavor, teachers everywhere might not be so bold in their defense of public education next time. So there I was, making last-minute edits to my forthcoming statement, filled both with the excitement of a scientist on the verge of a great discovery and with dread that the experiment could go terribly wrong.

A couple of teachers utilized the last of the masking tape roll to secure the microphones of the major news outlets in the area to the conductor's podium we had borrowed from the choir room. A group of teachers representing the various academic departments assembled in the front of the room. They were joined by Associated Student Body Government president Obadiah Terry (also the past president of the Black Student Union), there to announce that the ASB had voted unanimously to support the teachers in their proposed actions.

I called the conference to order with our school's salutation, "Welcome to the Doghouse"—an allusion to our fearless purple-and-white mascot, the Bulldog. Then I heard myself stammer out a brief script I had hastily thrown together between signing permission slips and heating up mac and cheese on my lunch break. I tried to explain to the assembled guests how we had attempted everything we could think of before taking this drastic measure. In 2010, I helped pass a union resolution, introduced by Ballard High School teacher Noam Gundle, condemning the MAP test (then new to Seattle) as inappropriate for rating either teaching or learning. Teachers had provided survey information to the school district informing them of the inadequacy of the exam. We tried asking for an audience with the superintendent about our opposition to the MAP.

"And so . . . " I paused, tugging at the purple baseball cap embroidered with a white "G" I had earned playing baseball at Garfield back when I was a student there myself. In those days, hitting line drives was the only validating aspect of school for me, as my standardized test scores had me convinced I was not an intelligent person. "The teachers at Garfield High School have voted unanimously to refuse to administer the MAP test."

## The Vote

Several weeks before, in the days leading up to winter break in December 2012, Mallory Clarke phoned my classroom to ask me to meet with her after school. Mallory is Garfield's reading specialist, heading the Read Right program designed to target struggling readers and help them make great gains in literacy. As a union representative at Garfield, I am accustomed to getting calls from colleagues with questions about the Seattle Education Association (SEA) union contract or district policies, so I assumed this was something about the collective bargaining agreement. After school, I climbed the stairs to Mallory's second-floor room. Upon reaching her room, she ushered me in, shut the door, asked me to sit, and then peered over the top of the worn partition by her desk, checking to see if anyone else was within earshot. I got the feeling this was not going to be a routine review of the contract. I was somewhat bemused by her precautions, but she certainly had my attention.

Her eyes widened as she got straight to the point. "I'm not going to give the MAP test." She said it with a delighted tone of defiance. "And there are others I have talked to as well." My first inclination was to jump out of my seat and pump my fist. But I managed to restrain myself, replying, "Wow, that's really exciting. What can I do to help?"

Over the next couple of weeks, Mallory and others set about organizing meetings of teachers in the tested subjects to see what they thought of the MAP test and what action they might be prepared to take. I participated in several of these sessions. When asked, teachers talked of losing days of class time to the test, the test not covering the material they were teaching, finding no value in the test results, students making random keystrokes during the test administered via computer. And while teachers appreciated their students' creative approaches to sabotaging such a mind-numbing exam, they bristled at having their pedagogical performance judged with such a haphazard method.

At one gathering in my classroom we discussed ways in which the MAP test exacerbated inequality and violated our students' civil rights. Teachers expressed dismay over how special education students' Individual Education Plans (IEPs) were disregarded by this test, and how English language learners, or emergent bilinguals, were being humiliated by a test that was not linguistically or culturally appropriate. I explained that as a history teacher I did not teach a subject tested by the MAP, yet my course and my students were nonetheless greatly impacted by the exam because the school library was shut down three times a year for weeks at a time while the test was administered on the library computers. This made it difficult to assign research projects because the students could not check out books or use the computers. I found that if I assigned a research project during MAP testing, the students without Internet access at home—predominantly low-income students and students of color—were at a severe disadvantage. I also passed out an essay, "Race and the (mis)Measures of Academic Progress," published on the *Seattle Education* blog, which I had written over a year prior to argue that the MAP test leads to the exacerbation of racial inequity because, like many standardized tests, it is used to rank and sort students into different tracks—not remove the barriers or provide the resources needed to close the opportunity gap that exists in education. Another teacher shared a document, written by Seattle Public Schools parent (and now elected school board member) Sue Peters, titled "15 Reasons Why the Seattle School District Should Shelve the MAP® Test—ASAP."[1] In it, Peters noted even the Northwest Evaluation Association (NWEA), the producer of the MAP, recommended against using their product to evaluate teachers.

At one meeting, Kit McCormick—a language arts teacher at Garfield revered both for her pedagogy and her humor—told us about her experience at a Seattle School District training she had been to the year prior where a district official had admitted to her that the MAP test had limited utility at the high school level as it had a higher margin of error than expected gains by the ninth grade. Then she relayed a story that made it clear the MAP was not properly aligned to the state standards that specify what must be taught at each grade level. Kit recalls explaining to us,

> After the MAP last year, one of my freshmen came and asked, "What is poetic en-jam-ent?" I asked where he had heard the term and he said it was on the MAP. He was referring to a poetic technique, "enjambment," wherein a line of poetry travels to the next line without a pause in thought or punctuation, usually indicating either an inevitability of action or a stream-of-conscious state of mind. The term is appropriately taught at the 11th or 12th AP level when readers should be concerned with style analysis issues. At the freshman level it's probably more appropriate to ask what the controlling metaphor of the poem is.

Beloved math teacher Mario Shaunette explained that he first realized the MAP was off course when he looked over the shoulder of one of his ninth-grade algebra students and saw a geometry question, which he analogized as if a Spanish teacher were to see a French question on the exam—"Sure it's foreign language," he said, "but it's not the same subject!"

One of our primary topics of conversation at these organizing meetings was about the possibility of facing disciplinary action. We discussed 2008 Seattle test-resisting pioneer Carl Chew, a well-known middle school teacher who on his own refused to give a state-mandated standardized test. He was suspended without pay and later pushed out of the district. We acknowledged the district could take the same action with Garfield teachers, but we also reasoned it would be harder for them if all the teachers stood together—firing whole departments would be logistically challenging, at the very least.

Once these small meetings confirmed that teachers in the tested subjects were united in opposition to the MAP test, we concluded our test boycott could only be truly effective if it were an initiative of the entire school. We then brought a proposal to boycott the MAP to an all-staff meeting and the bulk of our school's more than ninety educators assembled in the library to discuss the prospects for taking this bold course of action. I began the meeting by explaining the process. We would hold an open discussion and then take a vote. I made it clear this was a personal decision for each teacher. Each of us faced different life circumstances, and regardless of the outcome, we would all still be one Bulldog family.

Kris McBride summarized why so many teachers were opposed to the MAP. Several teachers shared stories corroborating Kris's overview. Teachers asked questions about what we would consider a valid assessment that could replace the MAP. Prepared for that question, I distributed the chapter from *Pencils Down: Rethinking High-Stakes Testing and Accountability in Public Schools* devoted to models of assessment beyond standardized tests that give educators a more holistic understanding of a student's abilities and thought processes.

Several teachers raised valid concerns about why it would be dangerous to refuse to give this test, providing personal testimony of how the district had acted punitively for far smaller transgressions of policy. These educators asked me what the consequences could be for boycotting the MAP. "If you refuse a directive, you can be labeled 'insubordinate,'" I explained. "We have a progressive discipline policy in the Seattle Public Schools, but ultimately your job could be on the line." Rest assured those were not the words that inspired the Garfield educators' boycott of the MAP. It was Karen Gunn, a highly respected mathematics instructor, who then rose to address the assembly. Her words sped up history: "I have something to say. This flawed test is going to label my students, and me, as failures because it isn't testing what I am teaching. I would rather be reprimanded for standing up for what I believe in than for doing nothing and letting this test take advantage of us."

When she sat down I knew it was time to call for the vote, and as soon as I did, the hands shot up. Garfield High School's teachers voted unanimously—save a couple of abstentions—to refuse to administer the MAP. The teachers then lined up to sign their names to a letter that read in part: "We, the Garfield teachers, respectfully decline to give the MAP test to any of our students. We have had different levels of experiences with MAP in our varied careers, have read about it, and discussed it with our colleagues. After this thorough review, we have all come to the conclusion that we cannot in good conscience subject our students to this test again." The letter then outlined our objections to the MAP, including the following points:

- Seattle School District staff admitted to a Garfield teacher that the test is not a valid at the high school level because the margin of error is higher than the expected gains.

- The test is not aligned to our curriculum.
- The MAP especially hurts students receiving extra academic support—English language learners and those enrolled in special education. These are the kids who lose the most each time they waste five hours on the test.
- Our computer labs are commandeered for weeks when the MAP is administered, so students working on research projects can't get near them. The students without home computers—predominantly low-income and students of color—are hurt the most.
- The MAP test is used in evaluating teachers. And yet the maker of the test, the Northwest Evaluation Association (NWEA), says that the test should not be used to assess teachers unless many safeguards—not present in the Seattle schools—are in place to achieve the highest level of reliability.
- Former superintendent, the late Maria Goodloe-Johnson, brought the MAP to Seattle at a cost of some $4 million while she was serving on the board of the company that sells it. The state auditor had already called this an ethics violation because she did not disclose it until after the district approved the company's contract.

The teachers at Garfield had not voted to oppose standardized testing in general. We had not even voted to denounce high-stakes testing in particular. In fact, while the vast majority of teachers at our school did believe to varying degrees that standardized testing had become overbearing, there were a range of opinions and varying levels of understanding about the usefulness or effectiveness of such exams. Some teachers favored replacing the MAP with a better standardized test. Others believed we had far too many standardized tests in the public schools and we should move toward portfolios, coupled with performance-based assessments, that could reveal and evaluate a whole range of abilities—such as the abilities to revise one's thinking after being introduced to new information, to research, to debate, to express passion for an issue one cares about, to incorporate ideas from peers into one's own unique answer, and countless more. None of those skills, nor the important factors of organization or motivation, are measured by bubble tests where success comes largely from the ability to eliminate wrong answer choices. Still, our active refusal to administer this one specific test, this one test we all could agree was irreparably flawed, achieved a new intensity in the debate on the massive "testing industrial complex" as a whole.

# Conquering Test Anxiety

My second son, Satchel Ray, was born two days after we had announced the MAP test boycott—on Martin Luther King Jr.'s birthday no less, which we took as a sign of good things to come. To see my four-year-old son Miles embrace his new baby brother for the first time—at the very moment my colleagues were birthing perhaps the nation's first all-school boycott of a district-mandated test—was a moment of true joy and possibility.

Yet the euphoria of those early days quickly waned as the first high-stakes test of our resolve came in the form of an all-district email from Seattle Public Schools superintendent Jose Banda to every educator in the district, declaring that the MAP test was not optional and he expected every educator to perform assigned duties. I know more than one Bulldog teacher's heart quickened—especially those in the tested subjects—as they realized this was meant as a warning that we could be charged with insubordination.

Within minutes of the superintendent's email, the lunch bell rang. Over the intercom, Kris McBride's voice was just audible over the din of students rushing to pack up their belongings, announcing that all Garfield staff should go to the first floor conference room to enjoy pizza sent by a school in Florida that supported us. Over slices of pizza, Garfield staff realized our struggle had become visible across the country. Educators from as far as Hawaii, people we'd never met, were counting on us to stand strong. Despite the threatening email, Doghouse teachers were not going to back down. Our determination was buoyed over the coming days as the chocolates, flowers, cards, books, donations, emails, photos of teachers holding "Scrap the MAP" signs, and resolutions of support came streaming in from around the country—and later from around the world.

One of the biggest boosts to our movement came when the Garfield High School Parent Teacher Student Association (PTSA) board voted unanimously to support the MAP boycott. Garfield's PTSA president, Philip Sherburne, an attorney and participant in the civil rights movement, was a strong supporter. In his statement, he wrote,

> The real issue is what the school district is going to do, starting early in a student's educational life, to help as many students as possible perform at grade level. Students should not be entering high school unprepared to do ninth-grade work. A major effort to get students to grade-level performance and to keep them there through graduation requires a level of focus and an investment of resources that we have not seen from the District or the Leg-

islature. It is this focus on improving student achievement and providing the resources to accomplish it that deserves all our attention.

Sherburne refused to let anyone mischaracterize our movement as one of teachers who did not want to be held accountable. He made it clear the teachers and parents of Garfield were not against assessing our students, only that we needed better assessments that were not wasting precious resources and time.

The next important step was that the boycott spread to other schools in the district. In some instances educators heard of our actions in the news and organized their own schools to participate. In others, organizers in the rank-and-file education justice organization, the Social Equality Educators (SEE), played a critical role in helping the boycott spread. We now felt the power of a growing uprising. At the urging of fourth-grade teacher Matt Carter, Orca, with grades K–8, became the second school to join the boycott, quickly followed by Chief Sealth High School and Ballard High School. Later during the spring round of testing, the Center School and Thornton Creek Elementary actively joined the boycott.

The task of organizing the boycott grew immense as we set about organizing rallies, spreading the boycott to additional schools, making alliances with community groups, issuing press releases, conducting interviews, writing op-eds, communicating with the school district, consulting with parents, and even holding staff events like "Bulldog Bowling Night" to keep up morale. At one all-staff meeting in the week after announcing the boycott, Garfield elected a steering committee for the boycott: Kris McBride, Jessica Griffin (math teacher), Mallory Clarke, Kit McCormick, and myself. Mallory and I then represented Garfield at the all-city MAP Boycott Coordinating Council that comprised educator representatives from the various participating schools.

Forces were amassing on the other side, too. Twice in January, *Seattle Times* editorialists railed against teachers for refusing the MAP and called on Superintendent Banda to be firm with us. The many education reform groups funded by the Gates Foundation were no doubt explaining to the superintendent the importance of disciplining those who would attempt to crumble the standardized testing edifice.

The pressure on the school district was clearly intense. In an effort to halt the spread of the boycott, the superintendent issued a statement on January 22 to principals instructing them to hold mandatory staff meetings to inform teachers of the potential of a ten-day suspension without pay for refusing to administer the MAP test. However, by then, a remarkable transformation had occurred that could not be undone any more than a butterfly can turn back into a chrysalis: the faculty at Garfield High School had lost its fear. At this point, every threat only emboldened educators who knew that any sanction visited upon the boycotting teachers would be met with overwhelming opposition from thousands of supporters.

When these bullying tactics only strengthened the resolve of teachers, Superintendent Banda issued a new directive to school principals, mandating that they begin overseeing the MAP test themselves if teachers wouldn't cooperate. This tactic was particularly insidious, as it was designed to turn administrators against teachers. The divide-and-conquer tactic, however, fell on its face. Both sides knew the relationship between the administration and the teachers were critical for the high functioning of our school, not to mention the success of the boycott.

On the day of the "test or else" decree, Seattle's superintendent came to Garfield with two other district officials to meet for a second and final time with the five of us on the steering committee. Kris McBride served as point person for this meeting and began by welcoming Mr. Banda to Garfield and thanking him for his time. I was truly awed by Kris's composure. She was responsible for administering the MAP at Garfield—and likely the most vulnerable to district charges of insubordination—and yet she looked these officials squarely in the eye, shook their hands, and spoke with an evenness that belied any uncertainties she may have had.

After a quick exchange of pleasantries, we got down to business. The superintendent told us his visit to our school represented a good-faith effort to start a dialogue with teachers. He told us that many teachers in Seattle used the MAP test and found it useful. He explained that in schools where the teachers took the test seriously, the kids did too, and the results were therefore more beneficial. He also told us that the best way to handle this situation was for teachers to participate in a newly formed district task force that would evaluate the MAP test and release a recommendation in the spring. Until then, he recommended we continue administering the MAP and revisit the question in the spring.

When he finished, our team of highly trained educators used our pedagogical expertise in an attempt to explain why the MAP test was an inappropriate instrument for assessing our students. We knew Superintendent

Banda was not responsible for selecting or purchasing the MAP test for Seattle, and as the new leader of our school district, we understood he probably
was not fully aware of the sordid history and many shortcomings of this
exam. We truly hoped our lesson plan for that meeting would help scaffold
an understanding of why he should "scrap the MAP," as our rally chant went.

Jessica Griffin began our lesson by explaining how the MAP was not
aligned to her curriculum and tested students on concepts she had not taught
because they were beyond the scope of the course. Utilizing her mathematical
expertise, Jessica then explained what it meant that the MAP had a higher
margin of error than expected gains at the high school level: it rendered the
test statistically invalid. She then checked for understanding by asking what
the superintendent's team thought of her criticisms of the test. There was no
response. Mallory, whose PhD in education focused on the literacy of urban
youth, explained the value of the formative reading skills assessment she used
instead of the MAP. She voiced the critical insight that even if MAP data were
a useful diagnostic tool, teachers do not receive any more resources to help
the students who demonstrate deficiencies.

Mr. Banda diligently inscribed our objections to the test on his yellow
legal pad, yet neither he nor the two district officials flanking him had a single
direct response to any of our critiques. At this point, I realized our visitors
were not really engaging with the "lesson" we had prepared on quality assessment, and if this class period were going to be salvaged, our only hope
was to employ an old teacher trick: the attention grabber. "Respectfully, you
are at a critical moment in your career," I said.

> You are new to this district and the decision you make in the next twenty-
> four hours will have a profound effect on your legacy in this school district. If
> you decide to carry out your plan to require administrators to remove students
> from our classrooms and take them to the computer lab, you will have made
> your choice to side with the corporate education reformers, some of the
> wealthiest people the world has ever known. They want the public schools to
> use standardized testing to evaluate teachers. Or you can cancel that plan and
> decide to stand with the unanimous vote of the teachers of Garfield High
> School, the unanimous vote of the student body government of Garfield High
> School, and the unanimous vote of the PTSA of Garfield High School.

I noticed as I spoke that Superintendent Banda rolled his pen back and
forth between his thumb and pointer finger with an increasing pressure that

slowed its revolution, no doubt a technique he employed to decelerate his rising temper. Under normal circumstances I am opposed to extrinsic motivators in education and I am a very strong proponent of fostering intrinsic motivation, but at that moment I got desperate and made this offer: "If you side with us, when CNN comes to interview us for our national day of action in support of the boycott, we would be proud to say that we have a real educational leader here in Seattle." Those words brought the meeting to a quick close as Mr. Banda thanked us for our time and moved to principal Ted Howard's office for a closed-door meeting.

From the beginning, the Garfield High School faculty had been impressed with Principal Howard's thoughtful approach to the boycott and his true understanding of our concerns. We also knew that he and other administrators were under immense pressure from the school district to make the boycott end. We hoped that behind that door plans were not being made to sanction any of us, but our true fear was that the school district had found the Achilles' heel of our effort and would successfully circumvent our boycott. If the MAP were successfully given to students by the administration, the lesson people would draw around the country would be that you can attempt to boycott a test, but in the end the test-pushers are too powerful.

At this point, if the boycott were to succeed, students—with the support of their parents—would have to go beyond a vote of support and become active participants. It was then that our social movement really caught fire. I had only read and taught about these moments in history, but I'd never experienced one myself. My parents had talked about their involvement in protesting the US war in Vietnam, the civil rights movement, and working to end apartheid in South Africa, but I had often wondered if I would be limited to teaching about mass struggles rather than participating in one.

Students, on their own initiative, produced a flyer that declared their right to refuse to take the test. Juniors and seniors—even those with the well-documented and seriously debilitating disease known as "senioritis"— got to school early and distributed the broadside to their younger classmates as they arrived. The PTSA simultaneously notified parents of their right to opt children out of the test. Emails were sent, phone calls were made, and the very day after our meeting with the superintendent, dozens of parents sent opt-out letters in opposition to the misuse and overuse of standardized testing.

Coerced administrators, however reluctantly, entered classrooms to read off lists of students who were to accompany them to the library to take the MAP, some for the second time this year (the third round of testing was scheduled for spring). Many students refused to leave their seats. They were enacting a sit-in in their own classrooms, exercising the right to refuse to be reduced to a test score. Other students marched off to the computer lab, only to express their creative defiance by repeatedly hitting the "A" key, completing the test in mere seconds and thus rendering their test scores invalid.

## Suspend the Test, Not the Teachers

In the midst of this collective defiance we organized a national day of action to support Seattle's MAP test boycott on February 6, 2013. We were overwhelmed by the show of solidarity. The Seattle NAACP held a press conference in solidarity with the MAP boycott, and James Bible, then the Seattle/King County president of the NAACP, joined rallying Garfield teachers to proclaim that the MAP test was part of exacerbating racial disparities because of its use as the gatekeeper to the advanced placement program that enrolled white students disproportionately as compared with students of color. Teachers at Berkeley High School in California held a lunchtime rally to support the MAP boycott and to speak out against the abuses of standardized testing. In Chicago, a parent organization called More Than a Score marked the day of action by petitioning parents at some thirty different schools to opt their children out of standardized tests. The student unions of Portland held a press conference to express their solidarity with the MAP boycott and assert the right of students to refuse to take standardized exams. Letters of solidarity and pictures of teachers who had assembled with "Scrap the MAP" signs came flooding in from around the nation. The presidents of the nation's two major teachers' unions, Denis Van Rokel of the National Education Association and Randi Weingarten of the American Federation of Teachers, sent letters in support of our boycott. I never felt so proud to be a union member. In concert with our day of action, we organized a mass email and phone call campaign to demand the Seattle School District "suspend the test, not the teachers"—and the superintendent's office was so flooded with calls that the greeting message for the district had to be changed to direct people to a newly created voicemail account for those callers with "questions about MAP testing."

# Education Spring

After successfully boycotting the MAP test in the winter, we had to gear up for another boycott during the third round of testing in the spring. If the district sensed the movement was petering out, the threat of consequences would become all the more real. We redoubled our efforts.

The district's task force to review the MAP got under way with little representation by actual educators. Meanwhile, a "shadow" MAP review organization was formed, led by two great Seattle teachers, Gerardine Carroll and Liza Campbell. Their Teacher Work Group on Assessment included more than twenty teachers who developed guidelines called "Markers of Quality Assessment." These markers defined authentic assessments as those that reflect actual student knowledge and learning, not just test-taking skills; are educational in and of themselves; are free of gender, class, and racial bias; are differentiated to meet students' needs; allow students opportunities to go back and improve; and undergo regular evaluation and revision by educators. The Teacher Work Group on Assessment concluded, "Quality assessments, at their base, must integrate with classroom curriculum, measure student growth toward standards achievement, and take the form of performance tasks. These tasks, taken as a whole, should replace the MAP because they grow from classroom work, are rigorously evaluated and respect true learning."

Later that spring, in celebration of May Day, International Worker's Day, the Scrap the MAP citywide coalition called for an international day of solidarity with the boycott. We received correspondences of support from parents, students, teachers, and labor unions from around the world, including Japan, Australia, Canada, Mexico, the United Kingdom, and communities across the United States.

We were emboldened as reports from around the country rolled in of people taking independent actions in opposition to their own standardized tests. We read of students walking out against the tests in Chicago. We learned of a parent Facebook page for Long Island, New York, that quickly garnered some eight thousand members, helping ignite an opt-out movement in that region. We heard about more than ten thousand parents, students, and educators in Texas marching in opposition to the then fifteen state-required standardized tests their students needed to graduate.

Even though I was thoroughly sleep deprived with a newborn baby at home, it was honestly a pleasure to get up early in the morning, check the education news headlines from around the country, and get to work to talk to my coworkers about our latest plans and the newest acts of resistance from around the country. Moreover, I had never been so engrossed in my lesson plans as I was that spring. As my AP US history class lessons engaged the 1950s and the era of the civil rights movement, the students approached the days' lessons with an uncommon urgency. Our reenactment of a debate between various constituencies of the Black population in Montgomery, Alabama, about whether to go through with the boycott of the segregated bus system took on an entirely new meaning from any civil rights lesson I had taught before. The passion and detail of the students' plea to their 1950s classmates to refuse to ride on those buses was something that just cannot be faked. My students were participating in their own boycott in a struggle for social justice, and this hands-on education brought to life for them struggles I was trying to teach them about from the past.

On the afternoon of May 13, at 2:06 pm, I was entering an assignment into my computer during the final period when a ping rang out from my computer, informing me of an incoming email. I spied a letter from the superintendent. I clicked it open and scanned the message. More platitudes about doing what's best for kids. But then, buried in the middle of the email there was one short sentence that caught my eye: "MAP will be optional for high schools for the 2013–2014 school year." I stood to my feet and yelled out, right there in front of the students, pumping my fist in the air, "We won! We scrapped the MAP!" I did nothing to attempt to regain order in the classroom for the last minutes of class. Students began whooping and spontaneous celebrations broke out as the news traveled that we had scored a historic victory over an illegitimate test. The only thing that tempered our exuberance was the knowledge that middle and elementary schools would still have to struggle to eliminate the test.

Our collective action not only produced a victory for the boycott of the MAP, it also transformed the culture of our school. Students and parents came to view teachers not as the maligned villains in the corporate drama about education quality so often portrayed in the media but as heroes willing to risk their jobs to improve education. Teachers could see in practice that students were not simply naïve youth who whose minds needed filling with our knowledge but powerful allies with ideas, convictions, and formidable capacities of their own. Teachers, too, saw each other anew, as they were now regularly escaping the usual isolation of their own classrooms and conversing about everything from the boycott to public education policy and advice about an upcoming unit. In my three years teaching at Garfield and during my four years as a Garfield student, I had never felt the school so alive with purpose.

## Possibilities

After I was done stammering through my introduction to the media at our January 9, 2013, press conference, others began sharing their stories. Kris McBride explained how the MAP did not align with the state standards, stating that when ninth-grade algebra students at Garfield take the math test, "It's filled with geometry, it's filled with probability and statistics, and other things that aren't part of the curriculum at all." My confidence in our action grew as Kris spoke, because, I thought, if the testing coordinator herself is spearheading this test boycott, we just might be able to pull this off. Next, Kit McCormick told how she was not allowed to see what's on the test, so she could not prepare the students to do their best. I winced when Kit said she was supposed to take her students for MAP testing the previous Wednesday, but she had already refused. I worried that her words could allow the district to single her out as a teacher who had already been insubordinate, discipline her, and then use her as an example to prevent the unity of our staff. My mind drifted from her address as I began to fixate on the numerous ways our staff could be vulnerable to attack and disquiet seized my nerves again. As cameras flashed, I tuned back into Kit's remarks as she continued, "I just see no use for it at all. And so I'm not going to do it. But I'd be happy to have my students evaluated in a way that would be meaningful for both them and me." Kit's self-assurance caught me off guard. I knew we had all voted to reject this test, but there was no way I could have known the staff would rise with such poise and determination.

Then, Mario Shaunette rose and approached the podium. He began speaking, deliberately pronouncing each impassioned word. "I work hard to try to build up the confidence of my students that they can be good at math." His unhurried pace then slowed to a full stop when his emotions swelled, disrupted his composure, and he fought to hold back tears. He then continued,

> Three times a year we have tests set up that make students feel dumb. And then we have to undo that. They feel like they should have known the answer. And they feel stupid. . . . Because the MAP tests students on things not in the curriculum. And then we have to undo that. It's not an accurate measure of what they can do, so they don't put in the effort. Absolutely we believe our students should be tested. We're all for that, and we do testing on a daily basis. But, if I don't step up now, and say this is a harmful test, who will? I'm teaching them by my example: I'm taking charge of what I do here.

Leaning into the microphone, as if to communicate to the assembled media not to lose these words in the editing room, Mario said of his students, "I'm teaching them that when there are things like that that are going on that are improper, that are incorrect. . . " He paused, looked down, shook his head and then, lifting his chin and looking directly into the eyes of one reporter, continued with his statement, "you have to step up and say something about it. . . . I hope everybody that has to administer a flawed test refuses."

# 2.
# DEAR BRANDON:
## AN OPEN LETTER TO A STUDENT ON WHAT THE MAP BOYCOTT MEANT TO ME
### Mallory Clarke

Dear Brandon,

I'm writing to let you know about the huge thing that happened to us at your alma mater, Garfield High, and to tell you about the role you played in making it happen. But first I want to start with an apology. I did something to you that I regret. You'll remember you were a senior in my reading class. It was the first year of the district's Measures of Academic Progress (MAP) test, and I was required to escort you to the computer lab so you could spend hours in front of a screen punching buttons in answer to test questions. I suspected the exercise was a waste of time. I knew I didn't need the test results and wouldn't be using them. As you know, you were tested daily in my classroom. Still, I was cowardly and allowed the district to decide how those precious hours of yours would be spent. Your senior year was your last chance to become a proficient reader before heading off to college, and brilliant as you are, it was taking you more time than the average student to finish the reading program.

If you had stayed in my classroom, I know you could have made significant gains in reading. Instead, I let your time go to waste. I don't know how your first year in college went, or even whether you were able to finish it, but I have thought many times since you graduated that I didn't do everything I could have to prepare you for the demands of your first college year.

If I had it to do over again, I would have simply kept you all in class. You are one of the important reasons I joined the MAP test boycott at Garfield last year, Brandon.

In the years after your class, I quietly failed to interrupt the learning in my classroom by refusing to take students to the testing lab. By that time, the district had informed us the MAP was invalid at the high school level, anyway. Remember Kris McBride? She was a math teacher, and then she became the testing coordinator. Last fall, she informed me that, given the new reporting procedures for the MAP test, I couldn't just quietly boycott the test anymore. I realized to continue my nonparticipation I'd have to do so publicly. Kris knew of one other teacher who had similar opinions, Adam Gish, in the LA department, and I hoped we could find at least one more to stand up with us. As stalwart as Adam was, I didn't want us to stand alone. I had heard stories of other teachers in the district taking similar solitary stands in the past, and they suffered bitter outcomes. Kris and I split the names of "tested subjects" teachers who would be required to administer the MAP and went off to contact our lists. Every teacher we talked to agreed to boycott with us—some enthusiastically, some reluctantly, and some only after serious reflection. We were surprised and gratified. Each teacher we spoke with told multiple stories of students harmed, indignities endured, and precious time wasted.

Many of us had voiced our opposition and been ignored. Our beloved librarian Janet Woodward had a disciplinary letter in her personnel file for talking to students about the test and posting videos of their varied opinions. The district conducted a survey of teacher views of the MAP, but results had been suppressed. Staff agreed we faced few choices if we wanted to be heard. By Friday before winter break, all twenty-four "tested subjects" teachers had agreed to boycott the test. I'll tell you, Brandon, I was so nervous and scared, but I was also excited and hopeful. Next I contacted Jesse Hagopian, one of our union reps (a Bulldog from the Garfield class of 1997 himself), to report what we were doing. I was pleased to see his enthusiastic response when I asked for his support. By the faculty meeting the following Wednesday, nearly 100 percent of the staff voted to support the boycott.

Then things began to happen. There was no more kidding around; this was serious. Were our jobs in jeopardy? Would this damage our careers? We had a new superintendent, and no one knew how he might respond.

We decided we needed a steering committee to lead the boycott, and I agreed to run. I had been stifling a growing feeling of frustration and helplessness in the face of a slow-motion tsunami of education policy that was hurting my students and my work life. Corporations and conservative foundations were creating policy that just didn't make any sense if you were a teacher or a parent. Did you know my daughter attended Garfield, too? Each time I was faced with one of their changes in our school, puzzling out the logic of it led me to discover that private individuals or companies were getting an awful lot of public money shifted to their bank accounts. The MAP test was the last straw for me.

For lack of funds, the district had just canceled summer school and night school—the only ways for struggling students to get a second chance to make up lost credits. Somehow, there were millions of dollars available for a test to evaluate teachers that even the test makers said we weren't supposed to use for that purpose. On top of all this, my profession seemed to be the popular spot to place blame for everything from lowered lifetime income to high crime statistics. I am very proud of the job I do in my classroom for students like you, Brandon. I think the results I get are impressive. My reading program can move students who come in reading at fourth-grade level or below to grade-level reading within a year or less. Yet every time I opened a newspaper or clicked on a link, someone was maligning my colleagues and me as lazy and incompetent. I'm not stupid, so I can figure out teacher-bashing serves the purpose of undermining our ability to protect schools from the incursion of profit motives. What might be even worse, though, is that the teacher blaming seemed to be distracting our attention from the real work of closing the achievement gap. Unfortunately, knowing it was a purposeful strategy didn't make it any less personally insulting.

The collected heat from all these insults created a steam engine effect inside my chest. I had to do something or explode. I joined the steering committee and then helped to start the citywide Scrap the MAP committee.

Jess Griffin, a math teacher on the steering committee, spearheaded creating a subgroup of all the teachers in "tested subjects": math, special education, English language development, and language arts. These were the teachers who faced losing our jobs or other disciplinary action. She dubbed us "The Necks" since we were the ones sticking our necks out. We met to talk over options and to decide the question of whether or not to continue the boycott at each turn of events. Some of us were older, more experienced teachers who mostly felt confident about keeping our jobs. We cracked jokes, traded wild ideas for boycott strategies, and kept our spirits up. I relied on Kit McCormick in particular. She was brilliant and hilarious. Some Necks were younger first-year teachers supporting young families. These families were living closer to the edge and felt the potential loss more sharply. Part of the job of the Necks group was to talk things through when we got nervous, listen to the younger teachers, and bolster our collective resolve.

When the existence of the Necks group was announced to the entire faculty, Wayne Miller, our Latin teacher, suggested nontested-subject teachers and staff would form a group called "The Backs" because they had our backs. I almost wept. Until that meeting, I had been seriously considering an offer of work in another school. Now I felt a part of something genuinely irreplaceable. Over the course of the next few months the support of the Backs was smart and unwavering. Jerry Neufield-Kaiser and Mario Shaunette, among many others, willingly jumped to the microphone at press conferences and wrote eloquently in the press. Brandon, I can't tell you how proud I was to be a part of the Garfield community.

When we first made the decision to not participate in this truly stupid test, Jesse suggested we write a press release to let the world know what we were doing. I was pleased, but frankly, I thought little would come of it. It felt as if we were huddled in the dark trying to start a small fire just to keep our students and ourselves warm. We expected a simple two-sided dialogue with our district administrators. Who knew we were kneeling next to a pile of kindling that stretched from Seattle all the way across the nation? Turns out, even teachers and policy makers in other countries noticed us! Within days of the public announcement of the boycott, letters, emails, and gifts started pouring in.

Teachers and families just about everywhere were fed up with being tested to death and wanted something to do to show their displeasure. We received drawings from small children, dozens of roses, boxes of chocolate, gift baskets, popcorn, and almost daily messages from teachers or parents from thousands of miles away who had found a random teacher's email address on our website. Teachers in Florida sent pizza for the entire staff! Those messages of encouragement made a huge difference for us. Whenever things got scary or hard, we would look at each other and say, "We have to keep going. We can't give the pizza back."

Those gifts and messages changed how I view the world. I began to see parents and teachers all over the country were feeling the same anguish I was and wanted to do something big about it. The sense that it was "me against the world" faded away. Brandon, we teachers often feel we are isolated in our classrooms battling against an unseen "corporate ed reform agenda." This boycott changed that.

Nowadays, I send letters of support to people all over the United States who are doing things I believe in and who might find themselves in hot water for it. It had never occurred to me to do that before the Garfield boycott. Now I know: simple letters of encouragement and praise are worth everything. The more I educate myself on the series of "reforms" being forced on our classrooms by foundations and corporations, the more I need my community. All during the boycott, the solidarity of teachers at Garfield and nationwide served that purpose for me.

When the district threatened us with ten days' suspension without pay, our first response was a bit of internal quaking and reassessment. On top of the damage to our careers and incomes, our ten-day absence would be a larger disruption to our students' education than even the MAP had been. We weren't sure we wanted to defend maintaining the boycott in the face of that. Within a few hours, Rachel Eells, another language arts teacher and I had simultaneously come up with the idea that we would volunteer in our own classrooms for those ten days. Someone mentioned we could be arrested for trespassing if we did that. That was a temporary wet blanket until we realized what a great photo op that would make if we were to be arrested trying to teach in our own classrooms. Fantasy actions like these boosted our morale.

But there were dark moments. I remember late one evening receiving word by email of a threatened act of retribution against Kris. I guess the district decided it wanted to make an example of one teacher whom they could label as responsible for what was clearly a collective action. My initial response at reading the email was to roll my eyes at the pettiness of it all and go back to reading my book. About an hour later, I noticed my stomach ached and my hands were shaking. I put the book down to take stock. Was I coming down with the flu? Nope. I was frightened. I was frightened for her, and I was frightened for myself. It struck me, in those moments, how powerful our opposition was and what we were risking to take this stand. I called Jesse and asked him to talk me down. Ten minutes later, I could go back to my book.

Many times during the boycott, the perspective of someone else saved me. I can only hope I provided that service for other Necks, as well.

Toward the end of the testing "window," the district issued an ultimatum to our administrators: Make that test happen tomorrow or lose your jobs! The administration called us together and explained their situation. They were willing to come to our classes and get the students. That way, none of us would be asked to directly support the testing and our boycott could be maintained. The steering committee met, emails flew, and dozens of water fountain debates took place. Late that evening, after proposing and discarding a hundred ideas (blockading the testing lab, walking out, deprogramming the testing computers, you get the idea) we had to admit that there was nothing we could do to stop the test without also stopping instruction. We weren't willing to do that, since our main objection to the test was that it obstructed learning for so many hours. We left for home, sad and defeated.

The next morning, however, parents and students greeted us at the doors, leafleting in front of the school. In front of every tested-subject classroom, a pair of students stood with armfuls of leaflets. Students knew about the test and their right to refuse it. Students realized they could respond to administrators' requests to walk to the testing lab by simply sitting quietly and respectfully and refusing to leave the room. I have never felt so thoroughly a part of an education community as I did that day. Hour after hour, administrators entered my room to invite students to the test, and students responded by looking at walls and holding perfectly still. Some English language learners felt that respect required doing as educators asked, and they were more likely to take the test. Students were just as good as teachers had been at ensuring that everyone, no matter their position on the boycott, was still a part of our community. Even so, only about one in eight students actually took the test.

Although it is difficult to discuss, I feel compelled to write about the role our union, the Seattle Education Association (SEA), played in the boycott. There was a clear division between the wonderful support we received from rank-and-file SEA members and the lackluster support from the elected leadership. The union representatives from buildings across Seattle voted to host a rally for the boycott. Our SEA president spoke at that rally and at a teach-in on assessment sponsored by the citywide Scrap the MAP committee. Union officials met with us to answer questions about possible steps in a disciplinary process. The president of SEA accompanied us when we met with the district administration. These were welcome demonstrations of support.

On the other hand, the SEA president also moved to block donations for supporting the boycott, out of fear that the organizing effort would move beyond his control. Twice he inexplicably took credit for starting the boycott. Moreover, union officials blocked access to contact information for union reps from other buildings by promising to deliver them but never getting around to it—no matter how many times I asked. Further, SEA officials met with the Necks to suggest we back down. They wanted us to declare victory in response to the national attention the issue received, and the district's decision to create a boondoggle "Task Force on Assessment," counseling that with these "wins" we should consider resuming administration of the MAP test until the task force made its recommendations. We fumed in private over this kind of obstruction, and personally, I still want a different leadership in our union.

Wonderful union members all over the district supported the boycott, however, and even took the boycott to their schools. Jesse was an amazing representative for us, fielding press requests and writing for publications. His wise counsel to resist being divided in any way, including from our union, saved the unity of the school, and made it possible for other schools to join us. I'll take that lesson with me forever, wherever I go. These union members deserve a stronger and less conflicted representative voice. So do I.

In June, the district caved, at least as far as the high schools were concerned. We never had to give the MAP again! But our victory was only partial, because elementary schools still have to administer it. It had been my job on the citywide team to tell other schools about the boycott and ask if they would join. I had met the staff at the boycotting elementary schools and at schools where a boycott vote didn't win, but many teachers supported us and despised the MAP. I had come to feel connected to them and had seen what stellar teachers they were. I was elated we won this much, but couldn't really celebrate until these people I cared about and their poor students were out from under the same suffocating weight of testing mania I had suffered under. Winning the MAP boycott is just the first battle. Next we're going to be faced with the Common Core exam, and it, from all reports, has many of the same flaws as the MAP.

Brandon, you and the rest of the students needing a little boost in high school are not a priority for the "reformers." They do their dirty business in your name and then the outcomes make things worse for you. Really, the only thing standing between you and schools seemingly designed to make you drop out are teachers and families who are willing to resist the nonsense. After this experience at Garfield, I feel almost no inclination to put up with the long list of policies that threaten my school: defunding; elimination of music, science, art and PE; gutting of teacher professionalism; even more testing; outsourcing curriculum and teacher education to businesses. These are just the first ones I think of, and they make me want to yell words not appropriate for school. The whole list is much longer. No one else is there to stand up for your little brothers and sisters, so I guess, as unprepared as we are, it has to be us.

# 3.

# "WELL, HOW DID I GET HERE?"
## THE MANY PATHS TO "NO"
## Barbara Madeloni

## Introduction

In the spring of 2012, I supported student teachers when they demanded the right to choose whether or not to participate in the field test, led by Pearson, Inc., of a national assessment of student teaching, the Teacher Performance Assessment (TPA). When, after months of wrangling and obfuscation, the administration of the school of education finally conceded that students be given informed consent, sixty-seven of sixty-eight student teachers refused to send their work to Pearson, Inc. This act of resistance to a national push for Pearson, Inc., to oversee student teacher evaluation garnered attention from the *New York Times* and led to my receiving a letter of nonrenewal.

In the months after the student resistance, during the battle for my job and since, I have met many people who say they admire my actions but that they cannot do the same because they see "what happened" to me. I feel so disconnected from the speaker each time these words are spoken. Others look at me and see a story of job loss, of pain, and isolation. But my internal experience is much more complicated, as rich with joy and freedom as it is fraught with anxiety and fear. It is confusing that the story of my resistance gets interpreted as a cautionary tale, when for me it is a story of the power and solidarity of activism. I realize that I need to not only tell the story of the action and its direct outcomes but also the history of its development and the fullness of what followed. If we are going to win this struggle for public education, economic and racial justice, and the flowering of the democratic project, we need to tell our stories of how we came to act in resistance.

When do we become the person who says *no*? From the outside looking in, acts of resistance can seem to emerge out of nowhere or from some trait of character akin to superhuman powers. "You are so courageous," I am told. But the words do not sit with my experience of myself. I am often frightened and uncertain. I know that I do not act alone, that others stand by me, that courage is not an individual attribute. Within the narratives of capitalism, which foster individualism and competition, activism is individualistic. The "hero" is the person who acts alone. This narrative not only denies the facts of organizing, but, even more perniciously, conceals the power of solidarity that fuels our courage and brings joy to the struggle. In joining with students to resist Pearson, Inc., I learned profound lessons of solidarity and hope. These were a culmination of years of building alliances and learning from the activists around me.

Before I was a teacher educator, I was a high school English teacher. I had come to teaching in middle age, looking at the classroom as a space to grow democracy, empathy, creativity, and the capacity to ask questions, speak, listen, and be an active member of the community. I came to education because I was afraid that the hopes for our democratic project were dwindling, and education seemed to be the space to save it. During the lead-up to the invasion of Iraq, when I was not yet tenured in the district where I was teaching, I angered the principal by telling her that she shouldn't laugh at students who were planning a protest of the US invasion. My speaking out about this, coupled with questions I'd been asking about what she meant when she insisted on "rigor" in our classrooms, led to a series of observations, which resulted in a poor evaluation. Her comments following the observations reflect a neoliberal vision of education: "When are you going to tell the students what the book means?" "I hope they realize this is not a democracy." "Too much emphasis on process and not enough on content." Without the protection of tenure, I had little recourse even as parents and students across the school community spoke up in my defense and demanded that I continue at my job. With union, parent, and student support, I would be able to return to the high school for a fourth year to be evaluated by the superintendent and a person of my choosing. Though there was every indication that I would be reinstated, I was offered a job at the university before the year was out and left the high school to enter higher education.

My initial dismissal garnered community and media attention. I was a popular teacher among parents and students. Reporters called for interviews. I deferred. I was blindsided by the job loss. Even though parents, students, and colleagues told me that the evaluation did not reflect my teaching, I found myself insecure and uncertain. I had not planned to run into trouble. I withdrew. I had entered teaching as a political act, as my space for activism. But I had not thought through or planned for the real consequences of teaching as activism.

I imagined that the university would magically offer me a space to engage my social justice work at less risk. I was wrong. While there was more freedom to acknowledge the horrors of US imperialism, the growing encroachment of accountability, surveillance, and demands for attention to "resource generation" was having its own silencing impact on teacher education, deforming our purpose and possibilities. It was only a matter of time before I would be faced with the choice to live in accordance with my conscience or remain silent.

There is not single linear path upon which to relate my story. From the time I left the high school to the moment when students in the student teaching seminar sat in deep solidarity refusing to send their work to Pearson, I traveled many paths at once. Together they brought me to the space of confidence and certainty of the rightness and necessity of my support for the students, at whatever risk.

## The Community Activism Path

The neoliberal policies that are deforming and undoing public education are wreaking havoc on wages, job security, health care, and housing. They are behind our endless wars and occupations, surveillance state, and increasingly limited possibilities for democracy. I left psychology to become a teacher in the 1990s, horrified by Clinton's dismantling of welfare and acquiescence to the racist characterizations of poor and working people. The stolen elections of 2000, the United States's nationalistic and militaristic response to the events of 9/11, and then the ongoing wars and occupation, brought me out on the streets and into meetings with longtime activists and newcomers: all of us trying to find our way to stop the violence being perpetrated in our name. I met some amazing people on this path. One, Frances Crowe, now ninety-four years old, was active in the struggle for divestment from South Africa back in the

1970s and '80s, was a leader of the antinuke movement, had been arrested dozens and dozens of times, and was still exhorting us to get out in the streets, connect with young people, take risks. In the aftermath of the US attack on Iraq, I worked with comrades to organize a teach-in, and then to bring a "budget for all" question to the town council and on local ballots across the state. I attended meetings of the fledgling Fund Our Communities and Not War group in Massachusetts. I watched and listened. I stood out and demonstrated. I took notes and passed them on. I wrote press releases and got people to sign petitions. I never did enough—my paid work pulled me away, but I was deeply inspired by the courage, persistence, and commitment to peace and love that I saw in my comrades. I knew I needed to do more.

At the same time, in the spring of 2011, a group of education activists came together to develop Education Radio. We started producing a once-a-week podcast that we made available to local community access station across the country, as well as distributing it online through Facebook and other sites. The work was intensive—interviews, project development, narration, working on sound, piecing together a story, getting it out there once a week. But it brought me into contact with amazing people, both those who were producing the programs and those I had a chance to interview. While I was too often sitting in meetings on campus where I found myself alone and isolated because of my perspective, outside of work I was talking to people who shared my outrage, were organizing opt-out campaigns, and speaking out against corporate deform and for public education.

## The Classroom Activism Path

As a teacher educator my social justice work focuses on raising the consciousness of the mostly white, mostly middle-class students with whom I work to understand the ways capitalism and racism unite to limit our lives and visions of who and what we can be. In my classroom practice I commit to building community, uncovering the naturalized discourses of individualism, competition, and commodification, challenging students about their privilege and schools as sites of reproduction, and helping them to imagine and enact liberatory education. It is not easy going. Many students who enter teacher education programs were successful in school and want to repeat that "success" in their own classrooms; white student teachers struggle to see how whiteness impacts themselves, their perceptions, and the students of color with whom they work; and all of us labor under the increasingly intrusive surveillance and accountability that make teacher licensure a series of obstacles to overcome rather than an educative experience. But my classroom is a place of good struggle, loving disagreement, careful listening, and deep uncertainty.

I taught a foundations course called "The Work of the Middle and High School Teacher." Graduate students usually took this course during the fall semester of the first year of the two-year masters program. The course was designed to peel back taken-for-granted notions of schools and education; to expose the ways power, privilege, race, and class impact how we fund schools; the kind of school experiences students have; and the ways we see our work and the young people with whom we work. The course requires a strong classroom community in order to engage questions that intersect the personal, the political, and our identities as teachers. Sometimes a group of students comes along that grows a very special intellectual community. In the fall of 2010 that group of students entered our masters program and this class. They included mothers and fathers who were balancing school and parenthood; recent college graduates who were excited about education as a space to ask questions; committed feminists and social activists; future teachers of Latin, Greek, biology, chemistry, history, mathematics, and English; and cautious philosophers. But they shared a spirit of questioning—each other and me—and a commitment to listening to our tentative answers. As a teacher I always work to build a classroom community based on trust, risk-taking, and vulnerability. For whatever reason, this group allowed itself to take chances that not all other classes had. Even as we disagreed about the relative impact of race, class, gender, and other oppressions or questioned each other about the nature of knowledge—the content to be taught and how we understood motivation and its relationship to learning—our arguments were infused with respect, with affection. In the spring of 2012, when the students refused Pearson, many of them were students from this class. They had experienced a sense of shared purpose and connection upon which to build their resistance to Pearson.

## The Personal Readiness Path

My experience at the high school had left me shaken and uncertain. On the one hand, I understood that my ideas about education practices were more radical than the norm. On the other hand, I preserved some faith that doing my job well would allow me freedom beyond the strictures of the growing neoliberal regime in education. I was not prepared to lose my job. Neither was I prepared to accept the support offered me. I was not prepared for the vulnerability of how public the attack was. And when I got to the university, this unsettled feeling stayed with me. I retreated to good work in the classroom but caution in the public space of my work. As contract faculty and someone who came to the university on a nontraditional path, I was insecure in my knowledge and status. These first years at the university were painful. I could not live with myself without speaking my voice, but I had been seriously burned by speaking out.

My partner and I spent many a long walk talking through my confusion and pain. These conversations became more emphatic as the accountability regime hit teacher education. I was walking two paths at once. On the one hand, the fear of job loss left me anxious to try to work within the rules of the academy, even as that meant actively participating in the refining of the accountability system. On the other hand, I was working on my courses and with my students to name the accountability system for what it was and to consider ways to resist, what resistance would look like and what risks we were willing to take. In the privacy of conversations with my partner and in my own mind, I feared and loathed each act of compliance and complicity. I felt the soul of my work slipping away. Fortunately for me, these talks led to a deepening commitment between my partner and me that we could not live lives of silent compliance. Over time, the conversations shifted to preparing ourselves for when we would stand up and one of us would lose our job or get arrested. We talked about the privileges we had and how to use them. We talked about working our way through the fear and about being strategic in preparing to live a smaller material life in order to live a more honest work life. That we did not have children made this decision easier and was a part of our conscious choice: we could do this at little risk to others beside ourselves.

## The Paths Join

I was teaching the Secondary English methods class in the fall of 2011 when Occupy Wall Street blossomed. I went to Liberty Plaza a number of times, interviewed people, came back, told the students stories, had them listen to my interview with the critical pedagogue Ira Shor that I'd recorded at Liberty Plaza, asked them to imagine the work of teaching as a political act. I went to local Occupy sites and continued to participate with local activists within the peace and justice movement. Some of the students in the methods class struggled to understand what this activism meant to their classrooms. We considered what we asked our students to read, talk about, and write; how we listened to them; what we knew of their lives; and how all of this fit or not with education for democracy and liberation. And in that struggle and within the conflicts, affection and courage grew.

At the same time, I found my voice and courage in department meetings. The Occupy movement was a part of this courage. Speaking with people in Liberty Plaza, marching to the Brooklyn Bridge, standing out in an early fall snowstorm in Springfield, Massachusetts, watching the police brutality when citizens across the country demanded their voices be heard: these added fuel to a soul already inspired by local activists. When my colleagues and I decided that our students should not have to participate in a field test unless they chose to, I willingly accepted the leadership role in demanding that this choice be given to them. In a concentration with many vulnerable faculty—either contract (such as myself) or pre-tenure—someone had to lead. While my role as coordinator and director of student teaching made me the logical choice, we all knew that this was a risky move. But it was a risk I had been preparing myself to take. One colleague from another concentration was increasingly anxious as I questioned the TPA and Pearson's involvement. One day she told me I "frightened" her. I was going too far. But I, as I told her, felt I was not going far enough—not compared to the women in their seventies, eighties, and nineties who were traveling to protest the Israeli occupation of Gaza, getting arrested at the nearby nuclear power plant, relentlessly knocking on doors and initiating conversations, and getting up each day to continue the struggle.

The school of education administration eventually relented to our demands and agreed that students had to be given the option to participate or not in the Pearson field test. The day I brought the forms for the students to sign and indicate if they were opting in or out of the field test the mood was both serious and joyful. Each student took his or her time to read through the information, to mark his or her form with care and conviction. Signatures had a force we had forgotten. And in the silence of the moment was forged a unity many of us had never before known.

I shared this story with the *New York Times* as an example of resistance to the corporate juggernaut.[1] The picture that accompanied the article speaks to the strength the students knew together. That I was targeted to suffer consequences is not unusual. Oppressors often single out one person as a fear-inducing example. But fear and a single person acting alone is not the lesson of this story. We stood strong together. I stood with people who knew me and who did not know me. I stand strong now with new comrades from within this struggle, including the student-community group Can't Be Neutral, which developed in the fight for my job and has grown to lead workshops across the country about resisting neoliberal policies in education. I have emerged from the nonrenewal and subsequent grievance as an officer of our local union and am running for president of our statewide teachers association under the banner of our progressive caucus. As I work to build an activist grassroots union, I experience again the joyful strength of the struggle. I see the multitudes of which I am a part rising up to either side and ahead of me. Each of us walking, along many paths, until we recognize we are not alone. This is how we come to say no. Together.

# 4.
# THE RISE OF THE BADASS TEACHERS ASSOCIATION

## Mark Naison

The rise of the Badass Teachers Association is one of most intriguing and startling aspects of the growth of education activism during the presidency of Barack Obama. At the time of this writing and editing (July 2014), the BATS—which is what most people call us—have more than fifty thousand members on our Facebook page, fifty state organizations, a Twitter account followed by more than six thousand, numerous themed subgroups (for example, BATS in Special Ed), and are involved in local and national actions several times a week to defend teachers, students, and public education. We have been publicly endorsed by Diane Ravitch—who has challenged us to be the ACT-UP of education activism—and are carefully watched and sometimes called upon for help by leaders of the national teachers unions. Elected officials and heads of the US Department of Education also know who we are, as we have organized many actions designed to influence their policies. The group with the name people love to hate is now a major force in social justice activism. SUNY Buffalo historian Dr. Henry Louis Taylor has described the rise of the BATS as "one of the ten most important stories in the USA in 2013."

Let me be honest. When education activist Priscilla Sanstead and I decided to create the Badass Teachers Association Facebook page on June 14, 2013, at 4:30 p.m., we had no idea that it would trigger a groundswell of teacher rage and activism the likes of which neither of us had seen. We knew teachers were angry but we had underestimated both the depth of that anger and the wellspring of creativity ready to be tapped if someone provided the right outlet. We also didn't realize that an approach to organizing we had both been exposed to during the great New York parents' test revolt of April 2013—one that allowed parents of vastly different political perspectives to work together—would prove to be so valuable in building a national movement. A defiant, in-your-face name; a unique multipartisan style of organizing; a pair of founders that included one who liked speaking in public (me) and one who liked creating organizational structures behind the scenes (Priscilla); and, as it turns out, perfect timing proved to be the kindling for a fiery protest movement that is still burning brightly.

Let's first consider two of the key elements in this mix, the timing and the name. In March 2012 more than a year before Priscilla and I started the Badass Teachers Association Facebook page, just before I was scheduled to speak at a United Opt Out protest in Washington, I helped the Bronx-based Rebel Diaz Arts Collective create a design for a Badass Teachers Association T-shirt and even produced a video to promote it. Neither the concept nor the shirt set the world on fire—Rebel Diaz sold sixty of the shirts, mostly to well-known education activists and to teachers involved with the remnants of the Occupy movement. And after Occupy DOE 2.0 in April 2012, the idea seemed to die.

So why did it take off in June 2014? What had changed? Here's my view. In March 2012, teachers throughout the nation still had hopes that the newly reelected Barack Obama would back off on testing and give teachers more respect and more input into shaping education policies. By June 2013, those hopes had been shattered. Not only did the president double down on Race to the Top policies promoting school closings and test-based teacher evaluations, he ignored National Teacher Appreciation week to celebrate National Charter School week and continued to give his full support to much-hated Secretary of Education Duncan. When you couple this with the actions of former Obama chief of staff Rahm Emanuel during and after the Chicago teachers strike, you can see why many public school teachers felt completely alone—deserted by the Democrats and put under direct assault by Republicans, who in most states pursued a privatization agenda coupled with vicious attacks on teachers unions.

But it was not just teacher rage and disillusionment that allowed the newly formed Badass Teachers Association to take off, it was also the approach to organizing that it employed. In April 2014, provoked by a toxic package of "reforms" forced through the New York State legislature by governor Andrew Cuomo, which included Common Core–aligned tests that were so long and difficult they resembled a form of child abuse to many—ten thousand families throughout New York decided to opt out their children from state tests and start a movement to push back against the testing. What made this movement so unique was that many of its leaders were Republicans and conservatives, some of them aligned with the Tea Party, who welcomed working with liberals, leftists, and leaders of local teachers unions. Never before in the state, or perhaps anywhere else in the nation, had a movement this diverse arisen to defend local control of public schools and fight back against uncontrolled testing. Keeping such a politically diverse group together was difficult, but two groups were created in the midst of the test revolt that were committed to that approach—Parents and Teachers Against the Common Core and the Badass Parents Association, formed with my help by a libertarian intellectual named Michael Bohr, who said only a "multipartisan" approach could defeat Common Core, one in which people kept their core beliefs but worked across the spectrum to defeat policies that threatened their schools and their children.

It was in these groups that I met the two key figures who would help make the Badass Teachers Association the force it is today: Priscilla Sanstead, whom I met in the Badass Parents Association, and Marla Kilfoyle, a Long Island teacher and parent who was a major force in Parents and Teachers Against the Common Core. While Priscilla and I founded the group, it was Marla's idea to have a recruiting contest on Sunday, June 16, that put us on the map. In one hour that afternoon teachers competing for the designation "Badass Teacher of the Month" drew more than a thousand members into the newly formed group. By the end of that weekend there was a buzz surrounding the group that began to resemble what Occupy Wall Street had inspired. For the second time in two years, a movement with an improbable name was moving to the forefront of social justice activism in the nation.

However, there the resemblance to Occupy Wall Street ended. Whereas Occupy Wall Street was committed to an anarchic, hyper-democratic governance structure, Priscilla and Marla, who were both organizational gurus, decided to create a complex structure that allowed for the creativity of the membership to find organizational outlets while clamping down hard on those who promoted positions that would split the group. Their first stroke of genius was to do everything possible to encourage members to use the arts to express discontent with current education policies—whether poems, songs, music videos, memes, innovative designs for everything from bumper stickers to T-shirts—and adopt the symbol of the bat, along with Batman imagery, to give the group a distinctive identity. The result was an explosion of creativity, much of it with a humorous edge, that made the Badass Teachers Association Facebook page an exciting, fun-filled place. What took place could be described as "the revenge of the arts teachers"—as the test-driven policies of the Obama and Bush administrations had succeeded in marginalizing the arts in public schools throughout the nation. Payback could be seen every day on the BATS Facebook page.

Another organizational innovation Priscilla and Marla introduced, with my full support, was to create a structure to carefully monitor the BATS Facebook page to delete posts that might prevent teachers of diverse political perspectives from being comfortable in the group or that took time and energy away from the group's political actions. We developed a team of trusted page administrators—now numbering sixty-one—to carry out this function, inspiring charges of censorship from those whose posts were deleted but allowing the fragile unity of all teachers committed to defending public education from attack—whether left, center, or right—to be preserved. To keep discussion on mission, we clamped down on any posts that challenged the name of the group; on posts that took a position on guns or religion; on posts that attacked the noneducation policies of either of the major parties; on posts that were racist, sexist, or homophobic; and on posts that used political clichés to demonize people on the right or the left. Many people predicted this approach would destroy the group; in fact, it may have made more teachers feel safe to join it, as discussion was generally kept focused on issues directly related to policies that affected teachers and their experiences "on the ground."

But perhaps most important of all, the group's founders—and this was more Priscilla and Marla than me—created a decentralized structure that allowed the incredible talents and energies of the teachers who gravitated to us to find an outlet. This took two forms: the creation of state BAT organizations that could mount actions based on local conditions, which varied greatly from state to state and region to region, and the creation of special-interest groups—BATS in Higher Education, BATS in Special Ed, BATS

Under Fire, Author BATS—which reflected the full array of issues teachers were passionate about and challenges they face. This allowed BATS to simultaneously have a strong, clear, national identity while giving members the opportunity to launch actions and discussions with smaller groups of people who shared their concerns. There is no other education activist group in the nation that has a structure like this—a national organization with over a hundred functioning subgroups working within it. In that respect, BATS has more in common with the ACLU and the NAACP than with Dump Duncan, Network for Public Education, or Parents Across America, although Save Our Schools has some similar features.

None of this could work without a passionate investment of energy by thousands of teachers around the nation who participate in the state BAT groups and BAT special-interest groups. Who are these teachers? Although I have not made a formal survey I would say the following: the vast majority are veteran teachers, with twenty or more years of experience, who are enraged at how they are being demonized, marginalized, and disrespected by those shaping current education policy. These are confident, talented people whose wisdom is being squandered and whose professional standing is being undermined. By giving these teachers—90 percent of whom are women—an organizational outlet, BATS has created a movement that education policy makers around the nation have learned to reckon with, and in some cases to fear.

But when all is said and done, more than all the discussion and support groups, all the memes and videos, all the BAT T-shirts and bumper stickers, it is the actions the group has taken, and its political statements, that have put BATS on the map. Ever since mid-July, under the guidance of general manager Marla Kilfoyle, BATS posts actions for the week on its national page. These range from Twitter swarms on Bill Gates, Michelle Rhee, Arne Duncan, the Koch brothers, and ALEC, demanding they stop demonizing teachers and promoting school privatization to organizing support for protests against school closings in Chicago, Philadelphia, Newark, and Camden; to bombarding elected officials around the nation with calls, emails, and tweets demanding they stop seizing teacher pensions, undermining teacher tenure, decertifying teachers unions, giving preference to charter schools and Teach for America, and rating teachers on the basis of student test scores. Because of such coordinated actions, teachers around the country, leaders of teachers unions, and education activists like Diane Ravitch now call on BATS for help whenever teachers and public education are under attack.

BATS has also produced important position papers on key issues in education policy—ranging from the Common Core State Standards to Teach for America—and members have testified at numerous hearings and policy forums sponsored by school boards, legislatures, and state education departments around the United States. Our next big steps will be organizing a teachers March on Washington (July 28, 2014) and running candidates for state, local, and union offices. Three of our BATS are running as write-in candidates for governor—in Florida, New York, and Connecticut—and scores more are running for school boards, city councils, state legislatures, and leadership positions in their teachers unions.

The explosion of energy this organization has triggered is unlike anything I have experienced in years of participating in social justice movements since the 1960s. The provocation has been education policies so profoundly misguided, destructive, and corrupt as to defy the imagination. But the response reflects the immense talent, energy, and idealism found among America's public school teachers—a group whose abilities policy makers have profoundly underestimated. The Badass Teachers Association is what those of us who grew up in neighborhoods like Brooklyn would call *payback*. America's teachers, truly a sleeping giant, have awakened and it turns out they are BAD TO THE BONE!

# 5.

# STANDARDIZED TESTING AND STUDENTS OF COLOR

## Brian Jones

I'll never forget the day that my students lost their science experiment. I was teaching fourth grade in East Harlem, and we were in the middle of a week-long investigation. Teams were assembled with trays of powders and liquids. Students were busy all over the room mixing and pouring, making observations and recording them. At one point in the proceedings my supervisor entered the classroom and told my students to stop what they were doing. As she held the door open, youngsters from another classroom delivered stacks of test preparation workbooks. My supervisor turned to me and explained that we needed to stop our experiment and immediately begin preparing for the upcoming state standardized tests. Assuming I misunderstood her, I suggested we would begin test preparation immediately following the experiment in progress—since it was in progress. She clarified: we were to clean up that very moment, and begin test preparation. No more science experiment.

There's something reassuring about the tests. Every student takes the same test, so there's an appearance of fairness. The poor and the rich are treated the same, apparently. Every student receives a score, so there's the semblance of transparency. Numerical scores provide an easy-to-grasp gauge of student progress: high scores are good, low scores are not. So it makes sense, on some level, for everyone—students, teachers, and administrators—to focus on raising test scores. If scores go up, that means students are learning and growing. It shows that teachers and administrators are doing their jobs. I don't entirely blame my supervisor for canceling our science experiment. Her action was logical. Our school was populated by students who traditionally have not done well on state standardized tests. Low scores or slow progress in raising scores could mean bad things for students, teachers, administrators; they could even herald the end of the school itself. So administrators are forced to prioritize raising test scores. In turn, teachers must force students to focus on raising their test scores.

The idea that standardized tests can be a lever of advancement for people of color has some powerful roots. There was a time when black people and other US "minority" groups were excluded from public sector employment, for example. Working for the government in transportation, social services, or education, you pretty much had to know someone to get a foot in the door. When civil service exams were introduced, many (but not all) people who had previously been excluded were now at least potentially included. To this day, bus drivers, firefighters, and many other public sector employees get their positions by taking a test. In most people's minds, a test is an opportunity, and believing in our children and encouraging our children means teaching them that they can pass anyone's test.

For people who have experienced racism in the schools, standardized tests can seem like part of the solution. In 2013 I participated in an event at a public school where parents, educators, and students came to discuss high-stakes standardized testing. It seemed to me that most of the attendees were already opposed to the spread of such tests, but at least one man was on the fence. Toward the end of the discussion, this parent rose to ask a question. He was dark-skinned and had an accent I couldn't place. His question, as I remember it, was something like: "I hear what you are saying about the problems of these tests, but what if a teacher doesn't like my child or discriminates against my child? Isn't the test more fair than the teacher's judgment?" From where that man was sitting, the choice between a standardized test and a prejudiced teacher was no choice at all.

I once asked the Chicago public school teacher Xian Barrett how he deals with these thorny questions. His advice was simple: "When parents raise those difficult issues, that's when you have to deepen the conversation." I thought of Xian when I was sitting backstage with a black parent at a right-wing television talk show. He was about to go on the air and talk about how great his kid's charter school was and why he supported school choice. I was about to go on to talk about how competition and choice were harmful to the universalist goals of public education. But instead of clashing backstage, we deepened the conversation. I asked him a lot of questions about his child's charter school and what he liked so much about it. As it turned out, the things he liked were the things public school parents have been fighting for all along: small class sizes, real arts education, science labs—in a word, resources.

Likewise, when we deepen the conversation about standardized testing, we usually discover that parents and educators want similar things for our children. If standardized tests are widely and loudly touted as an antiracist measure of opportunity and fairness, some parents who are desperately searching for some measure of fairness for their children might latch onto that. Those of us who are opposed to high-stakes standardized testing shouldn't moralize with people, or disparage their viewpoints or their experience. Rather, we have to validate their experience and find a way to deepen the conversation.

In my mind, we can find a lot of common ground on resources and curriculum. Of course, I think teacher training is important. It is absolutely essential that teachers be trained to respect the languages, cultures, and viewpoints of students and their families—and engage them in the learning process. But this should never lead us away from demanding the kind of educational redistribution that this country refuses to take seriously. My experience as a student has convinced me that resources are central. On scholarship, I attended an all-boys' private high school. As one of the few students of color (let alone black students), did I experience racism and prejudice? Absolutely. However, there are aspects of my education that I wouldn't trade for anything—the opportunity to read whole novels and discuss them in small classes, the opportunity to participate in several sports teams, to put on plays, to engage in organized debates, and to practice giving speeches. If, for my own child, I had to choose between an amazingly well-resourced school with a fabulously rich curriculum staffed with some prejudiced teachers, on the one hand, and a resource-starved school with progressive, antiracist educators who were forced to teach out of test-prep workbooks on the other, I hate to say it, but I would choose the resources every time.

Our society is currently spending untold sums to create more tests, more data systems, more test preparation materials, ad nauseam. And then they have the audacity to tell us that these are antiracist measures! Of course, all this focus on testing is a huge market opportunity for the private companies that provide all these services and materials. What is never under serious consideration is the idea that we could take all those same millions of dollars and create for all children the kind of cozy, relaxed, child-centered teaching and learning conditions that wealthy kids already enjoy.

It's not just that my students lost their science experiment. Science is about asking questions and learning how to find your own answers. It turns out that's not a bad way to approach literature, or mathematics, or history, or art, or social studies, or anything else that you want to learn about. But formulating your own questions and then trying to figure out what you might do to answer them takes a great deal of time. And when you're dealing with a population of students whose natural intelligence, curiosity, creativity, and brilliance tend not to register so well on standardized tests, then, if the stakes attached to those tests are high, time is one thing you don't have. The survival of my school required us to spend a ridiculous amount of time in test-preparation mode. From that perspective, tests—and the high stakes associated with them—were most definitely not a measure of fairness or of justice or redistribution but actually meant my students spent even less time working with the resources they did have.

When I was a student in public elementary schools, I definitely took tests. I took tests created by the teachers and I even took some standardized tests. However, I never remember anyone encouraging me to prepare for them. I certainly do not remember feeling that my future, or the future of my teachers or of the school, hung in the balance. Tests were just tests. I took them to show my teachers how I was doing, with almost no pressure attached. When I began my career as a public school elementary teacher in 2003, things were very different. A breaking point for me was the idea—presented to the staff in a professional development session—that the test itself should be the object of a genre study. Our reading and writing units were more or less organized around genres. One unit on poetry, another on memoir, the next on informational texts, and so on. Now we were to insert a new genre—the standardized test. Studying this genre required students to get into the head of the test-maker, understand their strategies for trickery, for offering false possible answers, for writing questions in a purposely confusing manner, and so on. And for the record: such lessons are effective. You can teach an eight-year-old how to do process of elimination in a multiple-choice test, and you can improve their scores by doing so. When wealthy students have to take a high-stakes test (the GREs, SATs, LSATs, or MCATs—and the value of even these are increasingly called into question), their parents often hire very expensive tutors who teach them the specific nature of the test. Do you lose points if you leave a question blank? If not, you might be better off leaving questions blank than attempting to answer them. That's important to know! Or is it? Should an eight-year-old learn things like that? Is that justice? And given the fact that it is precisely those students who have the least resources who will inevitably have to spend the most time in preparation for these tests, we have to ask: is that fair?

My child is not yet eight, but when she is, I sincerely hope that she does not have to learn to think like a standardized test writer. I hope she gets to dance, and play pretend, write what's on her mind, and ask great questions. Among other things, I also hope she gets to conduct real science experiments. And while she's at it, I hope her teachers' supervisors wouldn't dare interrupt her.

# 6.
# TESTING NIGHTMARES

## Karen Lewis

The Chicago Teachers Union (CTU) is the third largest local after New York's United Federation of Teachers (UFT) and Los Angeles' UTLA (United Teachers Los Angeles). Many people do not know that it is Local 1 of the American Federation of Teachers (AFT). Chicago is where it all started. It started with teachers demanding the wealthy town fathers provide sanitary conditions for students. When the CTU went on strike in 2012, teachers, paraprofessionals, clinicians, parents, and communities across the nation found common ground with our struggle. It was a full-blown resistance to the corporate reform movement that demoralizes students, their teachers, and their families. Chicago has been at the epicenter of the corporate school reform movement from the "reconstitutions" in the early nineties, which included breaking up large high schools into smaller schools, to "turnarounds" where the entire faculty is fired and forced to reapply for their jobs. Those models and full-out school closures were adopted full scale by the federal government when Arne Duncan, former CEO of Chicago Public Schools (CPS) became the secretary of education. (By now everyone knows that Duncan has never been a teacher, principal, or administrator and is not qualified in any state to be so.) His nonpartisan acceptance and promotion should have been seen as a harbinger of the disrespect for trained educators that would flourish under his administration. All those policies were prescribed punishment for doing poorly on standardized tests.

School closures have never worked in Chicago as a means to improve student achievement. While it sounded good as a part of No Child Left Behind, this concept of closing schools so that students could go to higher-performing ones has been researched thoroughly and found lacking. More often than not, students went to lower-performing schools. Many children were met with hostility because the receiving schools knew those children would lower their scores. School closures in Chicago also had the disadvantage of forcing children to cross dangerous gang boundaries. This policy drove thousands of children as young as nine or ten out of schools and into the streets rather than face an even more dangerous walk. It also directly contributed to the tragic death of Derrion Albert in September 2009, less than a year into Secretary Duncan's tenure. The policy of test and punish is an abject failure. In the following pages, I'd like to share my own experiences with testing as a student and as a teacher.

When I was little, I desperately wanted to learn to read. I craved the autonomy because my parents controlled how many bedtime stories I got. I was sure that once I unlocked that key to reading, nothing would stop me from expanding my world. There was no place I couldn't go—no friends I couldn't make—because the realm of an only child is often bathed in loneliness. My mother, trained in primary education, could have taught me to read, but she didn't. She didn't think it was developmentally appropriate. In those days, we weren't taught to read until first grade. I came home crying after my first day of kindergarten because my teacher hadn't taught me to read.

Reading developed my vocabulary. In fact, my cousins told me later in life, as far as they were concerned, I was never a little kid. In addition, if you wanted to be a part of the conversation at our dinner table, you had to be able to talk politics, current events, and geography. The maps of the world and United States were hung above the table and used to punctuate or prove arguments and were the basis for impromptu quizzes. Our meals were always a time to recall the events of the day and answer the question, "What did you learn in school today?"

My parents never thought the entire responsibility of education was on the school system. They were clear that piano, ballet, and art lessons were on them. They even bought me a German Berlitz book that contained *The Three Bears* and *Little Red Riding Hood*. From the very beginning, I knew that school was about socializing me (some might say "civilizing"), the three "R's," and a new adventure every day. Fortunately, my parents never pressured me about grades and tests. They always asked me whether I had done my best.

Of course, I never had. Those new adventures and new friendships were extremely important. I had to learn to share, to play in the sandbox without assigning architectural tasks, and to close my eyes and pretend to nap. I had to learn to stand on a square without wiggling or breaking out in song. I had to learn that some people lie, cheat, and steal. I had to learn that when I was wrong, my parents would not side with me, but that when I was right, they would find a way to deal with the problem without my knowledge.

Testing was never a problem for me. I did well on the weekly spelling tests (the hard candy for getting a perfect score was an incentive to make me slow down and pay attention instead of rushing to be the first to turn in my paper). I don't remember classroom reading tests. I remember reading groups and using the big, black pencils to write sentences on primary paper. Arithmetic (we didn't call it math then) quizzes were never my strength, but I wasn't terrible either. The first standardized test I ever remember taking were the "Iowas." They were given every spring and I always scored way above grade level. There was a small group of us who shared our scores and we discussed what it would be like to take classes with the kids in the higher grades. Those tests seemed to have the right answer just screaming at me.

All that changed my sophomore year when I took the PSAT. I was stunned when I got my results. If I remember correctly, I got a 43 in Reading and a 39 in Math. The prediction was that I would score a 430 in Reading and a 390 in Math on the SAT. That was way before writing was added to the test. My initial reaction was that there was something inherently wrong with the test. Once the shock wore off, I was shaken. I questioned what it meant to be smart. Especially when I had been told, "You can't study for these tests." Whoa—an entire industry sprang up to coach kids to do well on these tests, because the National Merit Scholarships were based on these scores. But in 1968, I don't know how widespread it was. I think the notion that I did badly on something I couldn't study for was problematic.

The following year I took the SATs and the Achievement Tests—in English Composition, French, and Latin. Unfortunately I don't remember those scores, but they were good enough to get me into Mount Holyoke and the University of Chicago as a junior. In the fall of 1970, I began my freshman year at Mount Holyoke. I transferred to Dartmouth when it went co-ed in 1972 and I do not ever recall taking a multiple-choice exam. I wrote in "blue books" where you had to "show all your work" and wrote papers, but I never took a multiple-choice, standardized exam for ten years. I remember having the conversation with one of my professors, Dr. Bernie Segal, one of the toughest teachers I ever had—because I was under the delusion that multiple-choice exams would be like the Iowa tests, with one screaming right answer, therefore much easier than Professor Segal's interminable blue books. He told me that in order to make a multiple-choice test in sociology valid and reliable, it would have to be so hard that people who knew the most could be penalized. That made no sense to me. He just looked at me as if I were the craziest student he'd ever had. Bernie didn't suffer fools gladly. He was demanding, rigorous, and intentionally with a reputation as the toughest professor in the department. Bernie would not let students express opinions that were not supported by the facts. He taught Durkheim, Weber, and Marx, none of which I remember, but I do remember his walking into class with his tie on backward and a shoe tied to his belt. I remember his discussing what the notion of convention was and how we break it, bend it, or work within it and why. For those students who were lucky enough to have him, may his memory be a blessing. I graduated from college, never having taken a multiple-choice exam.

By 1981, I was thinking seriously about going to medical school, and in 1983 I embarked upon my quest to retake all my science classes. This time I took the Kaplan course. I found the people running it a bit smarmy, smug, and not as helpful as I thought they should be. In addition, it was expensive, which made me think that kids who already had advantages would now have even more. The good news is that I got in to med school. The bad news is that I flunked out two years later, after never being able to master the art of multiple-choice test-taking.

In 1987, just months after "leaving" med school and the longest-ever teachers' strike, I started subbing. Having had no teaching experience or education courses, I was only allowed to sub in elementary schools, even though I was only interested in teaching high school chemistry. While I found it a challenge, I, fortunately, knew more than the kids; I simply followed the instructions the teachers left for me. I learned what I absolutely had no aptitude for—teaching pre-K and kindergarten. I found those the most mentally and physically exhausting jobs I had ever done. Add to that working three nights a week and Saturday mornings in a video store and tutoring algebra—I was quite busy. All this while taking courses two nights a week that included methods and a student-teaching stint during the summer of 1988. In order to get into the consortium summer program (six area universities cosponsored it), I had to take an entrance exam covering reading, grammar, basic math, and the Constitutions of the United States and Illinois. The only one that concerned me was the Illinois Constitution, because I hadn't even thought about it since eighth grade. I remember having a meeting with one of the professors who assured me the university would provide extra help if I hadn't passed the math. When he pulled up my scores, he seemed somewhat surprised. Not only had I passed the math portion (which had some algebra, a bit of geometry, and one trig question), I had done quite well.

Somewhere between then and 1991, CPS stopped certifying teachers and handed that over to the state. Let me explain how strange this was. For decades, CPS was the highest-paying district in the state. In order to become certified, the CPS Board of Examiners administered a three-pronged exam. The first was written, which included some multiple-choice and essay questions, a practical (depending upon what grade and subject—primary teachers had to be able to play the piano, lab teachers had to design and set up labs, and so on), and an oral focused on "How would you deal with?" situations. This rigorous exam had a high failure rate, especially for those not trained at the Chicago Teachers College. Many folks went to the suburbs or even Indiana, where the exams were easier. As a result, CPS had its pick of teachers. It also didn't offer subject exams every year. There was a lot of attention paid to supply and demand, but most exams were offered on three-year cycles. Those who didn't pass were allowed to teach, but only as Full-Time Basis (FTB) subs. There were some folks who spent their entire careers as FTBs, which froze their salaries on the fourth step of the pay scale.

By the time I started teaching, the state had taken over the certification and instituted a Basic Skills exam consisting of vocabulary, math, and writing in addition to a subject test. There were no rigorous pedagogy questions whatsoever, which I found stunning. The format mirrored that of the entrance exam to the consortium. I also thought the test was disgustingly easy. Here is a question I will never forget.

1. The auditorium is _____ than the gymnasium.
    a. biggest
    b. bigger
    c. more bigger
    d. most biggest

There were no algebra problems on the math portion and the writing section asked the only semi-pedagogical question: What new or innovative tool do you use to engage students in learning? Ugh! When I got my results, I was stunned to see that I had gotten a 98 percent on the math test. I kept wracking my brain to figure out what I could have possible missed. I think I got a 100 percent on the reading, 80 percent on the writing (because I was extremely sarcastic by that point in the test and wrote about how excited my students were to see that I used different colored dittos to make one assignment sheet). I thought this test was very easy—perhaps sixth-grade level—and had no problem with increasing the rigor of that test. But here's the thing. It did not make me feel smart. It did not make me feel as if it had accurately assessed my ability to teach and herein lies the issue with all these tests.

At the beginning of my teaching career, I saw how much emphasis was placed on standardized testing, so I wanted to be able to prepare my students for the world they were about to face. I remember being stunned when I gave the first multiple-choice test that came with the textbook. The white boys did extremely well. It was uncanny. I even had a long conversation with one kid who was doing very poorly in my class. He said he was never going to do much work and that he skated by being able to take the standardized tests. He even considered it a game as to how lazy he could get away with being, knowing the test would save his grade. One of my best students, a very bright African American girl, was devastated by her results. I spent a lot of class time going over why the wrong answers were wrong, because I thought it would help, but it didn't matter. She internalized the scores as somehow reflective of her value and potential. I knew that was garbage and immediately decided to make sure that these tests would carry no more weight for the total grade than quizzes, labs, or homework. It solidified my belief in multiple measures.

In 2002, I became a National Board Certified Teacher (NBCT). One of the reasons I did this was to finally get some sort of real evaluation of my skills. I had been rated "superior" in all my years of teaching, yet I did not have real feedback as to how I could improve. I always felt there was something missing from the "drive by" or "no by" [no administrator comes by] observations. I never had a problem with classroom management and basically felt that's how I was rated. I liked that the tests that asked for content knowledge and pedagogy were essay questions. You got to write everything you knew about a topic. In the section where you had to demonstrate your content knowledge of chemical concepts, I got a 4.25! That was the highest score possible, and it was due to the fact I got to truly demonstrate my knowledge. I also spent a couple of summers as an assessor. NBCT assessors are all experts in their fields. I was among a group of very bright, engaged chemistry teachers who were well trained and eagerly worked hard to assess properly. I am horrified that Pearson has taken over the assessment of NBCTs. I doubt it will be for the better.

When No Child Left Untested became the law of the land, a friend of mine got a job with one of the test-producing companies. They were looking for test item writers. I went through the two-day training because I thought I would a) learn to write better multiple-choice questions than the ones from the textbook; b) I would discover the key to eliminating bias; and c) I could develop a bond with a community of science lovers who would support one another and collaborate across the country. Needless to say, the bias training was not nearly as instructive or intense as it needed to be. It consisted of reminding yourself to use "she" instead of "he," including nonwhite-sounding names like Tran, Maria, Juan, and avoiding terms and activities that could draw attention to different socioeconomic levels. Don't write about going skiing or vacationing in Europe. There was nothing about using language in a clear and straightforward manner. They even taught us the difference between "good distracters" and "bad distracters." When I asked, "Why can't we just write questions that have one clear, correct answer?" I was told—not rigorous enough. I wrote a few questions, but the time it took ultimately was not worth the $25-a-question paycheck.

Sometime in 2009, the Illinois State Board of Education (ISBE) wanted to raise the cut score—the score that determines who passes and who fails—on the Basic Skills Test for students entering colleges of education. At the time I had been appointed to the Illinois State Certification Board and was fully in support. I remember the concern expressed by one of the members representing higher education who protested vigorously that doing so would lead to a significant drop in teachers of color. One of the other black teachers (who taught at a rather affluent suburban school) said that should not be a consideration because we wanted the "best" teachers. What I did not know at that time was that the Basic Skills Test had been changed significantly from when I took it. Imagine my horror when I found out a year later that ISBE was going full steam ahead with its plan. I testified against it at the General

Assembly hearings, but my words fell on deaf ears. Needless to say, the pass rate dropped to 21 percent for black and Latino teaching candidates. Hovering around the process were the same people who would push through the school reform agenda that has plagued the state since then.

When I was elected president of CTU, my students were sophomores. The following year they took the ACT. My former principal could not wait to tell me how well my former students performed. He even told me two of my students had scored in the 30s. Without missing a beat, I told him who those students were. I knew one was a middle-class girl in my first-period class whose parents were going through a divorce and who barely made it to class on time, understood almost every concept without my having to explain anything to her, and who could zip through a "book" test without batting an eye. The boy in my seventh-period class, also middle-class, did the minimum amount of work but could pass each test with flying colors. I didn't feel as if I could take credit for the good, the bad, or the ugly. These tests told me about my students before I ever got to teach them.

Looking back at over fifty years of personal experience with standardized testing, I have come to the following conclusions: The tests are still extremely biased in favor of upper-middle-class white males (I'm not even sure what "middle-class" means nowadays, but it certainly isn't the working-class and poor children who overwhelmingly populate Chicago Public Schools). The use and misuse of standardized testing to measure what students know is still a farce, and that America's obsession with numbers, data, and the like will continue a practice that has so little merit is almost laughable. The more mind-numbing the curriculum becomes in order to satisfy the insatiable god of numbers, the more the children who should have joy in learning will come to hate school. And that is the worst possible outcome I could ever imagine. The members of the Chicago Teachers Union will continue to work to change the political and economic landscape that allows the devastation of public education to happen. This fight is not nearly over and it will take us standing side by side in solidarity with our students, their families, communities, and other folks who are on the educational frontlines across this country to win. A movement starts with one small step. Let's join together and take the leap.

# 7.
# DEFENDING YOUNG CHILDREN
## Nancy Carlsson-Paige

I entered the field of education at an exciting time. It was 1972 when I started graduate school, just after the extraordinary social change and unrest of the 1960s, a time in history when many young people like me were so hopeful about the dawning of a better world. Through the Great Society's War on Poverty, families were receiving employment and welfare supports and the child poverty rate was declining. There were intensive investments in under-resourced schools as legislators took steps toward achieving their national goal: equal educational opportunity for all children. Words like *equity, poverty, segregation,* and *equal educational opportunity* filled the air—spoken by movement leaders, political leaders, and the media. It was at this time that many young people, myself included, went into education because we thought this was a career path that would allow us to help create a better, more just society.

I threw myself into my education studies, devouring readings in educational philosophy, history, and pedagogy. I learned about children—their development, how they learn, how to create classrooms to foster genuine understanding through active engagement. I was fascinated by how the dynamic interaction between children and their world was at the root of learning. It was wonderful to find a calling in life I loved this much.

Now, it's forty years later. And I am struggling to come to terms with how much things have changed in these few decades. When politicians and policy makers talk about education today, they no longer use words like *equity*, *poverty*, and *equal educational opportunity*. What we hear instead are these words: *accountability, evaluation, data, measurement, competition, choice, "race to the top."* The direction I thought we were taking as a nation to give all children an equal chance for a great education morphed in three decades into a cold-hearted call for measuring outcomes while at the same time ignoring the in-equalities that children are born into and that shape their lives.

And here I am, after decades of working as a teacher educator, looking at these education reform policies. They are not based in the research or sci-ence of the education field; they are driven by opinion or politics—by the views of people: policy makers, politicians, philanthropists, most of whom aren't in education and never were. Education reform policies, of course, should be based in the research and theory of the field; they should address the underlying inequalities in the school system such as the root causes of the achievement gap.

The focus of my work in teacher preparation has been in early childhood education. In recent years, I have watched the testing fixation and the pressure to teach academic standards pushed down to younger and younger children, even to kindergarten and pre-K, increasing the direct instruction children re-ceive and reducing their opportunities for imaginative, engaged, and devel-opmentally appropriate learning.

## How Do Young Children Learn Best?

Young children learn actively through hands-on experiences in the real world. They need to engage in active, playful learning, to explore and question and solve real problems. As children do this, they build concepts that create the foun-dation for later academic success. And perhaps even more importantly, through active, play-based, experiential learning, children develop a whole range of ca-pabilities that will contribute to success in school and life: problem-solving skills, thinking for themselves, using imagination, inventing new ideas, learning social, emotional, and self-regulation skills. None of these capabilities can be tested, but they are life-shaping attributes that are ready to develop in the early years.

There has been a consensus in the early childhood field for a long time that testing young children is not valid or reliable and often causes children undue stress. Young kids develop concepts and skills over time through a long, slow process that's often not linear and can't be quantified. The best way to assess young children's learning is through observation, done by experienced teachers who know what to look for and how to interpret children's activities and behavior. Assessments are really for teachers—to help them understand children and help them learn.

In recent years, I have sat in classrooms where four-year-olds, who should be actively engaged in play-based, hands-on learning, are sitting in chairs parroting back answers to teachers who are using a scripted curriculum that is aligned with tests. I have seen principals who enter kindergarten classrooms unannounced to make sure the teacher is teaching from the exact page of the curriculum at the exact right moment. In one kindergarten classroom I visited, a place barren of materials and without activity centers, the teacher was testing a little boy at the computer while the other children sat in imposed silence copying from the board: "Sit in your seat. No talking." One little boy was crying. When I looked at his paper, I realized he wasn't ready to write letters. Many kindergarten children are not yet ready to read or write conventional print and it's wrong and damaging to ask this of them. There is no research showing that learning to read and write in kindergarten has any long-term benefit.

## Resisting Bad Practices

When I first began seeing these alarming practices in early education, I tried to find colleagues to talk with about them. But comrades were hard to find. It has taken a long time for the early childhood community as a whole to wake up to what is happening. It is not easy to build a strong, unified voice among early childhood educators. It's an eclectic community—one that includes public school teachers, day care teachers, Head Start teachers, family child care providers, private preschool teachers, and teacher educators. Each of these groups has different experiences, needs, and perspectives. Many early childhood teachers receive low wages and have no union, while others have decent salaries and more secure jobs. Some are almost untouched by policy mandates and others, mostly in those programs receiving public funding, are under great pressure to comply with them.

We also have great diversity in the education and training of early childhood teachers. There are those with graduate degrees in early childhood education and others who have had little or limited access to education themselves. Most of the voices resisting education reform policies today are of early childhood educators who have strong backgrounds in the field and know the harm that comes from pushing academics and testing on young kids. But the less prepared teachers follow the mandates more willingly. Often they don't know how inappropriate and destructive they are or what alternatives a teacher could offer instead. When I read in the paper how a Teach for America teacher raised test scores in a classroom of young children, I shudder. I know just how he or she did it.

When the Common Core State Standards (CCSS) came out, many of us in early childhood were alarmed. There had not been one K–3 classroom teacher or early childhood professional on the committees that wrote and reviewed the CCSS. We could see that the standards conflicted with the research in cognitive science, neuroscience, and child development that tell us what and how young children learn and how best to teach them. Ed Miller of the Alliance for Childhood spearheaded a petition drive to oppose the K–3 Common Core State Standards. More than five hundred early childhood professionals signed it. The petition stated that the K–3 standards would lead to long hours of direct instruction, push active play-based learning out the window, and intensify the demand for more standardized testing. Of course, all this has come to pass. But the petition was not even acknowledged by the writers of CCSS (it was hand-delivered to them), nor was it mentioned in the summary of "public feedback" posted on the Core Standards website.

Many of us in early childhood education continued to be aghast as the steamroller of CCSS kept driving over us. The standards were written to begin in kindergarten, but federal policy began reaching into even pre-K. The US Department of Education announced its Race to the Top grant competition, the "Early Learning Challenge." The competition rewarded states agreeing to implement standards for pre-K that aligned with the Common Core Kindergarten standards and comprehensive systems of assessments aligned with the standards. This quickly led to a dramatic increase in didactic instruction and testing. The pressure on young children to learn specific facts or skills increased, even though these expectations are unrealistic, inappropriate, and not based in research or principles of child development.

Slowly some of us in early childhood education began to organize. We started a project called Defending the Early Years (DEY, www.deyproject.org). Our goal was to mobilize the early childhood education community to speak out against the education reform mandates negatively affecting young children. Our ongoing online survey has helped us stay connected to early childhood teachers across the country and to what is happening in their settings. We've organized early childhood teachers at conferences and through social media. Three of us from DEY wrote the early childhood platform for Save Our Schools and we collaborated with United Opt Out in writing a brochure to help parents advocate for young children who are just starting school. We write position papers and op-eds in which we call for new K–2 guidelines based on principles of child development to replace the CCSS; we advocate for policies that will address the problem of child poverty. Currently, we are developing an early childhood activist toolkit that will be accessible through our website and will contain fact sheets on corporate education reform and child poverty, videos of model classrooms, a PowerPoint presentation illustrating good practice, a guide for school principals to know what to look for in visiting early childhood classrooms, and many other resources for the activist teacher. We've accomplished a lot with our shoestring budget and limited time, but that's partly because so many early childhood educators are worried about what is happening to young children and are looking for support and strength through unity.

When I started my graduate studies in education in 1972, I moved with my two little boys into a one-story apartment next door to two extraordinary people who would become lifelong, beloved friends: Rosalyn and Howard Zinn. Having Howard as a close friend and political mentor for thirty-five years is one of the greatest gifts of my life. Howard had complete faith in the power of ordinary people to create social change. In fact, he believed that was the only force that could move the world toward greater justice. Time and time again over the years, Howard told me that as a historian he could say with confidence that change comes from the bottom up. Not from politicians, but from people. The politicians follow. Howard refused to get discouraged and he urged others to stay hopeful.

I think we are at a point now where our hopes are beginning to be realized. The tide is turning. People are waking up to what is happening in education in this country. There are rumblings—from parents, teachers, principals, and students who are not willing to accept a top-down system of test-based, standards-driven schooling or relinquish public education to the private sector. Increasingly, the media, so slow to catch on, are beginning to cover education in a way that starts to reveal the deeper issues.

As awareness grows, more citizens will awaken to the reality that No Child Left Behind and Race to the Top have failed to improve the quality of US public education and are in fact threatening its existence. More parents will opt out of standardized testing. More teachers will refuse to give tests. More principals will sign petitions and speak out. More early childhood teachers will stand up for young kids. More citizens will vote to reclaim a thriving and just public education system. Howard Zinn said it so wisely and well: "We don't have to engage in grand, heroic actions to participate in the process of change. Small acts, when multiplied by millions of people, can transform the world." I am lifted up by the many small acts I see each day, taken by more and more people who care about children and who long to live in a nation where children are loved and respected, and where not just some but all are given an equal opportunity for a great education.

# 8.
# "DREAM BIGGER"
## Interview with
## Mary Cathryn D. Ricker

*This interview was conducted on January 4, 2014, and has been edited and condensed.*

**Jesse Hagopian:** I thought we'd begin with your own history with standardized testing, either as a student or a teacher, that helped shape your views on standardized testing.

**Mary Cathryn Ricker:** Yeah! It's funny you ask that question because in the last year or so as I have gotten more fed up with standardized tests and fought back, but I personally was a fabulous test-taker. I was! I loved running home with all my school scores from the Iowa Test of Basic Skills and showing them. I had no fear of taking the PSAT in high school and it was probably around the time I took the GRE, started studying for that, when I started to question in the back of my mind, "Why am I studying all this vocabulary—how is that measuring the aptitude I have for graduate school?"

**JH:** Right, I was a bad test-taker, but I remember those SAT prep classes improving my score just enough to get into college.

**MCR:** There are all sorts of places that teach you how to game the system, you can take Sylvan classes, or you can take GRE classes, or you can buy books.

And I'd say in the last year my thinking has evolved about standardized testing—and I really have to give credit to you guys in Seattle with the MAP test boycott. I had already noticed that no one came into parent-teacher conferences asking me how their child could get a better standardized test score. They did want information, either they did have questions about "How can my child be a better writer?" or "How can my child get a better grade in your class?" but never—I would have one parent in thirteen years ask me—what do you think my child can do to get a better standardized test score?

**JH:** Right, smart parents.

**MCR:** Yeah, exactly. And then it was after, really, this national discussion started, kind of waking us all up saying, yeah, we can. I remember hearing Alfie Kohn once, oh gosh, this was probably in 1998 or something, when he was talking about standardized tests, where he says, "Don't give the standardized test, teachers! Don't break the shrink wrap!" And at the time I'm a younger teacher thinking, *I can't do that, oh my gosh!* But then starting to see people stand up and object, that's what started connecting with me as I started reading everything about why people were objecting. The research was backing up their objections too, which I felt was really compelling. That's when I started reading more about the cultural and racial bias historic in standardized testing and that kind of became my Jean-Paul Sartre nausea moment, when I realized that participating in standardized tests was participating in modern-day eugenics.

**JH:** That's powerful—I'm so glad you know that history. Not enough educators know that the idea of standardized testing in schools, which they are telling us are the key to "closing the gap," actually originated from proud white supremacists.

**MCR:** I realized I was playing the role they wanted me to play in establishing and reestablishing white supremacy. And then I started thinking, well, no wonder I did well on those tests as little second-grade Mary Cathryn and fourth-grade Mary Cathryn and fifth-grade Mary Cathryn. They were written for me! You know, they were written to reflect my culture, my lifestyle, you know, my values, whatever. And so then last spring we had an incident that drove this point home.

**JH:** Can you explain?

**MCR:** Last spring we had this incident in Minnesota with a mom and a daughter here in St. Paul that just sealed it for me. If I had any lingering doubts about the value of standardized tests or lack thereof, or of these tests reinforcing dominant cultural norms, they were all put to rest. A friend of mine is Native American, has been dancing in powwows for years, and she's also been taking her daughter for years, so they're both incredibly well versed in the culture of powwow and the meaning behind all the dances. One day her daughter comes home, she's a fifth grader. It was after one of these standardized tests, the Minnesota Comprehensive Assessment [MCA], and they're having dinner and her daughter says, "Mom, I was really bothered by one of the test sections today." And you know, her mom's hair stood up on the back of her neck. She said, "What do you mean?" Her daughter said, "There was a section on powwow." And at first her mom's like, wow, who would have thought they would ever pay attention to a Native American powwow in a standardized test; this is interesting. Mom said, "Well, what bothered you?" and she said, "Well, some of the things they said were just not true." So her mom stopped what she was doing and she sat down across from her daughter and she said, "what do you mean?" and so her daughter gave a few examples. "They called the regalia that they wear at powwows costume. Mom, we don't wear costumes!" She said, "A costume is what you wear at Halloween." And her mom responds, "No, absolutely. That's our regalia honey; that's not a costume," and it bothered her that they called it a costume. Then the daughter said, "And then they called the shawl dance"—which is one of the dances this mom happens to do—she said, "They called the shawl dance a *wild dance!*"

**JH:** Ugh. Same old tired, racist narratives being reinforced.

**MCR:** "—It's not wild, mom. *Wild* means there's no meaning to it and the shawl dance has meaning."

**JH:** Wow. Good for her for saying that!

**MCR:** I mean, you can imagine this mom, Jesse. On the one hand, her heart is breaking that her daughter's culture is being challenged, and on the other hand, her heart is totally warmed that her daughter has been absorbing all that is good about powwows to be able to know that what she was being told was wrong.

**JH:** These are the stories of resistance to tests that need to be told.

**MCR:** And so she named a few incidents in this passage that bothered her and the mom let me know, and I said, you have to file a complaint with the state of Minnesota. And the district started getting all freaked out because the mom had put something on Facebook that, "Oh no, we're breaching test security." But get this, the district had a choice to make at this moment. They could have decided to use a lens of racial equity and look through the lens of equity and side with the child, and protecting the child at all costs, and instead they chose to protect the test at all costs.

**JH:** Great point. So how did you handle it?

**MCR:** Well, to make this very long story short, the commissioner of education for the state of Minnesota personally called my friend and let her know that she was going to have a culture of bias review. She had said all these things had been bias-checked, but you know, "I'm really sorry your daughter had this experience and it'll go through another bias review." And my friend was happy with that answer, at least the commissioner of education was taking it seriously when the district was not friendly or accommodating to her daughter at all. We don't hear anything, don't hear anything, don't hear anything. I call the commissioner in August and ask, "Whatever happened to that bias review?" and she says, "Oh, we decided after talking about it that I would remove that section from the test because she had this Native American expert look at it and the person did say that yes, you could see those things could be offensive to the Native American community, so . . ." And I said, "Well, can I tell the mom and daughter—are you going to?" Like, someone should let her know. She just won!

**JH:** Amazing. What a powerful story!

**MCR:** Maybe it's a small victory, but in some respects it's a huge victory!

**JH:** Yes it is.

**MCR:** So that is some of my experience with standardized tests that really led me to this point of trying to rein them in.

**JH:** I'm glad you shared that. When we spoke before, I was absolutely fascinated by your approach to preparing for the current contract negotiations you are in. Can you lay out how you engaged your membership and the wider community in the struggle for the campaign you called "The Schools St. Paul Children Deserve"?

**MCR:** Yes, so to give you an idea of why we prepared for bargaining this way, if we go back to the year 2009, across the river in Minneapolis we saw that there were a bunch of parents taking advantage of the state's open meetings law to attend teacher negotiations and they were live-blogging from the negotiations, and they were not friendly—at all. St. Paul is just across the river from Minneapolis; we assumed that sooner or later we would have parents wanting to do this in St. Paul as well. And so, we started training all of our members who wanted to be contract action team members—those are the folks trained to be in negotiations, although anyone could come—we wanted members who were actually trained to understand it so that way they could talk to folks in the audience about, well, here's X language, here's what a memorandum of understanding means, you know, it helps demystify the process for people in the audience. And at our very first open bargaining session we had eight people observing us, which is a modest start. At our largest open negotiating session, we had over a hundred people observing. And at the end of negotiating when we had settled our contract and we had won enforceable class-size language, we won enforceable case load limits for our special ed teachers, we won improved teaching quality language in our peer assistance and review portion of our contract, which we call teaching and learning for career educators.

So fast-forward to 2012 as we began getting ready for the 2013–15 round of negotiating. And I had become familiar with Barnett Berry's work *Teaching 2030* and I was really intrigued with the idea of him taking this group of accomplished teachers across the country and having them incubate ideas about the future of teaching. And I had become more familiar with and more of a fan of José Vilson's thinking and attitude toward teaching, and I saw that he was one of the people who had worked on Teaching 2030. And we were so close to Chicago, I actually sent one of my organizers down for the whole week to go help them out—

**JH:** During their strike, you mean?

**MCR:** Yeah, and then another local leader and I went down for two days and just helped. Whatever grunt work they needed, handing out fliers, copying and collating things, whatever they needed, and so I became familiar with their message, "the schools Chicago students deserve." And so it was the fall of 2012 when I went into one of my organizer's offices and said, Here's what I want to do: I want to have these study groups or book clubs made up of teachers who aren't negotiating, rank-and-file teachers, and I want parents, I want community members. And I want to ask them what they want in our contract and rather than have this blank slate, let's use a couple touchstone texts to help spur some of their thinking. And so before I even picked a bargaining team for the 2013–15 contract, we put out a call for anyone interested, using connections we had to invite people to be a part of two study groups, one focusing on the teachers St. Paul students deserve and the other focusing on the schools St. Paul students deserve.

We kicked it all off in November 2012, we actually brought Barnett Berry in to lead these study groups. There were ten or twelve people in each study group, made up of equal number of SPPS [St. Paul Public Schools] team members and parents and community members; and one group had the book *Teaching 2030* and the other group had the book by Alfie Kohn, *The Schools Our Children Deserve*. And they were encouraged and invited to bring in any additional material they had, an interesting story in *Newsweek* magazine or a letter to editor in the *Pioneer Press*, or some legislation coming up in the Minnesota legislature.

**JH:** That's brilliant.

**MCR:** Yeah, and it ends up being really, really interesting. We also hired a facilitator so that they would be talking to a community leader who's facilitating it and not an SPPS leader, because we didn't want them to have the feeling that, you know, that Mary Cathryn, the president of the St. Paul Federation of Teachers, was push-pulling them to give the answers she wanted to hear them give.

**JH:** Right.

**MCR:** So I stayed out of these book clubs and we hired a community leader named Dr. Roz Carroll, who was a retired professor at Hamline University. She is also a lawyer, trained in racial equity conversations and racial equity work. And then because the book clubs were obviously small, 'cause you can't have a large book club, we actually had two different listening sessions where the members of the book club invited other parents, teachers, and community members and students in to wrestle with the same questions. And so we did one on December 10, 2012, that attracted—and of course the weather was horrible—but it still attracted forty people, which we were pretty excited about.

**JH:** I wish I could have been there to hear the conversations.

**MCR:** And then we held another one, I think it was March 2, 2013, and what we told folks in the book club was that they were going to put together a series of recommendations of what they wanted, sort of contract language that they wanted to see for "the schools St. Paul children deserve." They would present it to us in April and then our executive board would discuss with them, maybe debate it. If our executive board adopted it, they would then direct our bargaining team to negotiate based on these priorities.

And so the book clubs asked three big questions of the hundred or so people total at the listening session and they were: What are the schools St. Paul children deserve? Who are the teachers St. Paul children deserve? And then, therefore, what is the profession those teachers deserve?

All of that got incubated and put together; we had a researcher working with them so when they would ask if there was any research that supported their ideas there would be support for that and that's how we created the document you saw, "The Schools St. Paul Students Deserve." It is essentially the booklet form of the priorities that were presented to us as an executive board by the study group book club participants at our April executive board meeting. Our executive board adopted their priorities as our priorities for negotiating then, and our bargaining teams were invited to the executive board meetings so that they could hear them too, and then May 2, when we officially opened the negotiations, we launched it with the contract language that supported the priorities in "The Schools St. Paul Children Deserve."

**JH:** That's great, an amazing process. Can you tell us what those priorities are? What they came up with, and then also, have you ever heard of this being done before or is this something that you guys kind of just came up with?

**MCR:** I had not heard it being done before. If it has been done before, then I probably subconsciously adopted the idea from someone. This really just came from one of those furtive nights where you're trying to ruminate on how do I connect the dots between the different things our schools need.

We had seven priorities: educating the whole child, family engagement, smaller classes, culturally relevant education, high-quality professional development, access to preschool, and teaching, not test-taking.

**JH:** That brings us to the current contract negotiation you're involved in, which you're helping to lead the St. Paul Federation of Teachers in, and I think it's one of the most important struggles of teachers taking a stand against the abuses of standardized testing anywhere in the country. It is an incredible example of the Education Spring, of this new uprising of people saying that teaching has got to be about much more than just testing. Could you give us the highlights of the contract battle, and tell us about how you decided to defy Minnesota law in doing what's best for the kids in St. Paul.

**MCR:** We launched contract negotiations on May 2, and the district ended up with a situation where their human resources director left for another job, and they were without a lead negotiator. So, they ended up really faltering at the beginning of contract negotiations even though we had amended some things, the way we did them last time in 2011–2013 to help accommodate them. For instance, they said it was too hard for them to ready every week to negotiate, they didn't have enough time to prepare responses.

So we said fine, we'll go every other week. And then they said it was too hard to get our issues as we were talking about them, they wanted all of our issues up front, and then they wanted the summer to dive into the issues. So we said fine. We would meet every other week instead, we would give them all of our proposals up front, so they would have all summer to research them and come up with their counterproposals, and then we could hit it hard again in August. So we did that, but then they lost their chief negotiator. Now instead of appointing their very experienced assistant human resources director as chief negotiator, or instead of appointing their very experienced labor relations manager, who also has a masters in industrial relations, as chief negotiator, they hired a lawyer from outside the district, who is essentially a mercenary, to be their chief negotiator. She has no history, and she acts like it. She punches in her time clock, sits down and does her work, punches out. And she, even though state law allows open negotiations, was incredibly uncomfortable with open negotiations. She was incredibly uncomfortable with talking in front of an audience. So she immediately started changing the tone, by asking for caucus meetings, so she wouldn't have to talk in front of the audience. Asking to start changing the location of the negotiations in order to disorient people. She started all these shenanigans to try to suppress community involvement in our negotiations. In the end, she got so frustrated that she finally petitioned for mediation. The only person who has the right to close negotiations in the state of Minnesota is the state mediator. That was her last resort. So they ended up closing negotiations because they did not want to have these conversations with the community, they did not want to have them publicly.

You can see on our Facebook page pictures where they were walking out of negotiations literally two minutes after they started on September 19, and then filing for mediation the next day. They said it was unproductive to have people testify, can you imagine that? It's unproductive to have people talk about the things they care about at the negotiations table. So yeah, in many respects you roll with it. I'm an experienced negotiator with a very experienced team. Here is what it is: we are going to continue to negotiate as publicly as we can. That is when we started these videos, so we could share firsthand the kind of testimonies we would be having at the negotiations table with anyone who would watch the videos. We started having online and physical petitions, we went door-knocking, asking people to sign on to the "Schools

St. Paul Children Deserve" priorities, and we did that online as well. We collected more than four thousand signatures and delivered them to the school board in November. And at the December mediated negotiations meeting meetings they said, "All right, fine, we'll negotiate some of these things," which they had previously refused.

**JH:** So how did you all decide to try to negotiate a contract without the use of the Minnesota Comprehensive Assessment test in teachers' evaluations? How is that struggle going?

**MCR:** One of the reasons we decided to oppose the MCA was that we had to get this balance back between teacher grading and student learning. And the obsession with standardized testing was not helping at all. We knew we had to do something provocative to get the conversation back on student learning and not "achievement," right? "Achievement" is just a code word for a scale score.

We had this experience with MCAs and the things that were off with them, like all the math tests being scored wrong one year and other incidents like the piece on Native American powwows being written in a culturally irresponsible way. We decided that at the end of the day we would get back weeks and weeks of teaching and learning if we stopped administering the MCAs. And we would save money. So we know we started with a provocative conversation, but no one is having this conversation. Everyone is blindly assuming that, "Well, if they tell us we need standardized tests, I guess we need to," and what we are seeing is more and more people across the country who are actually saying, "You know what, I am starting to think that the emperor has no clothes either, I'm starting to think that I have a voice and a say in this." Like Jerry Brown in California, we have Joshua Starr in Montgomery County, we have Don Coon in Texas. And the latest example that warmed my heart is a superintendent in Kentucky who wants to go to portfolio assessments for her students. Instead of having a finger waved back at her, saying, "Shame on you, you're breaking the rules," she has the state commissioner of education who says, "Yeah, I want to find out how we get out from under this federal mandate because you're doing something creative for kids." It warms my heart, on the one hand, but it also makes me disappointed at the incredible, profound lack of vision of the education leaders in our state, when my superintendent's only answer when we wanted to opt out of the MCA tests was, "But we have to do them." There is no dreaming there. There is no dreaming of a life after standardized tests. There is no dreaming of a balance coming back, which is so disappointing because there is a lot of energy in Minnesota to rebalance our approach to standardized testing, and they are not taking advantage of that. They think they have gone far enough—we finally got rid of the grad rule, which was a big victory.

Last year in Minnesota legislature there was this test that you had to pass, a math test, in order to graduate. It didn't matter what your grades were for the four years, you had to get a passing score on a test. And of course the test cut score that they picked was completely arbitrary. It was just like, "Let's put it here." So despite kids getting passing grades, kids weren't graduating because of this one grad test. Finally we got that grad test taken out of the student expectations, and a student no longer has to pass it in order to graduate. We do have this energy, we have people starting to think sensibly and starting to move in really sensible directions. We are very clear with our school district that we want to make progress on this language. We don't necessarily expect them to walk into negotiations one day and say, "All right, we'll take your language on testing wholesale and let's just be done with negotiating." We expect them to come back with something that helps us make progress, like what good argument could we make—only testing in fifth and eighth grades. for example, and starting to put some parameters on the amount of time our children lose to standardized testing.

**JH:** Instead of working with you and seeing the new discussion both in Minnesota and around the country over testing, didn't they just walk out of negotiations when you proposed not administering the test?

**MCR:** Right, well, on September 19 they walked out because it was unproductive to have people at the negotiating table testify about why they cared about issues, including testing.

**JH:** OK, so testing was part of it. So what do you say to people who say, "What you are advocating for in refusing the MCAs in your evaluation is illegal, and so, how can you do that?"

**MCR:** It's the school district that is saying that, but they're not dreaming. All through history we've seen really bad laws changed by people who have decided to take illegal action. Because they couldn't act on a law as it was.

**JH:** Who are you inspired by in history?

**MCR:** My most immediate inspiration is Local 28, my union. In 1946 there was women's union and a men's union. The women's union was Local

28 and the men's was Local 43. The women's union went on strike and the men's union decided to join them in November 1946. And it was illegal to strike back then. They did on November 26, which was not the warmest time to be walking a picket line in Minnesota. They called it "the Strike for Better Schools." Do you know what they were fighting for? They were fighting for modern textbooks, they were fighting for kids to not have to have classes in the boiler room, they were fighting for a way for the district to provide shoes for kids who came to school shoeless. I look back at the things they were fighting for, and they were fighting for the same things we are fighting for now, schools our children deserve.

**JH:** I am pumping my fist in the air right now!

**MCR:** So I would say that is my most local example. I have a number of other examples that I sort of personally use, when I look at the relationship, the friendship that Frederick Douglass had with Susan B. Anthony. They were both suffragists, they were both abolitionists and you know they had these serious of arguments. Voting wasn't legal for either black men or any woman. And slavery still existed when they struck up this friendship, two things that were institutionalized in our laws. These two struck up this friendship, this camaraderie, to fight them both. And I'm sure people told them that "slavery is in the law, there is nothing you can do about it," and "Women will never have the right to vote," and "Black men will never have the right to vote, that's just the law." Their friendship is one of the most intriguing relationships in American history, for me. Here were two people fighting. I don't look at our work to fight standardized testing as monumental, perhaps, as ending slavery or for universal suffrage. Yet at the same time they inspire me because they agitated each other, they dreamed with each other, they didn't stop, they didn't lose hope.

The other thing that really intrigues me is people who are far, far less famous. When I look at pictures from the civil rights movement, I am inspired by all the people whose names I don't know, who are siting at a lunch counter getting sugar poured on their head, and getting coffee poured in their laps, and we don't know the names of those people. But segregated lunch counters were illegal, and they decided to defy that. Sure, they had people who said, "Hey, that's just the way the world works, don't fight it." Of course they did. But they had this power of dreaming, that this doesn't have to work that way. I just think, we don't know their names. We don't have monuments to those folks in Washington, DC, or anything like that. But those are the folks who really did it. Those were the rank-and-file social justice advocates who really started changing hearts and minds. It was that nameless person who walked back to her community, with sugar and ketchup and mustard and pepper and coffee all spilled on her dress. Everyone in her community saw that, and they were changed by the courage that whoever she was had. I believe that "It's the law" is one of the hollowest arguments you could make. Give me any other argument, but don't give me one that is so lame as "It's the law."

**JH:** That to me is so inspiring, that those are the people you look to in terms of transforming American society, and that you're able to use the lessons of history and struggles for social justice and implement them for teachers today who have become, sort of, the "invisible man" that Ralph Ellison wrote about—not consulted at all about education, right? We are the last who are consulted . . .

**MCR:** Not even acknowledged to be in the room!

**JH:** . . . and billionaires, people who have never been to public schools, are the first to be consulted about what changes should take place. And students, parents, and teachers are the last. And so I really wish there were more union leaders like yourself and I wonder what you think the role, in general, of teachers unions is in the struggle against standardized testing, but also in the larger struggles for social justice.

**MCR:** I actually think that in many respects we need to reclaim the roots of our union movement. The roots of our union movement were rooted in social justice work. Our fight for a fair wage was all about lifting people out of poverty, and all about decent housing, and it was about ending discrimination. It was about lifting up a whole community when people, when all work, was treated with dignity. So in many respects we need to go back to the roots of our union movement and look again. I feel very strongly that as the president of our union, I have an obligation to carry on in that spirit and that history of standing up for what is right for students and their families, and for a teaching profession that we deserve. I read stories from 1946, and I read about sugar beet workers who stood up for our teachers, and I read about how the AFL stepped in and helped support our teachers, and I just think that we understood community back then and we understood the Paul Wellstone adage that "We do better when we all do better." I think that it's our union's responsibility to tap back into the social justice work that birthed the union movement. Our history in the civil rights struggle, our history in ending discrimination and understand that there is place. . . . Obviously, that is my big "warm my heart" vision that gets me out of bed in the morning.

I will give you the most pragmatic first step I would recommend for any other union leader—that our contract is the most powerful document that we can use to get our point across. I can fill school board meetings with teachers until the cows come home, and there is power there, but it is limited power. Or it is temporary power. We might get them to swing a vote on one thing, but our contract the only place that we have enduring power. As a union leader, if I want to send a message that I think is right, for students, families, and the future of our profession, the place I send that message with a sonic boom is our contract.

**JH:** That's right.

**MCR:** That is what is pragmatic for me. It's the ability to negotiate language that improves teaching and learning.

**JH:** I've been so inspired by the Chicago union for taking up the fight by building community but by bringing it into the contract, by your struggle, and in Portland, they are in a similar fight. There seems to be a new upsurge in rank-and-file teachers who want to reclaim the profession from the corporate education reformers. I wonder what you think the future of that rank-and-file upsurge is, because as much as I defend our unions all the time against the corporate education reformers, I also get frustrated by some union officials who are stuck in an old model that isn't working in this current onslaught of attacks.

**MCR:** Right, in some respects, I don't know how this comes across, but I'll say that I think that I am a manifestation of that insurgence. I was someone who came from a union background, and when I decided to run for president in my union in St. Paul I had no reason why I really had to. I loved my classroom, I had just finished my National Board certification, I was the district model classroom of secondary English language arts, so people were coming through all the time and I was leading great professional development. I had no reason to want to do this, except that everything I saw, back in 2004 to 2005, started crumbling around me. That was the way teachers were starting to be treated, the way the profession was seen as a starter profession, and in some respects I had every reason to want to stay, but if I don't do this now, then I have to accept that this is what is going to happen. So I think that we need more people, and it's not going to happen overnight for some people, but I think getting involved in your union that is already established and that already has a structure—you're able to tap into a national network and sometimes union leaders who look more resistant to be more bold really just need more people to stand with them, because what I found is that being a local president is lonely. But being a teacher is lonely, too, only different. You don't have a lot of peers, you don't have a lot of time to meet with those peers, because teachers have so much time on task with our students, so it is pretty lonely.

I can't say that it is my leadership that has made SPFT successful, it is only because I have found people who wanted to stand alongside me and I wanted to stand alongside them that has us promoting ideas like the parent-teacher home-visit project, and ending standardized testing, and promoting culturally responsive parent-teacher conferences, and teachers of color who say, "We want a role in diversifying the profession." In the contract discussion I talked to you about, this whole plan, I would have never have pulled that off if it wasn't for people who wanted to do that together.

One of those things that I would say is spend time with your union leadership to find out what you could do if you knew you could not fail. Find out what they say. If they say something crazy provocative, awesome, and off the wall, then you know you've got the right person. They just don't have enough people around them to pull it off. But if they say something like, "Well, you know, I'd like to get us a 2 percent raise and improvement in our health care," then you know you have someone that is only interested in old-fashioned, transactional union politics. The message I would have for union leaders out there is this: don't be afraid of leadership from the members. You don't have to be the person at the microphone all the time, or the person in front of the camera all of the time, or the person who is coming up with all the ideas. I will tell you that so many of the successful ideas that we have had in the St. Paul Federation of Teachers have been ideas that other people have come to me saying that they want to do. Like having our own professional conference every March. That was two of our members coming to me saying that they want to do this; that was not my idea. It was a brilliant idea. I figured how much it would cost, the budget, figured out the logistics, but they ran with it. That's awesome! Members came to me wanting to start the parent-teacher home-visit project. That was awesome and I said, "Yes, we will find the money in our budget to do that." It's your work, and you are the leader in this work.

The two most important things I would say to union leaders is: 1) think of the contract as our most powerful weapon in the struggle to defend public education and push back against the testing madness, and 2) don't be afraid of the leadership power of the members alongside you.

# 9.
# SALT OF THE EARTH SCHOOL
## "THEY CAN'T BREAK US"
## Interview with Jia Lee

*This interview was conducted on May 30, 2014, and has been edited and condensed.*

**Jesse Hagopian:** I know that the struggle around stopping the standardized testing obsession at the Earth School started before your recent dramatic announcement of the boycott, and I wanted to get the background of what happened last year in the parent organizing effort at your school. What happened last year and how did that get organized?

**Jia Lee:** It started with realizing—myself and the parents at the school—what was going on in other schools: there was suddenly a pressure, you know, that this year's test scores would need to rise and that we needed to do some more test prep. As an insider at the Earth School—I'm both a teacher and a parent—I just started talking to parents and saying, "This is really concerning because it undermines our work of looking at children as whole beings, as different kinds of learners, you know, and makes it hard to do the kind of work that we would normally do with our students." I found out that there were some meetings going around in the city with a group called Change the Stakes, with members who were resisting the use of field tests on their children. I went to a meeting and asked if people wanted to opt out of the actual test and not just the field test. And when that question was raised, maybe three hands went up in a room of about twenty-five or so. So I said, Let's do this. I mean what more powerful action can we take than saying we're going to deny the data? So the parents at three schools started organizing against the national and state tests that were coming up—and I think we only had three weeks until the ELA [English Language Arts] test.

**JH:** What were the stakes for this test?

**JL:** At that time it was being used for the promotion of students, and determined school grade reports, with the Annual Yearly Progress [AYP]—which then determined whether or not schools were placed on a special list. School closures were happening based on that.

With all that information I really knew we had to act. . . . So we decided in one week we were going to have a testing forum at the Earth School, and I said, "Why don't we just make this a citywide meeting and invite as many people as possible?" And sure enough we had this opt-out forum at my school and people came from all over the city. We had no idea it would be such a draw in such a short amount of time and that it would spark so much conversation. The forum was called "The Schools Our Children Deserve" and I think it was about a week before the test.

**JH:** What a great panel that was.

**JL:** You came out to speak and we had Jenny Fox, who is a member of Change the Stakes, [Jane] Hirschmann from Time Out from Testing, and Brian Jones, and I moderated. And the next thing you know, at my school we had 30 percent of the kids being opted out!

**JH:** Amazing.

**JL:** But it was difficult to organize because we teachers had a gag order at that point. I guess they got wind of stuff going around; they said teachers are not to speak to parents about opting out. "We can't protect you if there's any disciplinary action, it's insubordination." I mean we got that e-mail and I was like—

**JH:** Wait, who sent that e-mail, the union?

**JL:** It was the New York State union teachers president at the time . . .

**JH:** Oh, wow.

**JL:** . . . who sent out that e-mail and . . . everyone was just so excited, but it kind of put a damper on other teachers talking about it. At this point though, parents had really taken it on . . . saying teachers are afraid . . . this is their jobs [on the line], so they are not going to talk about it. We as parents have to take on the task, and so I said, I don't care. I'm out already. I'm a parent. My son was in the fourth grade and we were opting out, so we went first and then we reached 30 percent of the school opting out in just one or two weeks.

**JH:** That's awesome.

**JL:** This year it went up to 60 or 70 percent.

**JH:** So you started last year at around 30 percent and now this year you got up to 60 or 70 percent?

**JL:** Seventy percent, yeah.

**JH:** Amazing. I can't tell you how it feels to know that the panel I was a part of played a role in helping spur this rebellion.

**JL:** Yeah, it was huge. But something else significant happened, and that was that the organization Change the Stakes went from thirty-some odd people three years ago to just over three hundred last year. This year in New York City, just over a thousand students were opted out. In New York City, school communities are very divided, so we realized we really needed to lay the groundwork and establish collaboration between the schools. So like Earth School, we were open to inviting parents from other schools to come talk about opting out when in the past parents didn't feel they had anywhere to go. They would talk to people and they would hear that someone talked with the Earth School. We heard there's an opt-out going on, what's that about? And the next thing you know that parent is planning something at their school.

**JH:** That's wonderful.

**JL:** Brooklyn New School was amazing—they went from I think five students last year to this year having way more students than us [opting out]. I think they have something like three hundred students [opting out] in their testing grades; they went up to 87 percent opt-out this year.

**JH:** That's great. So how did you go from parents opting their students out of the test to a much more severe and bold step of teachers willing to risk their livelihoods at the Earth School to refuse to administer the tests? How did you organize the teachers there, what has been the impact of your stand to refuse to administer it, and what consequences are you facing or what gains are you making?

**JL:** We had to make a stand and just stop the testing obsession and you know we're not going to do things that are going to negatively affect our students, so we became consciousness objectors. Everything that we understand as educators about childhood development and culturally relevant teaching made us want to save the culture in our school. . . . I mean there is definitely support from almost all the teachers [for the testing boycott], but only three of us signed the letter that we then sent to Carmen Fariña, the new chancellor [of the New York Public Schools]. When we put it out there some teachers were still worried about the consequences, but we did get some staff and supporters, and ultimately three of us did not administer the test.

**JH:** What was the chancellor's response and has there been any backlash?

**JL:** There hasn't been any response. And we aren't waiting for a response. At the Earth School we believe that education is a profession that needs autonomy, and in order to do our work with students and do right by them teachers need to have the autonomy and flexibility to work collaboratively and to work outside of test scores, outside of very rigid standards. One size does not fit all. And in order to provide a culture of engagement rather than compliance, we have to push back against these policies that are coming down. We realized that the things our school is really all about will not be possible if we follow the mandates. I think people understand the need for a strong collaborative culture and that if we stick together with our parents and with other schools they can't break us and force us into compliance.

# Teachers of Conscience Letter to Chancellor Carmen Fariña

*The ongoing wars, the distortions of truth we have witnessed, the widening gaps between rich and poor disturb us more than we can say; but we have had so many reminders of powerlessness that we have retreated before the challenge of bringing such issues into our classrooms. At once, we cannot but realize that one of our primary obligations is to try to provide equal opportunities for the young. And we realize full that this cannot happen if our students are not equipped with what are thought to be survival skills, not to speak of a more or less equal range of literacies. And yet the tendency to describe the young as "human resources," with the implication that they are mainly grist for the mills of globalized business, is offensive not merely to educators, but to anyone committed to resist dehumanization of any kind.*

—Maxine Greene, *In Search of a Pedagogy*

Dear Chancellor Carmen Fariña,

We are teachers of public education in the City of New York. We are writing to distance ourselves from a set of policies that have come to be known as market-based education reform. We recognize that there has been a persistent and troubling gulf between the vision of individuals in policy making and the work of educators, but we see you as someone who has known both positions and might therefore be understanding of our position. We find ourselves at a point in the progress of education reform in which clear acts of conscience will be necessary to preserve the integrity of public education. We can no longer implement policies that seek to transform the broad promises of public education into a narrow obsession with the ranking and sorting of children. We will not distort curriculum in order to encourage students to comply with bubble test thinking. We can no longer, in good conscience, push aside months of instruction to compete in a citywide ritual of meaningless and academically bankrupt test preparation. We have seen clearly how these reforms undermine teachers' love for their profession and undermine students' intrinsic love of learning.

As an act of conscience, we are declining the role of test administrators for the 2014 New York State Common Core Tests. We are acting in solidarity with countless public school teachers who have paved their own paths of resistance and spoken truthfully about the decay of their profession under market-based reforms. These acts of conscience have been necessary because we are accountable to the children we teach and our pedagogy, both of which are dishonored daily by current policies.

The policies of Common Core have been misguided, unworkable, and a serious failure of implementation. At no time in the history of education reform have we witnessed the ideological ambitions of policy makers result in such a profound disconnect with the experiences of parents, teachers, and children. There is a growing movement of dissatisfied parents who are refusing high-stakes Common Core testing for their children and we are acting in solidarity with those parents. Reformers in the state department of education are now making gestures to slow down implementation and reform their reforms. Their efforts represent a failure of imagination—an inability to envision an education system based on human development and democratic ideals rather than an allegiance to standardization, ranking, and sorting. State policies have placed haphazard and burdensome mandates on schools that are profoundly out of touch with what we know to be inspired teaching and learning. Although the case against market-based education reform has been thoroughly written about, we feel obliged to outline our position at length to address critics who may see our choice of action as overstepping or unwarranted. You will find a position paper attached to this letter. We are urging you, Chancellor Fariña, to articulate your own position in this critical and defining moment in the history of public education. What will you stand for? What public school legacy will we forge together?

Sincerely,
Colin Schumacher, Fourth/Fifth Grade Teacher, PS 364, Earth School
Emmy Matias, Fourth/Fifth Grade Teacher, PS 364, Earth School
Jia Lee, Fourth/Fifth Grade Teacher, PS 364, Earth School

# 10.
# ICE THE ISAT
## BOYCOTTING THE TEST UNDER MAYOR RAHM EMANUEL'S REGIME
### Sarah Chambers

It was testing day. I had just read the directions, which instructed my students to fill in the bubble of the letter that corresponds to the best answer choice and the students had dutifully began reading passages and darkly shading bubbles with their number-two pencils. All the students had begun except for one of my eleven-year-old boys at the end of the row of desks, who had stalled and was slouched over his test booklet. I watched as he plucked out his black eyelashes one by one, agonizing over a standardized test that would determine, in part, my efficacy as teacher and contribute to the overall rating of our school. In that moment, I thought to myself, *This over-testing is child abuse.* I cannot inflict this mental and emotional harm on one more student. That's when the word "boycott" first flashed across my mind. This is the story of how an emotion became a movement in which the parents, students, and teachers of Maria Saucedo Scholastic Academy organized to reclaim the classroom and demand that students are more than a test score.

Boycotts do not just happen—they are organized. The testing boycott at my school was strategically planned with a multifaceted approach that included teacher, parent, and student support. Although the planning and implementation of this strategy occurred in a one-month span, the agitation around over-testing and employee power in the school organizational structure was built over a couple of years.

Saucedo Academy is a large public elementary school on the southwest side of Chicago, with a dense immigrant population and a high percentage of students from disadvantaged socioeconomic backgrounds. Because Saucedo is an academy, our students must apply and are accepted through a lottery system. Saucedo is a Level 1 school with some of the highest test scores in the area. The intention of this boycott was not to remove tests that "lowered our school's level," but was instead motivated by much larger goals.

Over the past several years, handfuls of parents across the city had already opted their students out of various assessments by writing letters and meeting with their children's principals. Chicago-based More Than a Score is one parent advocacy group spreading the "opt-out gospel," and began by hosting forums with parents addressing the problems with high-stakes standardized assessments and explaining how to opt out one's child from a standardized test. Several colleagues and I began going to their forums to learn how to share the concept of opting out with more parents.

Previously within the Chicago Teachers Union (CTU) and the social justice caucus within the union, CORE (Caucus of Rank and File Educators, union caucus), we had discussed the many ways over-testing was damaging education but hadn't spoken of concrete steps and strategies to combat these tests as teachers. We brought More Than a Score's fliers on over-testing and opt-out letter templates to CORE's monthly meeting. CORE's testing committee also created a boycott checklist/timeline that included the steps necessary to lead to a successful boycott and massive opt-out of a test (see the checklist/timeline on the following page). During this CORE meeting, the members of the CORE testing committee presented a strategy to spread the opt-out movement to schools throughout the city. We explained that for a school to organize for a teacher boycott, they must simultaneously organize a schoolwide student opt-out campaign. CORE members brought thousands of letters to their own schools and nearby schools that had a growing testing resistance movement.

At Saucedo Academy, we hosted our own information sessions for parents on high-stakes testing and how to opt their children out before passing out the opt-out information. The parents were shocked by the number of tests and by the amount of instructional time lost, which most schools rarely publicize. Parents asked many questions and were disturbed to learn the spring 2014 Illinois Standards Achievement Test (ISAT), which would take away one to two weeks of instruction time, was already being phased out and was no longer even tied to the same high stakes of promotion and school leveling for which it had been originally created. Families quickly embraced the idea of opting out of this exam.

The most effective strategy for educating parents on an issue is to have other parents, rather than teachers, discuss with them. Parents place the greatest trust in other parents, especially parent leaders, because they know that they have the same interests in mind. At our information session, we identified a number of parent leaders who were especially eager to take on the ISAT. Before long, these parents were leading their own information sessions. Soon, students began to lead meetings as well, educating their parents and peers about high-stakes testing and the opt-out process. We continued to have these sessions four to five times at various locations before and during the boycott. These sessions not only helped build toward the boycott but also continued through the boycott itself, helping to correct misinformation.

In addition to group information sessions, one-on-one meetings were important for building support around the idea of a boycott with faculty. During these meetings, I spoke with teachers before and after school, during lunch and in passing about the opt-out movement nationally and locally, as well as the "big picture implications" of over-testing, such as the firing/layoffs of quality experienced teachers, public school closures, and the agenda to privatize our school system. Sprinkled in these discussions was the word "boycott." Up to this point, it was still too early to fully discuss a boycott of a test, but I wanted to plant the seed in people's minds, especially among some of the most respected teacher-leaders in the school. Through our staffwide personal email listserv, I sent articles on over-testing and issues with the Common Core State Standards and dates of informational sessions and panels led by organizations, such as More Than a Score, against excessive testing and guided parents and teachers on how to opt out children.

In Chicago, unlike every other school district but one in Illinois, the board of education is appointed by our mayor instead of being democratically elected by the residents of the district. Mayor Rahm Emanuel's board of education has controlled the schools with an iron fist, laying off experienced teachers, slashing budgets, and enforcing strict discipline on teachers. Because of these conditions, I knew that we had to have a tight strategy to opt out as many students as possible in a short period of time if we were going to be able to challenge the mayor's education policy. Two weeks before the ISAT was sup-posed to be administered, I prepared a union meeting at Saucedo to launch a massive opt-out campaign. We made copies of the opt-out flyer and template for each Saucedo student from third through eighth grade. I knew the stakes were high for this effort—if CPS got wind of such a massive opt-out opera-tion, they would try to swiftly shut down all opt outs at our school and across the city.

At the union meeting, we had a discussion about the implications and lo-gistics of a massive schoolwide opt-out of the ISAT exam. One of the major obstacles to disseminating information about opting out is political. We took precautions to ensure that no teacher was passing out "political materials" while on the clock. We were all to pass out the opt-out fliers and templates before or after school by picking up our class five minutes early or dropping them off five minutes late. The teachers told their students to return the opt-out letters to their homeroom teachers rather than to the administration so that the administration wouldn't catch wind of the campaign. With the signed letters in their hands, teachers could make copies and turn them all in on the same day. This also protected the student in case the letter happened to be "lost" by administration.

Once the students received the letter templates, opting out spread like wild-fire. Almost the entire student body did not want to take this tedious standard-ized test, so they urged their parents to opt them out. Within a week, we had around 50 percent of the students at our own school opting out of the ISAT exam. We set a date to turn all the opt-out letters in to the counselors. By then, the administration at Saucedo already knew about it. At that point, they were not opposed to students opting out because the CPS central office hadn't threat-ened their careers and force-fed them lies about loss of school funding.

A week before the test, over half of our students were opted out of the ISAT. This was a great start, but at this point the other half of the school was still officially required to take the test. The missing opt-out forms were un-signed in part because many parents working multiple jobs couldn't attend an informational session and, therefore, were probably wary of signing the opt-out papers for a test that their children had taken for years. Because these students did not have signed forms to opt out of the ISAT, teacher leaders and I began to talk to teams more seriously about boycotting the administra-tion of the exam so that not a single student at our school would be subjected to the test. In our professional opinions, the ISAT would provide us with no information that would inform our instruction, robbed our students of two weeks of instructional time, and belittled the intellects of our students, whose multifaceted skills cannot be measured by the process of eliminating wrong-answer choices. We also believed that beyond Saucedo, the test was not useful for students at any school and we knew that without the attention to the abuses of high-stakes testing that a teacher boycott would generate, the opt-out movement would fail to spread to other schools. The only way to launch this dialogue against over-testing and to strike a blow against the privatization agenda was to boycott the test. And that is exactly what we did.

On Tuesday, the week before the ISAT exam, a core group of Saucedo teachers who wanted to organize the boycott scheduled an "important union meeting for Saucedo teachers." We chose a Tuesday because fewer people take off after school on Tuesdays and we had four to five days before the test was scheduled for the boycott to snowball to other schools.

The key to having an effective boycott vote is to ensure that all staff in the testing grades actually attend the union meeting, which is a serious hurdle for many schools. The Chicago Teachers Union strike in 2012 taught me that to achieve 100 percent attendance at a meeting of overworked educators, it helps to have multiple forms of advertising and announcements—and serve food. We advertised the union meeting through our whole staff email listserv, posted signs on the punch-out clock, placed notes in everyone's mailboxes, and called all the teachers through our staff phone tree. With the support of our UNITE HERE! union brothers and sisters working in the cafeteria, we bought breakfast for everyone.

At the union meeting, we had everyone sign in so we could easily see if there were missing staff. Team members found others not in attendance and brought them to the meeting. The meeting began with teachers and CTU organizers discussing the boycott, both the benefits and the possibility of severe consequences such as discipline or termination. We had a rich discussion of the pros and cons among the teachers right up until the vote.

Before the boycott vote, we explained the paper ballot we would be using, with its three options: 1) Yes, I will teach rather than give the ISAT; 2) Yes, I will teach rather than give the ISAT if 75 percent of the staff votes yes; or 3) No, I will give the ISAT. Each staff member voted individually and submitted his or her ballot anonymously. We counted the ballots in front of the staff and

100 percent of the ballots were for boycotting the test! The results blew me away. The room exploded with excitement and cheers. Although we had done so much to organize for this moment, I had not known the amount of courage that we would find in that room. The Saucedo staff had pledged to refuse to inflict harm on their students from these draconian tests.

Right after the meeting, my heart was pounding with excitement and nervousness anticipating the weeks to come. I immediately contacted the CORE communications team to set up a press conference with a diverse group of teachers, students, and parents. After school, teachers, parents, and students converged for the press conference. Surprisingly the mainstream media, which was often not in support of teachers or the union, allowed us to share our story without any negative spin. It was difficult for them not to support the boycott when teachers, parents, and students were all in agreement that students should be learning, not being over-tested. From then on we were bombarded by the media almost every day—before and after school and during our lunch breaks—sharing our stories of resistance and hope for better assessments.

The day after our announcement of the ISAT boycott there was a complete shift in the administration's attitude toward the teachers and the opt-out movement. Suddenly, they did not support students opting out nor did they support the teachers' stand. CPS officials met with administration and threatened their careers unless they "fixed" the situation. The CPS central office sent an email to all employees stating that we would be disciplined, fired, or possibly lose our teaching licenses for our actions if we went ahead with the boycott. We had expected threats of termination but not the extreme threat of removing our teaching licenses.

The threats became more real at Saucedo when members of the administration went to every teacher one by one when they were alone in their rooms and told us, "You will lose your job if you boycott," "You will be replaced," or "You will be disciplined." Due to this intense pressure, we held meetings almost every day with multiple people from the union offices, such as CTU lawyers, organizers, the head of the grievance department, our field representative, the head of staff, and the officers, including CTU president Karen Lewis.

Not content with bullying teachers, CPS soon began attacking our parents. Administration members called parents every day, hosted what we called "mis-information" sessions, held one-on-one conferences with parents, and sent home letters to convince parents to opt their child back in to take the ISAT. The administration regurgitated lies that CPS fed them about our school losing funding, which could lead to losing our renowned band program. We combated these scare tactics by having parents, retirees, and other supporters pass out daily fliers with the correct information: ISAT scores are not connected to funding, Title 1 funding is not connected to ISAT scores, our music program is not connected to ISAT scores, ISAT has no bearing on selective enrollment entry, leveling of the school, or student grade promotion.

Parents and teachers weren't the only ones under siege; students were also bombarded. The CPS central office announced that all students, whether they were opted out or not, must be given the test booklet. These actions were intended to get students to reverse their (or their family's) decision and take the test. To counteract these absurd rules, supporters passed out "students, know your rights" cards that explained their right to refuse the exam. These cards proved to be extremely effective. Some students in rooms that had all opted out were told, "Your parents changed their minds, they opted you back in. You need to take the exam." Students yelled back at administration, "That's not true! He's lying," or "We refuse!" Students were the victors since the administration could not force children to take the test.

Yet it was not all victories, and some battles were lost in the over-testing war. Due to the scare tactics of CPS and the administration, some teachers overturned their decision to boycott the test. Every day leading up to the test, we utilized our phone tree to let teachers voice their concerns, support them with expressions of solidarity, and gauge their levels of support for the boycott. During these calls, we ranked boycotters from low to moderate to strong levels of support for the boycott. We split the list of low-to-moderate boycotters among union officers and leaders to call for one-on-one conversations. Many had long discussions with teachers, calming their concerns and expressing the significance of their actions.

The day before the ISAT was to be administered, we held a final boycott count by calling each teacher to ask them directly if they still chose to teach rather than give the test. A number of teachers dropped out, but twenty-five stayed strong. A group of non-tenure teachers—the most vulnerable educators among us, who could be terminated without cause—met with administration and stated that they refused to give the test to students who had opted out but would give the test to non-opt-out students. The administration agreed to their demands. This was a moment of extreme bravery for our non-tenure teachers because they could be "non-renewed" with the click of a button and risked losing their jobs the following year.

Our movement received the joyous news the week before the ISATs that another school, Drummond Thomas Montessori School, had announced their own boycott of the ISAT. They had a handful of boycotting teachers and a large percentage of students opted out of the ISAT. It's important to note that CPS's oppressive tactics to opt in students at my school were not applied at Drummond. Drummond has a large percentage of white, middle- to upper-class families. CPS's opt-in campaigns were only utilized in schools with high populations of brown or black students. We had seen these racist attacks occur in the past when 90 percent of the school closings and actions were in schools with a majority black population.

Although Drummond students were not harassed to opt back in to take the ISAT, CPS had other severe and reactionary actions for Drummond. CPS sent legal investigators to Drummond to interrogate children as young as eight years old to manipulate them into "telling on" their teachers so CPS could discipline them in the future. Enraged Drummond parents, many of them lawyers themselves, stormed the school's office to stop the investigations, declaring the illegality of interrogating their children without parental consent.

After hearing about Drummond's interrogations in the media, the Saucedo staff prepared for interrogations. The minute we found out that interrogations of students and teachers were taking place at our own school, we contacted parents by phone, mass text, and email. Parents flooded the phone lines and stormed the office, demanding that the school not interrogate their children. Student interrogations ended as quickly as they had begun, but intensive teacher interrogations continued for the rest of the day. The interrogators tried to scare teachers into naming other teachers leading the opt-out movement. They asked one of my colleagues, "Was this led by a Ms. Lambers [meaning Ms. Chambers, my name]?" They used this strategy to get teachers to correct the absurd name they created, and say that "Ms. Chambers" led the campaign. This malicious treatment of staff continued during ISAT week and was more than we could have ever anticipated. Walking into Saucedo on the first day of testing reminded me of the scenes from Little Rock, Arkansas, during integration battles. There was security everywhere and unknown individuals from CPS central and network offices. They were extremely rude to teachers, students, and administration, often yelling at them and slamming doors.

During the ISAT days, teachers were given a sheet with rooms listed as opt-out rooms and testing rooms with teachers' or staff members' names attached to a room number. Many of the boycotting teachers did not have their names attached to any room and were not given directions about what their duties were supposed to be. Many of the boycotting teachers had a majority or 100 percent of their students opted out, yet CPS did not allow them to teach their own students during testing time. CPS staffers monitored many of the opt-out rooms and had the students sit silently for hours, not providing any instruction. CPS wanted to further demoralize boycotters and send a message that students who do not take the test cannot receive more instruction.

On the first day of testing, CPS even refused to give breakfast to many of the students in opt-out rooms. After a media blitz on this inhumane treatment, they provided breakfast to the students, but some students did not have utensils and had to eat with their hands. Other students were packed in rooms with between fifty to sixty other students and were forced to eat on the floor due to the lack of chairs and desks.

This abuse was not only forced upon general education students but also on students with disabilities. I am a special education teacher and all of my students opted out. I was only allowed to be with two of my students with cognitive delays; the rest of my students were placed in large classrooms with teachers without special education certification. After a couple days, they scheduled one of my Spanish-speaking students with a cognitive delay to be relocated to a room with a teacher who was not certified to provide specialized services and did not speak any Spanish. Furious, I buzzed the office and blurted out, "My student is not with me and has pullout special education minutes. He is currently not being provided his pullout minutes, which are in his legal individualized education plan. His mother will not be happy when she hears this. I strongly recommend you return him to my classroom immediately." Within minutes, he was returned to my classroom, where I was able to teach him for the entirety of the testing weeks. In my own classroom, during the boycott, I immediately felt a sense of freedom in my instruction and curriculum. I felt like I could fully teach in a way that I was passionate about. My shackles were off. They had already threatened to remove my teaching license, what more could they do to me?

Where teachers had opt-out classrooms, they told me, they taught wonderful lessons of other resisters and activists in history, such as Gandhi and Rosa Parks. The students related these activists' civil disobedience to our act of civil disobedience in boycotting the test. These students were engaged in learning instead of stressing over a standardized exam.

During this time, the support from around the country also kept our spirits high. For multiple days throughout the boycott, we received lunch and desserts with letters of support from across the city—from parents, teachers and others in solidarity with our boycott. Each boycotting teacher received a vase with a note thanking us and telling us to stay strong. Every single day, for weeks, we received letters, union resolutions, blog posts, and media support from all over the world, including a letter from Diane Ravitch, an all-staff picture from Garfield High School (that had led a successful boycott of their own against the MAP test) holding a sign that read "Ice the ISAT!," and a resolution of support by the entire Chicago Federation of Labor. This ubiquitous support kept us strong until the end.

Largely because of the overwhelming solidarity, no disciplinary measures have been taken against any of the boycotting teachers. Yet while we stayed strong, CPS's threats prevented more schools from joining the ISAT boycott. Our act of civil disobedience did not spread to schools other than Drummond, but through our organizing efforts and press conferences, our message spread throughout the nation, our story even reaching National Public Radio and the *Wall Street Journal*. Our actions have spurred a significant number of discussions around Chicago and the nation about the detrimental effects of over-testing our students.

These boycotts and the opt-out movement will only spread in the coming years. To all the teachers reading this, you won't truly feel free as an educator until you stand up unconditionally for your students. This year, I did not have to see a student pull out his eyelashes, anguished with the burden of a high-stakes exam. This is the first year that a student did not cry in my class from the stress of standardized testing. Brothers and sisters, lose your shackles. Boycott the test!

# 11.

# THE INTERNATIONAL [HIGH SCHOOL]:
## ARISE YE OVER-TESTED TEACHERS
### Rosie Frascella and Emily Giles

On May 1, 2014, in a small high school in Brooklyn, twenty-seven teachers and five support staff refused to administer the New York State English Language Arts exam. It was the first time that New York City high school teachers had organized a boycott of a state standardized test. So many factors came together to make the boycott possible that, looking back, it feels like an organizer's dream. But it wasn't a dream or a miracle. It was the result of patient organizing; the anger, frustration, and resentment built up over years of then New York City mayor Bloomberg's testing regime; and a test that just didn't make an ounce of sense for our students. These pieces came together and the result was an urgent desire to act. Teachers at the International High School at Prospect Heights had bemoaned the havoc wreaked by standardized tests on their students' confidence and learning and their classrooms for years, but this test pushed them over the edge.

Our opt-out story really begins in October 2013. Bloomberg had one foot out the door, and his department of education would soon be replaced. A progressive Democrat, Bill de Blasio, was poised to win the mayoral race and all signs pointed to the appointment of a chancellor of education who actually liked teachers and students. You could feel the entire school system—teachers, students, and parents—ready to breathe a sigh of relief.

Our school is the kind of school where people come to stay. It's a small school that most of us consider a second home, a tight-knit family. Our student community is made up of predominantly English language learners, many of whom have missed several years of school (often due to trauma) prior to arriving in New York City. Students feel at home in our hallways. Often, the school is one of the first places they feel comfortable and at ease in a new country. Both the students and the school staff work collaboratively to do classwork and make school decisions. Teachers are passionate about their students' rights as learners and as citizens, and put valuable time into building relationships with students and their families.

After negotiations between the city and the teachers union over a new teacher evaluation system failed in 2013, the state imposed an evaluation system for teachers based on test scores and observations. The evaluation system mandates that 40 percent of teachers' ratings be determined by test scores. The other 60 percent is determined by observations based on a rubric of teaching and learning. With the birth of a new evaluation system came the creation of new exams—the misnamed Measures of Student Learning, or MOSLs. The sole purpose of these tests is to evaluate the teachers. The tests are not connected to what we are teaching. For students, the tests don't count for anything.

That fall, schools around the city worked to understand and implement the new teacher evaluation system. In practice, at our school, the collaborative staff portfolio process was overrun by the need to comply with the new regulations. A team of teachers and administrators was selected to sift through a menu of tests that could be used. The menu provided the illusion of choice—in reality, the "options" were between one bad test and another bad test. Many teachers would be evaluated based on the scores of students they had never taught; others, on subjects they didn't teach. As a staff we considered our options and ultimately decided that it was most important to stand united against what we all agreed was a punitive, divisive, and ineffective evaluation system. We chose the "solidarity" option, which meant everyone would be evaluated on the same exams whenever possible.

In early October, ninth and tenth graders took the ELA (English Language Arts) performance-based assessment exam. This initial assessment was used to provide a baseline for our students and to place them in a peer group so that the city could evaluate the "growth" of their English teachers. On paper this seemed harmless, but in practice it was demoralizing to both the test takers

and test givers. The test was more than four pages of rigorous nonfiction reading in twelve-point font and an essay prompt. The majority of the students
were beginner-level English speakers and readers, and many were preliterate
in their native languages. The test was simply beyond the reading level and
comprehension of our students. The idea that a test so wildly inappropriate
could provide any meaningful information about our students was just absurd.
And to think that we would then be scored on their performance on that test
was downright appalling.

Like any students, our kids wanted to do well on the test. We did our best
to explain to them that the test didn't count and would not hurt their grades,
but they wanted to succeed and feel validated. Instead they were devastated.
Humiliation ran deep on both sides. Students looked at teachers with puzzled
faces that seemed to say, "Why would you ask me to do something you clearly
know I can't?" One of the ninth graders was a tiny, quiet student brand new
to Brooklyn and the United States. She didn't speak a word of English, and
was intensely dedicated to school and her work. She sat staring at the test.
She asked one of us for help over and over in Spanish. She just looked helpless
and sad.* After trying to make sense of the test, and realizing they couldn't,
many students put their heads down. Some cried. The majority of our students, even those who could read and write above a sixth-grade reading level,
scored a zero on the test. When talking to one of our tenth graders about
how she felt about the test, she said, "I felt really bad after. I knew I didn't do
well." This is a young person who has managed to master English in less than
two years, reads constantly in her spare time, and helps other students self-
lessly. She simply doesn't deserve to feel that way.

For many it was the first experience of testing in which they would be
told that they are not good students; that they are not smart enough; that
they do not have what it takes to succeed in school. Testing is a part of high
school life for most public high school students in New York City. And our
students, new to English, new to the testing culture, quickly learn the lessons
that high-stakes tests teach: you are not the right kind of smart, you cannot

---

* This student is one of the most independently motivated and curious learners I have
worked with. She got a zero on the test in October, and her father opted her out of it
in May. I will have her as a student again next year, and am so grateful to work with
her again. —Emily

do well, you will not succeed. For too many students, it is a test that keeps them from graduation year after year—not their ability to think critically, to analyze a text, or do a valid science experiment, just a test. The difference with this ELA performance exam was that it meant nothing for students—it was not a gatekeeper, not for credit or promotion, but only to measure their teachers. After it was over, several teachers vowed never to put their students through it again.

A few months later, stories circulated of parents around the city opting their students out of high-stakes tests. "Opting out" gained prominence even in the mainstream media, with stories like that of Castle Bridge in Washington Heights making the news (see chapter 20). The numbers for opt-outs around New York State were growing as well. At our school, the buzz didn't fall on deaf ears. The school was already deeply engaged in a conversation about how to get our students out from under the burden of the tests.

We had been on the waiting list to become a New York Performance Standards Consortium school for years to no avail. But this year, the talk around the city was that more schools would be let in, and most likely we would be one of them. The consortium in New York City is a group of schools that have state exemption from the Regents exams—these exams are the blood and guts of most schools' curricula, as students must pass them to graduate high school. For our students, recently arrived emergent bilinguals, the Regents exams are the major roadblock between students and graduation. Moreover, the Regents exams do not adequately measure our students' understanding of content or their ability to think critically and creatively. As a school, we have been thinking deeply about the alternative assessments and the creativity and rigor our curricula would embody once freed from these oppressive exams.

The fall then was shaped by two factors: 1) a punitive and absurd teacher evaluation system that had pushed people over the edge; and 2) what the consortium represented—the prospect of creating our own assessments based on the curriculum we taught and that truly prepared students to be college ready and provided them with practical life skills. Together, these factors created the fodder for resistance—we knew what we were against, and we knew what we wanted. Water-cooler chats of opting out became a common occurrence. As more teachers became agitated, the possibility of resisting a test became more and more a reality. An ad hoc group of educators began having more serious conversations and hosting organizing meetings among the whole staff.

Teachers were not the only ones talking about the opt-out movement. Parents discussed testing requirements for their students in a PTA meeting. Our administration made sure they understood what each test meant for their children and what their rights were as parents. Students too joined in the discussion. The student government set up a table during parent-teacher conferences to give parents information about the tests their children take throughout high school, the stakes attached to those exams, and their rights. Parents began submitting opt-out letters for the ELA assessment exam. During parent-teacher conferences, teachers had the opportunity to talk to parents about their thoughts on the tests. One parent put it very clearly: "Why should my student spend class time on a test that doesn't matter for her?" Another parent at first took the position that it wasn't really that big a deal. Then as she talked, she stopped and said, "Unless it's a bad experience for the students. I don't want my child being put through that test if it will make him feel bad—he already feels insecure about speaking English." Our administrators, along with Chancellor Carmen Fariña, supported all parents' right to opt out. A week before the exam more than 50 percent of parents had opted their children out of the performance assessment.

As the test date grew closer, and more opt-out letters came in, teachers began to think about what we could do as educators to stand up against this test. A handful of teachers had already stated their intention to refuse to give it, and the idea was catching on. While we stood firmly against the test, we were also nervous and afraid. After all, refusing to give a test is an act of insubordination that could carry significant consequences. The opt-out movement was growing around us, and it certainly gave us strength, but the movement was still in its beginning stages. We felt very much like we would be out on a limb and on our own.

We also understood that as a school, we were in a better position than most to take action. The turnover rate in most New York City public schools is high, but our school has a staff of almost all veteran teachers and only three teachers who did not yet have tenure. That meant we were uniquely positioned to speak up, as tenure provides the necessary protection we would need from undue punishment or unfair treatment. Our administration is wonderfully supportive of teachers, truly trusting that we know what is best for our students, which is sadly rare. And what's more, they stand firmly against the high-stakes testing reforms that are dismantling public education. Most teachers do not enjoy these circumstances. Because of that, we felt that we were in a better position than most to bring attention to what was happening to English language learners all over the city. It was our time to stand up for what we knew as educators was right for both our profession and our students.

Another factor worth mentioning is that the staff had experienced collectively standing up for what they believe. The year before, the school had created a scholarship fund for undocumented students. The scholarship fund provides money to students who can't access state and federal financial aid due to their immigration status, and, as a result, often can't go to college. In addition to the personal relationships that teachers have at the school, there is also a foundation of politics and organizing.

In the two weeks before the test, we had lunch conversations and phone conversations and after-school conversations and morning conversations, and more conversations! So many questions that could determine the outcome of our boycott were raised at these meetings. Not all of our parents opted their students out, so did that mean that we shouldn't stand up against the test? Would that position us against some of our parents? What if every teacher didn't want to refuse to give the test? How would we make sure people wouldn't feel pressured to act? But how would we make sure people would feel empowered *to* act at the same time? What about our untenured teachers? We wanted to protect them, but wouldn't want them to feel excluded or isolated. Would we go public with our action? Would that give us more protection or make us more vulnerable? What *would be* the consequences? Would the UFT (United Federation of Teachers) stand behind us? And the big one . . . how would we tell our administrators?

The questions just kept coming. Slowly though, we began to work through them. But organizing among teachers isn't easy, because we're all so busy! Finding a lunch period that we were all willing to give up instead of planning or working with kids was not a small task. So we found other ways. Our staff is divided into teams. We assigned one person on each team to be the point person. It was that person's job to gather the thoughts and questions from their team, then as many of us would come together as we could to share what we learned. In retrospect, this resulted in a lot of unevenness—some people were very informed and others felt like things were moving too fast.

We decided that of course we wanted to respect the wishes of all our parents, but as professionals we had an obligation to speak up about what we knew to be damaging to the young people we serve. We realized that parents and students must lead the opt-out movement as the stakeholders, but as the ones in the classrooms giving the tests we cannot just stand by and wait.

We learned that the best way to empower one another was to talk to each other, listen, and seek advice and help from the activist community around us. We drew strength and inspiration from the Seattle MAP test boycott. Reviewing their story reaffirmed our convictions about what we were doing. Jesse Hagopian graciously took time to have long conversations on the phone talking through next steps, giving advice, and offering solidarity in any way he could. Jia Lee and Colin Schumacher, New York City teachers who had refused to give an elementary test shortly before, made themselves available to help in any way we needed. On the day of the boycott, they sent us a fruit bouquet to celebrate. Those chocolate-covered strawberries and pineapples on sticks got passed around the entire school, lifting people's spirits and building our confidence. We'd never seen people so happy about a bowl of fruit! Conversations with other activists helped us keep perspective and remember that the movement is bigger than our school. And mostly, they showed us that we may be out on a limb, but we certainly were not on our own. Following the Scrap the MAP model, we decided that publicity would give us strength and protection. In that spirit, we announced our decision not only to Chancellor Fariña but to the entire city. We scheduled a press conference for May 1, the morning of the test, and launched our website: www.standupoptout.wordpress.com.

Sadly, we also learned that our union, the UFT, did not have our backs. For the past two years, as the opt-out movement had grown and it became more and more clear that these tests cause more harm than good, the UFT had been on the wrong side of the debate. While the UFT officialdom completely abandoned us and distanced themselves from our action, other organizations embraced us, supported us, and made our action possible. MORE, the Movement of Rank and File Educators, a UFT caucus that many teachers in our school are part of, helped us tremendously and stood with us. We knew they would be there if we needed backup in any way. NYCoRE, the New York Collective of Radical Educators, built us a website and made sure that we could see every amazing message of solidarity that came through from around the country.

CTS, Change the Stakes, taught us what they knew about the media and helped us navigate it. These groups and the people in them demonstrated true solidarity and made clear what a unified fighting rank and file is capable of.

Finally, organizing is hard work and everyone moves at his or her own pace. The decision to boycott the test had to come from each individual. A little over a week before the test, our chapter leader sent an e-mail to the chapter. He laid out what he believed to be the possible consequences, including loss of employment and denial of tenure. Then, he explained that, being fully aware of the consequences, he planned to sign his name to the letter refusing to give the test. At that point, there were about seven teachers who planned to refuse to give the test. Over the next week we discussed what it would mean for only a portion of the staff to sign. We learned that everyone has unique circumstances, and some of us are in better positions to stick our necks out than others. Standing in solidarity means understanding that, trusting in each other's decisions, and giving people space to participate in whatever way they are comfortable. For us, this meant that not every teacher signed the letter refusing to give the test. As a staff, we made a decision to keep our untenured teachers' names off the letter, but they stood with us publicly at the press conference—a brave and bold act. In the end, finding that true sense of solidarity—one not based in righteousness or moralism but rooted in our collective decision to act in whatever way each of us could—made our action possible. During the few days before the test, people signed on one by one. At the end of the day Monday we had about ten signatures, and then Tuesday it snowballed with every teacher signing but four. During that same staff meeting we voted to go public with our action and to hold a press conference on Thursday morning.

On Wednesday, April 30, we sent our letter of refusal to Chancellor Fariña and notified the media of our press conference the following morning. As hard as it was to get to that moment, it was really the next twenty-four hours that were the most trying and, at the same time, the most affirming. We were confronted with a request from the DOE to call off our press conference. Our administration worried that we were publicly making enemies of a new city administration that wanted to be our ally. More urgently, they also worried that our action would destroy our chances of getting into the consortium, something we all believed in and wanted. These worries were valid. Our administrators did not threaten us with disciplinary action; instead they were honest about their fears. And the reality was those fears were also our own, but we weighed our options and chose to act in spite of them. It was in those moments when we were forced to articulate our thinking about the test— what it did to our kids and its political significance in the bigger picture of education reform—that we finally overcame our fear and felt absolutely confident in our decision to boycott and go public. Because what we realized was that while the new DOE *was* our ally in a way that Bloomberg's never was, as teachers we were in a position to take a stand that they would not. If we didn't say enough is enough and draw the line in the sand, it just wouldn't happen. The forces on the other side are too strong and constantly pushing. Someone had to push back. And in that moment, that someone was us!

On the morning of May 1, we got to school very early. By 7 a.m., press vans were already lined up outside. We gathered our handmade posters, press releases, chant sheets, and Prospect Heights T-shirts and headed outside. We were excited, really nervous, and shy of the cameras and reporters. Thankfully, supporters from NYCoRE, CTS, and MORE were there to buoy our energy and confidence. We started with a chorus of "We're fired up! Won't test no more!" And then we read our letter to the press. After all the work that went into that moment, it went by so fast! We walked back into the school and started our teaching day, but it felt like we had this really exciting secret that wasn't a secret at all. Solidarity messages started pouring in immediately. We ate lunch together, projected statements of solidarity on the Smart board and shared our fruit basket. We were giddy and really proud of the stand we had taken.

That day the students of the International High School at Prospect Heights had a full day of learning. They collaborated and discussed. They read books together and practiced their writing. They worked hard in math class as usual. They laughed and had fun with their teachers. They did not spend three hours of their day staring at a meaningless test. They did not feel like failures or cry over text that was too difficult for them. And that was a victory.

We have yet to receive an official response from the chancellor or the department of education, and we don't expect one. The same day of our boycott, the city and the UFT released news of a settled contract after years of failed negotiations. With the desire to sell the proposed contract as teacher-friendly, the DOE was positioning itself as being on the side of teachers. Reprimanding a group of teachers for boycotting a test that even the DOE admits is ill-suited to our group of students was not high on their list of to-dos. What's more, the outpouring of support showed that we were not alone. If we were disciplined, it wouldn't stay quiet.

At the end of the school year, we got great news. Our school, along with every other International school in the city, has been granted a waiver from some of the Regents exams. This waiver is not the same as the consortium's; it is better. It acknowledges that students who are learning English have different learning needs and therefore require different assessments. It is a step in the right direction, but there's a long way to go. It is clear that the testing regime is meeting resistance even from high-ranking officials like our chancellor, but we can't leave it to them to dismantle the web of privatization and high-stakes testing that has taken over our schools.

As we celebrated the news of our waiver, we also began to think about the new challenges we will face. Common Core still looms over our heads, setting standards that do not reflect what our students need. Taking away the pressure of the tests is a good thing, but it does not address every problem in our public school system. Teachers in our school dream of classes driven by the needs and interests of our students, fully functioning science labs with a working greenhouse, and the time and space for teachers to work collaboratively with small groups of students. Without the externally imposed "standards" of the tests driving our curriculum, we will teach to much higher expectations: our own. And to meet them we need so many things—smaller classes, more space, native language support for the more than thirty languages spoken by our students, more teachers, more art, more time to plan interdisciplinary projects, more guidance counselors, and the list goes on. We teachers don't agree on every detail of what our perfect school day would look like, but we do agree that the last thing teachers or students need is one more minute of our time spent giving, taking, grading, preparing for, or thinking about another standardized test.

# STUDENTS

# 12.

# TESTING ASSUMPTIONS:
## ZOMBIES, FLUNKIES, AND
## THE PROVIDENCE STUDENT UNION

## Cauldierre McKay, Aaron Regunberg, and Tim Shea

Passersby in downtown Providence jumped, startled, as a ghoulish-looking crowd of young people turned the corner of Kennedy Plaza. Green skin shined, sunken eyes stared, and torn, "blood"-spattered clothes dragged as they shuffled down Westminster Street. These dreadful-looking young men and women gathered at the entrance to the Rhode Island Department of Education (RIDE), where, instead of battering down the door in search of brains, these zombies showed they had plenty already. One demonstrator stepped forward, megaphone in hand. "We are here to protest the use of high-stakes standardized testing, and the zombifying effects it is having on our state's young people," he proclaimed. "To base our whole education, our whole future on a single test score is to take away our life—to make us undead. That's why we're here today, in front of the RIDE, as the zombies this policy will turn so many of us into. We're here to say: No Education, No Life!"

Our organization, the Providence Student Union (PSU), has been organizing against high-stakes standardized testing in Rhode Island since 2012, when the state department of education began implementing a new testing-based graduation requirement. By 2014, students must score high enough on the New England Common Assessment Program, or NECAP, to receive a high school diploma, regardless of grade point average or other evidence of scholarly success. PSU members, while recognizing creativity was not an important skill for the test, nonetheless felt it might serve us in opposing the new graduation policy.

The youth-led PSU organizes around a mission "to build the collective power of students across Providence to ensure youth have a real say in the decisions affecting their education." Students have consistently agreed with supporters of high-stakes testing that it is time to raise expectations and standards in our schools. But we were outraged at the narrow-mindedness of those who believed that simply slapping a high-stakes standardized test onto the end of our twelve years in crumbling, underfunded schools was going to magically solve the poor educational outcomes of low-income districts like Providence. For us, it is an issue of equity: this policy disproportionately puts low-income students, students of color, students learning English, and students with disabilities at high risk of being denied a diploma.

In essence, high-stakes testing punishes individuals—youth!—for systemic failures. In doing so, it makes an implicit argument that educational challenges are not the result of larger economic or political problems but rather the fault of these kids who were too dumb to pass their NECAPs, and of their teachers, who were too lazy to teach them properly. In fact, students and their teachers are currently the only people in our state being held "accountable" for our education system's failures. Not RIDE, which is in charge of setting education policy; not our school district, which has failed to create the engaging learning communities we need; and certainly not our state's elected officials, who have consistently underfunded our schools and social services while cutting taxes for Rhode Island's wealthiest citizens multiple times in the last decade. Arguably, the latter group is most responsible for the fact that forty-two thousand Rhode Island children, or about one in five of the state's kids, live in poverty.[1] Yet the logic of high-stakes testing implies that the ones to blame and to be punished for the failures of the system are the very people who are doing their best to teach and learn in difficult circumstances.

Even worse, this policy has vastly increased our schools' obsessive focus on raising test scores, with disastrous results. The Rhode Island Department of Education has framed this as a good thing: "We're finally giving students the extra supports they need to pass the tests," the department has repeatedly claimed. But what this actually means is that friends of ours are getting pulled out of their classes to do "NECAP boot camp."

Two PSU members had been talking all year about how much they loved their computer class and how useful it was. One day they came to our meeting with frowns—they had been taken out of that class and put into a test-prep class with all the other students who had scored "below proficient." Other PSU members began arriving with more horror stories: time was being spent during history classes and gym classes to do math remediation, interesting class projects were being replaced by test-prep computer modules, and on and on. Students most in need of engaging instruction and creative learning were being squeezed into narrower, less individualized, less active classes focused on test prep and basic math skills. In short, the scope and depth of our entire education were being sacrificed for the sake of correctly answering five to eight additional questions on the standardized math exams to get students across the pass line.

Rhode Island students are familiar with this story. But the average person—and especially the average elected official—in our state had no understanding of these concerns when we began our campaign in the winter of 2013. High-stakes testing is a complicated issue, and if people had heard of Rhode Island's new policy at all, it was likely through the distorted cliché that "testing will raise standards, and we all agree we need higher standards." Our organization knew we needed to correct this misperception by getting the matter on the public's radar and changing the frame through which people saw the issue.

But how? We had already organized a "normal" rally at the RI State House (the usual kind of protest with a crowd, some speeches, and so on) and spoken at a number of state board of education meetings, but we needed to get more creative if we really wanted to vault the issue into the public eye. Then we had our brainstorm.

We were having a conversation about what high-stakes testing does to students when PSU member Cauldierre McKay mentioned that it basically turns students into test-taking, unthinking zombies. A collective light went on. We all agreed the zombie image was a perfect symbol for our message about how this policy undermines real student success; it was a metaphor we knew the public would be able to grasp quickly and easily. In addition, we knew zombies were hot—the *Walking Dead* show had 16.1 million viewers for its season four premiere to become the most-watched drama series telecast in basic cable history—and we figured that dressing up like zombies would be fun and attract students. So why not organize a zombie march against the Rhode Island Department of Education to demonstrate to the world exactly what we felt we were being turned into?

Countless amounts of talcum powder, red food coloring, corn syrup, eyeshadow, and ripped shirts later, the protest was a big success. Students had a great time and we attracted a lot of local news coverage. After all, what reporter would want to miss the scoop, "Zombies Converge on Downtown Providence?" In the following weeks, pundits turned their attention to the broader issue, and new organizational allies stepped forward.

However, our zombie action also brought increased pushback. RIDE officials began a talk show blitz and testing supporters published op-eds hawking the absolutism that anyone who was against high-stakes testing was against high standards. A number of commentators tried to discredit our activism, saying we should stop wasting our time with gimmicks and instead focus on studying. After all, if we weren't so lazy and just did our work, we should be able to pass the NECAP.

Once again, we needed to reframe the conversation. PSU member Kelvis Hernandez was particularly upset by one adult commentator who showed his ignorance of this issue by claiming that students should be able to pass the test easily. "If they think it's so easy, why don't they take the test and see for themselves?" Kelvis said. A new idea was born: This time we decided to debunk the "high standards" messaging by pointing out what this test actually measures, what it misses, and how "easy" the tests are.

After the success of the zombie action, we knew we could get attention using untraditional tactics. We assembled a very brainy, well-dressed crowd in the basement of Providence's historic Knight Memorial Library. Our accomplished group of about fifty volunteers included state representatives, state senators, city council members, senior aides to the mayor of Providence, accomplished attorneys, directors of major nonprofits, Ivy League professors, a former Democratic nominee for governor, an NBC news anchor, and a scientist or two.

A buzz of anxious conversation filled the room until a group of youth stood up to collect the adults' attention. The students quieted the crowd, read instructions, and distributed test booklets and answer sheets. At last, PSU member Monique Taylor announced, "You have one hour to complete the first section. You may begin now." Pencils up, heads down, they started filling in bubbles.

The plan for the "Take the Test" event was simple: get as many successful adults as possible to take the NECAP. Of course, we encountered some complications. For one, it is illegal to have an actual copy of the NECAP, so we created a sample, mock exam using the questions RIDE releases every year. We did our best to approximate the same ratios of kinds of questions regarding content, format, and "depth of knowledge" assessed in the real test. Second, we found our biggest detractors were least likely to be willing to risk failure by taking the test. All members of the Rhode Island Board of Regents who had voted for the testing policy declined to participate in the event, as did the director of the state's Teach for America, the spokesperson for Rhode Island Democrats for Education Reform, and others. When asked, commissioner Deborah Gist responded that since she has a doctorate and has taken many tests, she did not feel the need to prove herself to anyone. (It is worth pointing out that PhD candidates are mainly evaluated with performance-based assessments; they are required to actually be able to think and do, rather than simply to fill in bubbles.) Fortunately, there were lots of other people who did have the courage to put themselves in students' shoes, and after several weeks of outreach to all the elected officials and successful professionals we could think of, we had a respectable group of test-takers.

As you might imagine, this event quickly became a media sensation. The next day newspapers were filled with pictures of the confused and frustrated adult test-takers struggling over their mock exams. When we called a press conference to announce the results of the graded tests a week later, every outlet in the state showed up to hear the outcome. They wanted to know: how many passed?

The results? Of the fifty successful, talented professionals who participated, thirty—or a full 60 percent—did not score highly enough on the mock exam to graduate under Rhode Island's high-stakes testing graduation requirement! The fable of the necessity of standardized tests to produce a "career ready" populace—a larger myth even, perhaps, than zombies—had been vanquished. As it turns out, test questions really don't seem to measure the constellation of skills, knowledge, and attitudes it takes to succeed in the world.

Of course, the NECAP didn't disappear right away, so we are still organizing against high-stakes testing in Rhode Island. But we did have some important and lasting successes. In the blink of an eye, a great deal of the framing around this issue has changed. We made it difficult for RIDE and its allies to argue students needed to pass the test to be successful in life, when so many clearly successful people had just failed it. It became easier to break through the shallow "They don't want high standards" frame, and to point out the arbitrariness of holding hostage a high school diploma for a single standardized assessment. And it taught our fifty volunteer test-takers a valuable lesson, too, creating many new important allies. Many of these elected officials subsequently were key to persuading the state's General Assembly to pass a resolution condemning the testing graduation requirement.

Since these actions, students have kept up the pressure. We held a major public forum on alternatives to high-stakes testing, held a sit-in at the department of education, met with Rhode Island's governor, and more. Through it all, we in the PSU have been inspired by the acts of testing resistance around the country, from Seattle to Portland to Chicago to New York and everywhere in between. These actions gave us the courage to raise our expectations, and we now feel part of an emerging national movement. We hope our story may inspire others to speak out for just, student-centered education transformations.

## Postscript

In June 2014, the Rhode Island General Assembly passed legislation placing a three-year moratorium on the use of standardized testing as a graduation requirement. During the debate on the floor prior to voting, many legislators explained that it was students' activism that changed their thinking on the issue. Members of the PSU—who have been working toward this for years—are excited. But there's no time to rest; we still have lots more work to do to ensure every student in Rhode Island receives the education they deserve.

# 13.

# 518-455-4767

## Amber Kudla

I'm from North Tonawanda, New York, a little city that no one has heard of between Niagara Falls and Buffalo. We have some decent schools, the graduating classes are about two hundred and fifty to three hundred students. It's not a very diverse or interesting city.

My disdain for standardized testing began in my junior year of high school, when I took AP Biology. It was the teacher's first year teaching the subject, and it seemed as though he was learning the material just a little before the rest of the class. It was basically up to the students to learn the course themselves if they wanted to cover everything that would be on the AP exam.

AP exams are written by the College Board and are one example of standardized tests. They are scored from one to five, where five means that the student is "extremely well qualified." I didn't initially have a problem with them because they are given once a year, and I thought they were testing the material in a reliable way. However, that year, I was feeling particularly unprepared for the exam. For the first time in my life I left entire essay questions blank and guessed on others. I got a five. That's when I started to realize that standardized tests weren't really testing intelligence, and they might just be rubbish.

By my junior year of high school, I had realized that I had a fair shot at becoming valedictorian, so I began contemplating throwing my grades in order to avoid having to give a speech at graduation. Grades are just numbers, right? Well, at that time I was also looking at colleges, and it turns out colleges think that grades mean something. And since I'd be paying for my own education, I needed all the scholarships that I could get. So I crossed my fingers and hoped I'd be third in the class, but I didn't throw my grades. And when senior year rolled around I ended up being valedictorian.

I am quite afraid of public speaking. When it is not a looming threat, I'm really confident. I'm sure I can get up in front of hundreds of people and put a lot of emotion into it and never stutter. But as soon as I found out that I would have to speak at graduation, I went to the principal's office to beg not to do it. I was still pretty confident at that point, sure I could get up there if I wanted to, and I just argued that I had nothing crucial to say. But I could hardly get a word in edgewise. He said if I didn't make a speech I would be disrespecting everyone, and then he said, word for word, "It's not that you don't have a choice, it's just that you have a very limited choice." He meant, *You have you do it, but you can choose what you will talk about.*

So I chose to speak about testing. I didn't like the idea of complaining at graduation, but I couldn't get up there and say, "I'll miss you all, these were the best years of our lives!" If I had to stand up there and talk, it had to be about something that I felt somewhat strongly about, and I'm not an overly sentimental person. I wrote eight drafts before I would let my English teacher revise it. Then I wrote four more drafts with her help. In the end she showed it to the principal, who was very angry about it. I had to remove all my attempts at levity. Jokes apparently implied disrespect. I was left with basically a political statement.

I hate politics. Sure, I hate testing as well, but I dreaded the idea of making a speech, and I dreaded the idea of making *that* speech. I begged my parents to let me stay home for graduation, asked my dad how I would go about incapacitating the car so we couldn't get there in time. I couldn't eat the entire day before. When I got to the park where the commencement ceremony was to take place, I ran into the principal. He told me he loved my speech, and if that was what I took away from high school, it was fine with him. I still don't know how to interpret that.

While waiting in line for commencement to start I was nervous, as our school of roughly 275 students had managed to fill a theater with thousands of people. On stage I would be surrounded by a wall of people staring at me. And my damn cap wouldn't stay on my head. I was so angry that I had to make a speech to please everyone, to avoid disrespecting anyone. I couldn't enjoy my own graduation day.

So anyway, I suffered through it and received two standing ovations. People really liked that the title was the state representative's phone number. I was met with no complaints. A lot of people came up to me afterwards crying, thanking me for doing it. Overall, it was an incredibly stressful experience, but if it gets the word out, I suppose it was okay. What follows is the speech I gave that night.

## "518-455-4767"

Mr. Woytila, Mr. Fisher, honored guests, parents, friends, families, and members of the class of 2013.

First and foremost, let's thank all of our families for their support and guidance over the past eighteen years, and for never giving up on us. We also owe our teachers and administrators many thanks for motivating us to try our hardest and for giving up their free time to help us out. They have all provided us with many great opportunities and have served as excellent role models.

Now I don't think I'm qualified to stand up here and give two hundred and fifty students advice, and I'm sure you have received enough motivation and insight from Mike and Mr. Fisher, so I'll just take the opportunity to voice an opinion. What I would really like to address here is the current state of public education.

This year, New York has joined four other states in following the Common Core standards. The goal is for every student in New York to learn the same things as every student in all of the other states. And in order to do this, we apparently have to triple the number of standardized tests that students take in exchange for state funding. This year we took assessments at the beginning, middle, and end of each course as part of this new system.

Some people think this will challenge our students to work harder, and help the US to rise above other countries in academic rankings. They say that once we adjust to the change, these tests will be beneficial. On the other hand many teachers, principals, and administrators across the state have felt the need to retire early, since their job descriptions have changed so drastically that they hardly consider themselves educators anymore. Most say that it has become all about tests and numbers and that there is very little focus on the students.

Whether you are for or against these assessments seems to depend on how you define learning. Perhaps it is your perspective that better test scores mean your child is understanding more. To me, testing has little connection to learning, and knowledge is not something that can be definitively measured with grades.

Regardless, these state assessments sit kids down for an exam on the first day of school, testing things that will take them at least a year to learn. That's pretty discouraging in high school and I can't imagine what that does to a first grader's motivation. Learning should be about discovery. Does it make sense to begin your discovery with a summary of the journey?

No, that's really just cheating yourself. You see, introducing subjects with the most difficult topics first is not a good way to get people excited about learning. We are students, not statistics. And these tests should have no effect on how we are taught. And they are affecting how we are taught.

The thing is, our educational system is built for the average student. Multiple choice means that answers need to be watered down, so they test the most general concepts. I believe that we all have far greater potential, but we are taught how to be average. And is that really going to help us when we enter the job market and we are vying for the same job as our brilliant exchange student, Quilin?

As for the argument that the assessments are challenging our students more, sure that's true. It's a challenge to fit the same amount of material into one year with more exams. It's a challenge to memorize loads of facts in time for the next test. It's also a challenge to eat a teaspoon of cinnamon in one bite without choking, but what are you really accomplishing?

How about some statistics? The dropout rate in some parts of the US is about 25 percent. In Finland, it is less than 1 percent. Why? Because in Finland, teaching is left up to the teachers. Standardized tests are few and far between. And guess what? They consistently outperform the US on international math, science, and literacy tests.

At this point, I'd like to throw a slightly relevant quote by a famous person into the mix to make my speech seem more legitimate. That appears to be how these things work. So Albert Einstein once said, "Everybody is a genius, but if you judge a fish by its ability to climb a tree, it will live its whole life believing that it is stupid." We can't judge someone's intelligence by how well he does in a small group of isolated classes. Everyone learns differently, so education is not something that can be successfully standardized.

Sure, we have to get a lot of people through the system, but there are more efficient ways of doing it. Maybe it's more cost-effective to have large impersonal classes, but to cram in so much meaningless information? We could learn a lot more if we could discover connections between biology and physics or English and history instead of memorizing lists of isolated facts just long enough to pass tests.

I mean, you all know that kid in math class who would always ask the teacher, "When will we ever use this in real life?" to which the teacher responds, "You'll need it on the final exam." No, that is not the answer. You are learning math because it has useful applications. Yet the nation's mentality seems to be that we are learning these things just to pass tests. And why do we need to pass tests? To evaluate teachers and get funding.

But what good is this funding if we are not learning the things that will help us to reach our full potential? I once had a teacher who, after I asked a few too many questions, told me, "it's not something you can understand, you just have to memorize it." Don't ever let anyone tell you that. You are capable of understanding anything you set your minds to. It may take time, it may take patience, but if you really want to understand something, get out there and understand it. You can't let people try to tell you who you are and what you are worth. That you aren't as smart as someone else because you scored ten points lower than him on a standardized test. That doesn't mean anything—grades are just numbers. It's better to learn and to understand than to get good grades. And no, one does not imply the other.

Anyway, this is why I tried so hard to get out of this speech. Not because I don't respect all of you, I do. It's just that "valedictorian" is a label and I don't respect what it stands for. I am not the smartest person in our class; I could learn something new from every single one of you. I'm good at memorizing things, but that's not so useful outside of the standardized world of high school. And I'm pretty sure a lot of you have been more successful than I was, unless your standard for judging success is a Scantron sheet.

Now you must be wondering why this is relevant. We're graduating, we're out of the system, it doesn't matter anymore. Well, it still matters to anyone you know that's growing up in New York State. School should not be about passing tests to get more funding. School should be about learning, understanding, thinking critically, and finding something that you are passionate about. Tell your younger siblings, friends, and neighbors to think, and to form their own opinions. To cautiously let their grades slide and do some actual learning.

Clearly my position is that most of the numbers you are given in high school are useless, but here's one that means something. The title of this speech, which you can find in your program, is the phone number of Robin Schimminger, our representative in the New York State assembly. You can use this to share your opinion with Albany, whether you are for or against the state assessments. Let your voice be heard and hopefully some day education will once again be about the joy of learning and discovery.

Well, that was the closest I could come to inspirational; I'm not very good at coming up with really deep stuff. So I'm going to end with one final quote from an author named John Green. He describes the one test, the only test in your life that matters. And spoiler alert: it is not a standardized state assessment. He says,

> The test will measure whether you are an informed, engaged, and productive citizen of the world; and it will take place in schools, and bars, and hospitals, and dorm rooms, and in places of worship. You will be tested on first dates, in job interviews, while watching football, and while scrolling through your Twitter feed.
>
> The test will judge your ability to think about things other than celebrity marriages, whether you'll be persuaded by empty political rhetoric, and whether you'll be able to place your life and your community in a broader context.
>
> The test will last your entire life, and it will be comprised of the millions of decisions that, when taken together, make your life yours. And everything—everything—will be on it. So pay attention.

Thank you and congratulations, class of 2013.

# 14.
# WALK OUT!
## Alexia Garcia

During winter break in December 2012, about twenty-five students crammed into one student's dimly lit living room for a general Portland Student Union meeting. We shared couches, chairs, and sat on the floor in order to squeeze everyone in. We called our friends to make sure all schools with unions had representation. We were to discuss our goals as a union, which would become our Five-Point Program. Everyone wanted one of our points to be about deemphasizing standardized testing—but to what extent was the question. A lively debate broke out. We discussed how testing is becoming higher-stakes and how it's used as a means of evaluation, students shared stories about how testing takes time away from actual learning and is irrelevant to many of our classes, and we discussed alternatives to both testing and evaluation. The solution became the area of disagreement. The discussion escalated, voices rose, and students even left the room in frustration. There was one suggestion that did receive a lot of support: "Why don't we refuse to take our tests?" Students liked the sound of that, an opt-out campaign; however, none of us would have believed that a month after this meeting we'd be leading a nationally recognized campaign and be part of a fight for educational justice.

When the Portland Public School district (PPS) attempted to apply for a $40 million Race to the Top grant in November 2012, the school district asked the Portland Association of Teachers (PAT) if they would approve the application. In order to apply for the grant, the teachers would have to agree to be evaluated based on their student's standardized test scores. The PAT disapproved the application, as they pointed to research that shows evaluations based on test scores does not improve teaching and learning, and therefore prevented the district from applying. The school board responded on November 21, 2012, saying that the PAT does not "adequately engage in solution-focused discussions" and when that does not happen, "our students suffer." The school board knew they needed to put out a statement as we were being flooded with emails from parents and community members who were upset by the rumor that Portland schools "turned down $40 million dollars." Where did this rumor start?

On November 15, 2012, the *Oregonian* published an editorial from the Portland Business Alliance (PBA), which claimed to speak on behalf of the students of Portland. The PBA called evaluation based on test scores a "reasonable set of . . . measures" and shamed PAT for their "obstructionist behavior." The PBA, which has been supportive of recent school bonds and other levies that do support children, made the public statement that they would no longer "support further funding requests." This is when students—not the "students" the Business Alliance claimed to speak for, but real students—joined the conversation.

In the 2012–13 school year, we had two student unions in Portland. The Portland Student Union and the Portland Public Schools Student Union. The Portland Student Union was formed out of students protesting budget cuts in May 2012. We are completely student-run and nonhierarchical. Each high school with an established student union met weekly at lunch to take on issues within their respective schools. The high school student unions would send representatives to frequent citywide Portland Student Union meetings. Students would share what their schools were working on at these meetings and talk about how we could support each other's projects, which would lead to districtwide efforts.

The Portland Public Schools Student Union (PPSSU) has been a longstanding student group. There is no cap on the amount of representation a high school can have; however, one student from each high school represented at the PPSSU will serve on the Superintendent's Student Advisory Council (SuperSAC). SuperSAC then reports to the superintendent on what the PPS Student Union is working on. SuperSAC also annually elects one student to serve as the Student Representative on the PPS School Board and lead the PPS Student Union. The district appoints one paid adult adviser, whose level of participation depends on the appointee. In recent years the appointee had a very present voice at meetings, and therefore the school district had great influence over the projects the PPS Student Union worked on. We organize around issues in our district and hold quarterly SuperSAC presentations for the superintendent on what the PPS Student Union has been working on. The student representative is also expected to represent the PPS Student Union at school board meetings. This group had provided a student voice at the district level and had historically abstained from "activism," especially any actions that opposed district policy. But this was about to change.

The Portland Student Union took swift action after reading the PBA's inflammatory editorial for the *Oregonian*. Our written response made it clear that the PBA was attacking the teachers union out of self-interest, not in defense of public education. We, like the PAT, would support getting an additional $40 million for our schools, but not at the cost of "reforming" education to reduce it to an endless string of standardized tests and increasing our teachers' workloads. We felt that if the PBA truly cared about Portland Public Schools, it would urge the city and the state to prioritize funding for education and comprehensive teacher evaluations that included students, parents, and other educators coming together, instead of only supporting high-stakes standardized testing.

These discussions led to a protest at the PBA's Holiday Open House and Food Drive on December 14, 2012. We turned our protest into a food drive as well, showing up with cans of pumpkin and cranberry sauce, singing holiday carols, and wearing the very best in high school holiday fashions. One student changed the words to "The Twelve Days of Christmas" for the occasion, tying together standardized testing, teacher evaluation, and school closures. We handed out leaflets to all who entered the PBA function as well as to passersby. Our signs and banner read "PBA Is Going on the Naughty List." Our whimsical approach to delivering a serious message attracted attention and energized our student activists, yet the PBA did not strike standardized testing off of its "wish list."

The Portland Student Union's "PBA/Race to the Top Committee" became the "Standardized Test Committee," and we put out a Five-Point Program with point three outlining authentic assessment and holistic learning:

- The emphasizing of a holistic educational structure and evaluation, while deemphasizing standardized testing.

- Immediate repeal of Senate Bill 290[1]

- Implementation of a flexible curriculum in classroom, deemphasizing textbook work for hands-on work, that is, learning by doing.

- Deemphasize college as the only gateway to success, refocusing of public education as a developing point in life, particularly in high school.

- We want good schools and teachers. We want an evaluation system that really speaks to a teacher's potential and habits: good and bad. To this we suggest a system that includes students, parents, and other involved educators coming together in evaluation, rather than abstract testing.

After all our work organizing students, attempting to educate the business elites, and proposing alternatives to the tests, we realized that it would take still much more to reclaim our education. So at one meeting in late December 2012 a student proposed that we all simply refuse to take our state mandated standardized tests. This suggestion won great support.

The PPS Student Union followed what the Portland Student Union had been working on with the PBA and Race to the Top. On January 2, 2013, we sent the following letter to the PBA board members and their CEO and president Sandra McDonough, who had submitted the PBA's letter to the *Oregonian.* A response was immediate and we set up a meeting with Ms. McDonough for February 13.

January 8, 2013, I asked PAT president Gwen Sullivan a few questions pertaining to the PBA, Race to the Top, and high-stakes standardized testing. Gwen told me that the PBA had never contacted PAT about Race to the Top to hear why they chose to prevent the Race to the Top application from going through. She also said that she opposed high-stakes standardized testing and would be opting her kids out. I told her students had briefly discussed launching a campaign to challenge standardized testing.

On January 9 I walked into the counseling office and asked about the procedure for opting out of the state tests. The question was not received well; however, one counselor brought me into her private quarters and started calling district testing coordinators. I felt like the counselors and testing coordinators were caught off guard by this request. I sat in this counselor's office for over an hour, missing my own classes, frustrated by this process.

I learned that in high school only juniors would be taking the Oregon Assessment of Knowledge and Skills (OAKS) in reading, writing, math, and science. Students needed a passing score in only reading, writing, and math in order to graduate. When students didn't pass, they would have the opportunity to retake the test two times. This meant students would be pulled out of additional classes. In some cases the vice principal would pull students out of class to teach them how to take the test before they went in to retest.

In the wake of my visit to the counselor's office, the testing coordinator sent us the criteria for opting out, which read: "The student's parent must submit a written request to the school district, listing the reasons for the request and proposing an alternative individualized learning activity for the student that meets the same goals that would be accomplished by participation in state testing." The acceptable reasons for opting out included "student's disabilities or religious beliefs." At the high school level, students could not simply opt out and still be eligible for graduation. Students would also have to demonstrate proficiency in an alternative way. These alternative ways included using PSAT, SAT, ACT, International Baccalaureate (IB), and Advanced Placement (AP) test scores or work samples.

Test scores evaluate schools by publicly labeling our schools as "Outstanding," "Satisfactory," or "In Need of Improvement" on the state report card. Schools are evaluated in a variety of categories, and if the school failed in one category, it would get an "In Need of Improvement" on the entire state report card. One of the categories was "participation," requiring 95 percent of students in every demographic to take every test.[2] This meant if enough students opted out, then our school would be labeled "In Need of Improvement" on the state report card. These scores would not affect the amount of funding our school received, but schools still didn't want to have a label of "In Need of Improvement" for fear that it would lower enrollment.

I brought this information to the Portland Student Union's Standardized Testing Committee meeting on January 10, 2013. Students at this meeting raised concerns that there was not equity in accessing alternative assessments, that by refusing the tests we could be contributing to the labeling of our schools as failing, and wanted to know more about what we hoped to achieve from this campaign. By the end of the meeting, we concluded that the best course of action was to work to achieve such high levels of students opting out of the tests that every high school in PPS would be labeled failing, thus rendering the label itself meaningless. In understanding that students did not all have the resources and ability to take PSAT, SAT, ACT, or IB and AP assessments, we concluded that we would encourage opting out of all the OAKS tests, offer to pay for students who needed additional support for these alternative exams, and then really push opting out of the science test as it's not required for graduation and therefore does not call for an alternative proof of proficiency. We also needed to respond to how all our schools would be labeled as failures. Our solution was to twist the label by saying "we know our schools are in need of improvement, and we don't need some incomprehensive score to tell us that. And in actuality, it's the system that's in need of improvement." We hoped to gain media attention and really contribute to the national conversation about standardized testing and its role in our education system.

That night, I received a Facebook message from PAT president Gwen Sullivan that read, "I'm not suggesting this, just sharing information," with a link to a *Seattle Times* article about Garfield High School's MAP test boycott that had been announced earlier that day.[3] This was one of the first moments when I realized the movement was greater than just some frustrated students; it legitimized what we were doing and gave us standing in future conversations with principals and district employees who were trying to break down the campaign. I was excited to be able to respond to Gwen with the Portland Student Union's proposed "Opt-Out Campaign" plan.

January 14, 2013, the first day of the writing test, my friend and I taped posters all over Junior Hall of Lincoln High School that read "JUNIORS: OPT OUT OF STANDARDIZED TESTING Informational meeting, Wednesday, Lunch Rm. 142." I was immediately called into the principal's office. All three of our school administrators sat there and grilled me about the campaign. I felt sure their goal was to be intimidating. They wanted to express the power they held over me and make me feel ignorant. Vice Principal Neal explained the process for administering the test. He said that when students do not pass, we pull them out of class to teach them how to take the test, then test them again. If that second test doesn't go well, then we work with them on work samples, which takes a lot more time. This was frustrating to hear. It was so clear that these tests were not about finding out how good our school was, but how "good" we could make it appear. I asked the question, "Is our school not in need of improvement?," which really frustrated them. Everyone in that room knew our school needed help. We are the most affluent public high school in Portland and still have overcrowded classrooms. That really brought up issues of integrity. Why was it so important that we took these exams? They so clearly were not a reflection of our school's ability to educate. Principal Chapman expressed her concerns about how a "bad" score would affect enrollment in our school, and expressed her concerns about equity, as many alternatives to OAKS were alternative standardized tests that cost money. I sat there wanting to cry out of frustration and anger that they had me cornered without other student union members there to support me. After this two-hour-long inquisition, I told them I'd pass along their concerns to the union, but I couldn't call off the campaign. That frustrated them. The students had made this decision together and were in control. I could tell that they were scared of how this campaign could impact our school. I immediately I called my friends, who reassured me this was a "good" decision. I also messaged PAT president Gwen, who directed me to Betsy Salter and Susan Barrett from Oregon Save Our Schools (Oregon SOS), saying that they could answer my questions.

January 16, I met with Betsy Salter from Oregon SOS; she was also comforting and reassured me that this campaign would be huge and we would be able to achieve the goal of contributing to the national conversation about high-stakes standardized testing. I asked her to attend the PPS Student Union meeting that night as I was planning on proposing the campaign to see if we wanted to cosponsor it. That proposal went over extremely well—even our district's paid adult adviser, Andrea Wade, spoke of how poorly standardized test scores are used.

It was settled—both groups would co-lead the PPS Opt-Out Campaign. The student representative on the school board submits monthly reports to the school board of education. This is an opportunity to publicly report to the board on what the PPS Student Union and SuperSAC have been working on. My next report was scheduled for January 28. I decided to include the Opt-Out Campaign in my report and kick it off that night. The board was completely unprepared for what I was about to present.

Never had I done anything too "radical" before in front of the board. Rarely had any student representative, especially during a student rep report at a televised board meeting, done so either. Not only did I confront the board about one of their recent antiunion acts but I also publicly encouraged the community to opt out of OAKS testing. This board report went viral as did the Portland Student Union's article about the opt-out campaign.

January 29, the Portland Student Union website had more than a thousand views. And within eight hours a thousand became two thousand. Then I received an email from Diane Ravitch that read, "I am posting this early tomorrow morning. Will reach at least 50,000 people across the nation." We were slowly finding out that this action had massive support from around the country.

January 30, Ravitch posted about us on her blog with the headline "Good News! Students in Portland, Oregon, Are Speaking Out." On that very day we learned of the Providence Student Union's campaign against their high-stakes, standardized New England Common Assessment Program, or NECAP, exam. Now we knew were not alone and this display of student power gave us a surge of energy to continue our struggle. Now we were rolling. On January 31, we got our first interview request from the *Oregonian*. On February 2, the *Oregonian* published a story of our movement on the front of the Metro section of the paper. On February 4, we sent out a press release further detailing our demands for a high-quality public education. On February 5 we presented the campaign in more detail to superintendent Carole Smith, who, of course, did not openly support us but understood our frustrations. That same day, representatives from our unions gave four interviews, one with *Democracy Now!* and three with local news stations. On February 6 we had a press conference at the Portland Public School District headquarters.

The press conference was very successful. Juniors who were opting out spoke about why they were opposed to the OAKS testing. Susan Barrett also spoke, as well as recently elected school board member and Oregon SOS organizer Steve Buel. Additionally, a few students' parents spoke about why they supported their child's decision to opt out. Finally, Lincoln's Black Student Union submitted a statement about why they supported the campaign, as high-stakes standardized testing contributes to inequality. The experience of all these groups working toward a common cause was truly exhilarating and gave us hope that we had begun the process of reclaiming public education for students, teachers, and parents.

The power of our coalition was quickly validated when, about a week later, the PBA president McDonough and two of her employees agreed to meet with the PPS Student Union. This was absolutely one of the worst, least productive meetings of my life. We opened up the conversation by thanking them for their support on past PPS bonds and levies, and then made clear that we opposed their stance on Race to the Top. Immediately an argument broke out. They were upset with the Public Employee Retirement System (PERS) benefits that were going to teachers, and they were very supportive of high-stakes standardized testing. Little did they know I had just spoken out against the proposed PERS cuts and we were leading an opt-out campaign that opposed exactly what they were pushing for.

We tried to reason with the PBA. We pointed to education systems like Finland's that are regarded the world over as highly successful. We explained that Finland's success was the result of an approach to education that values the whole student, provides wraparound services for their students (and general populace), and does not include a single high-stakes standardized test in the entire K–12 system. Ms. McDonough responded with curt condescension: "Have you ever been to Finland?" So there it was; all our points were invalid. We walked out of that meeting shocked and confused, but with a greater understanding of the fight we were taking on: you cannot just reason with business interests and the profit motive, you have to build a base of power to challenge them.

Our next action: a walkout on March 14 in solidarity with the Colorado Student Power Alliance (COSPA) walkout happening that same day. In Colorado, the students would be walking out and then traveling to their state capitol building to demand action surrounding high-stakes standardized testing. We would replicate this. Jefferson High School was testing that week, and Jefferson had talked previously about an action that would unite their school's struggle with the other schools from around the district. The plan was to bring PPS Student Union and Portland Student Union members from around the city to Jefferson High School to greet students as they walked out. We would then travel to Salem, Oregon, to speak with our representatives about high-stakes standardized testing. Representative Lew Frederick, a Democrat from District 43, had created House Bill 2664 that, if passed, would require the Oregon Department of Education to call into question the role standardized testing should play in public education. His House bill did not have teeth behind it, and therefore would require the community to keep an eye on the department of education to make sure that testing was truly being scrutinized. We decided to speak in support of the bill and planned to be there later to ensure the department of education would be held accountable.

Restarting our movement in the spring hinged on the students of Jefferson, one of the most exceptional schools in Portland. In the last ten years the Jefferson High School cluster has had more school closings than all the other PPS clusters combined. It is the only majority African-American high school in Oregon and 76 percent of its students receive free or reduced lunch. It has a 35 percent graduation rate, the lowest of PPS's "traditional" high schools. OAKS tests have a huge impact on this low graduation rate, as a passing score is required to graduate and this has resulted in spiking numbers of students being denied a diploma. Moreover, as a direct result of the federal education policies of No Child Left Behind (NCLB) and Race to the Top (RttT), Jefferson has been labeled a "Focus and Priority School," which results in an extreme emphasis on measures like OAKS testing—and less attention to art, music, and other programs that enrich education. As a result, these students have a lot to fight for. Yet the Jefferson High School students decided against participating in the walkout after being pulled into the principal's office and being told that the negative label the school already had would be perpetuated if students walked out on the test. This left us with the dilemma of having a walkout we had already called for but no school to anchor it. In the rush to switch locations and go on with the show, the Portland Student Union began to break down.

Students argued over who would take on hosting the walkout. It was concluded that it would be Grant High School. However, controversy erupted as the Grant Student Union did not want to take responsibility for it. In hindsight we should have called it off, regrouped, and developed longer-range plans to build on our successes. But we didn't, which led to low turnout on the day of the walkout and many students being rightfully upset by the process.

Many of our more involved students quit the Portland Student Union after this event. Sometimes I despair that it was my fault for pushing to have a walkout that did not have enough support. Other times I think people simply took this frustrating time period as an opportunity to back away from the group and enjoy other aspects of their lives. At least no one can say that we made the grave error of remaining silent about our own education. Whatever mistakes I and other leaders may have made, the Portland Student Union continues and undoubtedly will regain its strength as more students are impacted by the test-and-punish policy.

Because the PPS Student Union was not as involved with these actions, it was not split apart by the bitter debates that surfaced during the walkout. However, the financial support we received from the school district was disappearing. Student trips to Salem that were easily funded by PPS in the past suddenly could not be organized. Our adult adviser, who once spoke in support of the opt-out campaign, began to aggressively insert her pro-OAKS opinion to stall organizing. When I reached out to her to find a way to work together, she refused to meet or to return my phone calls and emails. Yet Andrea would send out emails to all the students, the board, and the superintendent about how I was "a child" and how there was "some type of relationship established with [me] and a few PAT members" and how we had an "agenda." My principal told me that she had heard rumors around PPS that I did not actually listen to students' voices, and that I was racist.

This hostile environment made it difficult for the PPS Student Union to proceed with the campaign. It showed that Portland Public Schools only cared for student voices when it benefitted them. The second we opposed their agenda we were belittled and financially cut off, and our opinions were dismissed.

We did our best to not let this faze us. The PPS Student Union continued on its quest for high-quality assessment. Students stepped up and financed sending five students to Seattle for spring break in late March to visit Garfield High School and talk with Garfield students about their experience with the MAP boycott. We sent students to Salem, Oregon, to lobby for a higher education budget and in support of House Bill 2664—three times throughout February and March. We were able to achieve a lot without the support from Portland Public Schools, although the open attacks from PPS left students feeling hopeless, divided, and frustrated to the point that some decided to leave our organization.

By the spring, the most stable Portland Student Union branch was the Cleveland Student Union. Cleveland High School's OAKS testing had yet to come and chatter of a walkout was increasing on the Facebook walls of student activists. We set the date for April 18 at 10:30 a.m. for Cleveland High School students to walk out on being reduced to a score and walk in to the movement for a student-centered education. When Cleveland's administration found out about our plans for a walkout, they mobilized. First they threatened to prevent students who walked out from running for student government. Then they sent notes home to parents about the importance of taking the OAKS tests. Students who turned in opt-out forms were denied their right to opt out. However, students simply refused to test in numbers so large that their administration was overwhelmed and did not take any further action.

Fliers were passed out, banners were made, and a PA system was set up outside the school. On the planned date and time about seventy Cleveland High School students walked out of their front doors chanting, "Hey hey, ho ho, standardized testing has got to go!" and carrying banners that read, "I Am a Student, Not a Test Score" and "Education Is Not a Commodity." After two students gave speeches, they took to the streets and lapped the school, chanting. It was absolutely amazing.

If there's one thing I've learned from our student organizing, it's that organizations do not necessarily care that a student voice is authentic as long as it can be used to further their own agendas. From Stand for Children, Students Matter, and StudentsFirst to Portland Public Schools, the list of organizations influencing and implementing policies in public education goes on and on. These groups are happy to claim that their standardized tests, their contract proposals, and their agendas of privatization and union destruction are what's best for students. They're happy to put students' faces on their materials and to have students volunteer for them. In the case of Portland Public Schools, PPS was more than happy to provide food, transportation, and adult advisers as long as PPS could exploit students to support their agenda.

However, the minute students begin to question the authenticity of such organizations, we are met with withdrawal of financial support, dismissal of our opinions, and complete disrespect. By simply asking for the teachers union's opinion, or proposing that students and teachers should not be evaluated based on how well students can pick A, B, C, or D gave PPS permission to leave us behind.

Our year ended there, but the battle continues. The PPS Student Union continues under the name "PPS Student Association," and the students are rewriting district policy to ensure the PPS Student Association officially exists under board policy. Andrea Wade, our adult adviser, was moved to a different department in PPS and has been replaced by PPS's political consultant Jon Isaacs. I've heard that whenever the actions taken by the PPS Student

Union in 2012–13 are brought up, Jon Isaacs changes the conversation. From what I can tell, PPS was successfully able to rein in those students. The Portland Student Union remains in its rebuilding phase. It ran an incredible PAT Solidarity Campaign in the 2013–14 school year during the contract negotiations between PPS and PAT. From walkouts to mic checks the students proved stronger than ever.

# 15.

# POEMS

## Malcolm London and Falmata Seid

## High School Training Grounds

Malcolm London

*He who owns the youth, gains the future.*

—Adolf Hitler

At 7:45 a.m.
I open the doors to a building dedicated to building
Yet only breaks me down
I march down hallways
Cleaned up after me every day by regular janitors
But I never have the decency to honor their names
Lockers left open like teenage boys' mouths
When girls wear clothes that cover their insecurities but show everything
    else
Masculinity mimicked by men who grew up without fathers
Classrooms overpacked like bookbags
Teachers paid less than what it cost them to be here
Oceans of adolescents come here to receive lessons
But never learn to swim

Part like the Red Sea when the bell rings
This is a training ground

My high school is Chicago
Diverse and segregated on purpose
Social lines are barbed wire
Hierarchy burned into our separated classrooms
Free to sit anywhere but reduced to divided lunch tables
Labels like "regular" and "honors" resonate
Education misinforms, we are uniformed
Taught to capitalize letters at a young age
Taught now that capitalism raises you
But you have to step on someone else
To get there,
This is a training ground
Sought to sort out the regulars from the honors
A recurring cycle
Built to recycle the trash of this system
I am in "honors" classes
But go home with "regular" students
Who are soldiers in a war zone in territory that owns them
When did students become expendable?
CPS is a training ground
Centered on personal success
CPS is a training ground
Concentration on professional suits
CPS is a training ground
One group is taught to lead and the other is made to follow
No wonder so many of my people spit bars because the truth is hard to
    swallow
The need of degrees has left so many of my people frozen

I had a 1.9 GPA
I got drunk before my ACT and still received a 25
Now tell me how I am supposed to act?
Homework is stressful

But when you go home every day and your home is work
You don't want to pick up any assignments
Reading textbooks is stressful
But reading doesn't matter when you feel your story is already written
Either dead or getting booked
Taking tests is stressful
But bubbling in a Scantron doesn't stop bullets from bursting
Our direction hasn't changed
When our board of education is driven by lawyers and businessmen
One teacher sits on our boards
Now what does that teach you?
We all know the drill
I hear that education systems are failing
But I believe they are succeeding at doing what they're built to do
To train you
To keep you on track
To track down an American dream that fails so many of us all

## Multiple Choice

Malcolm London

*There are two primary choices in life: to accept conditions as they exist, or accept the responsibility for changing them.*

—Denis Waitley

every morning in the third grade
I stood to pledge allegiance to a flag dangling in the front of my class.
I had not learned yet how crushed windpipes hanging
in the same fashion
were pendants of freedom, too.
before freedom was a choice to cross the street alone,
eat candy for breakfast or not bathe . . .
before I knew Santa Claus was a black woman
scraping together her last to see a smile sled

across her son's face on a winter morning,
i've assumed every problem must have a multiple-choice solution
every year since the third grade my future has been led
by the tip of a number two pencil shading in
alphabetized answers on a Scantron
to determine what class i might end up in,
by inhaling test-prep booklets lower, upper or middle
since the third grade I've inhaled test-prep booklets
commanding me to "concentrate,"
"be patient, careful, to choose the correct solution"
or "eliminate answers you know are wrong"
and since the third grade it seems Chicago has choked
on all of the above
except the *process of elimination.*

when a board of ed ignores the voice of the throat it plans to close
it shows we are number two
pencils shaven to fill in
applications for Walmart, or boxes of prisons, or row houses
or apartments pushed outside the city,
flushed out, we are number two
to boards of education who are better at plumbing than their
        namesake
the school-to-prison pipeline drains so many, so well
when a mayor bullhorns to a city of unions on big shoulders,
and says "no choice, no funding" stiff as a neckache, says eliminate fifty
        schools
and in the same breath heaves public dollars on a new stadium for DePaul,
and in the same breath regurgitates a request for more charter schools
he suffocates and strangles classrooms packed like sardines,
reeking of sweat & one teacher with merely two hands
not wide enough to hand out quality education
the only cutting in line students fear
is from their district's budget
we are blaming public schools for being stumped
without looking at the root causes

since the third grade fed the illusion we have multiple choices
but when an unelected board
closes schools
in black and brown neighborhoods for the past decade
it is from new lumber we are hanging
by a thread sewn around our necks
what choices are we given then,
except to become pendants of freedom, too

a closed school means a door may block our entrance
but our people were born at the exit,
we stand, we fight back, and we organize,
even after tested by people who control our schools
who have never been inside of them, will never send their children
    there
because we have numbers, too.
because Santa is a black woman somewhere
wrapping her son's gift to place it under a tree
not see a city hang his future from one
for our schools are pillars, not to be pillaged for capital gain
for our choice will not be determined by a Scantron,
or by politicians who make squad cars out of school buses,
or by developers who displace communities cloaked in an urban
    renewal banner
or taken away by a board of education unveiling its splinters.


# Modern-Day Slavery

Falmata Seid

The things that I found and will say
sway the opposition in ways that make you reassess your accusations.
We're told the key to success is education, but what's displayed in their
    legislation is intuitions designed to keep us chained in cages.
Pass back the fact that being black means you can't match white wages

Pass back the fact that it's always Goldman Sachs that drains your life
   savings
Pass back the fact that it's all done in stages
Please open your eyes; this is modern-day slavery
I've come to the conclusion that these tests are an illusion.
A disguise, a mere mirage for their lies, their crimes, underfunding education, while at the same time feeding potential Einsteins
to school-to-prison pipelines.
It's the system that I'm trying to undermine so if you don't mind
please, let me state some of my own finds:
The US ranks seventeenth in education in the world,
but what we're not told
is that it also ranks number one for the most people incarcerated—2.3
   million.
Overcrowding jails to the point where there are more inmates
than there are beds to sleep in.
It costs 63 billion dollars a year to continue paying these businesses
   that profit off the exploitation of people?
Why is it that 37 percent of black males have not completed high
   school?
Why is it in Seattle there is a plan under way in my neighborhood to
   build a 210-million-dollar facility
for the incarceration of more youth like me.
It doesn't make sense. To combat naïve crimes that are oftentimes
   nonviolent
with a hostile environment.
Instead we should help these youth by creating programs
that offer jobs that actually will hire them.
Programs that let these youth pursue an education because the public
   ones don't let them back.
And I'm not talking about creating more of these loosely regulated alternative schools where the only thing they do is groom these students to come back to the prison system because that's cruel.
Start cutting 60,000-dollar costs per inmate and increase the state's
   spending per student from 7,500 dollars.
See, Washington state spends over 80 million dollars a year on stan-

dardized testing. Administer exams like the MAP this spring but
   can't exactly explain what the test brings?
It's amazing.
These exams are the ones where teachers have no say on how to cater
   the test to a student's learning
These exams are the ones measured by a metric decided by people who
   have never faced adversity in their life
These exams are the ones that belittle the hopes and aspirations of kids
who were told to dream big.
These exams are Malcolm X's teacher that told him he couldn't achieve
   his dreams.
See, Malcolm X dropped out of school at the end of eighth grade.
He was later known by the name Detroit Red.
Now, everything Malcolm did was to accumulate the bread
because he had listened to what his teacher said.
His dreams of becoming a lawyer were, "No realistic goal for a nigger."
In Malcolm's case he became much bigger
Than that worth his teacher slapped on the sticker.
But tell me, how much different are these tests? No really, how are they
   different?
They tell a student that despite his many talents if he does not shade in
   the correct bubble on a test,
that supposedly defines his intellect,
he is doomed to fall,
so next fall,
he contemplates whether he wants to come back at all.

# 16.

# BEING A FUTURE TEACHER IN THE MIDST OF THE MOVEMENT

## Stephanie Rivera

*How can you go into the field knowing what is happening to it? Why don't you just stay away?* Like most teachers going into the field, I chose to pursue this profession years ago to make a positive impact on students, similar to how my teachers have made an impact on me. Yet, with about two years being involved in the movement, I have been able to articulate my reasons for continuing to enter into the field with a more clear and concise reasoning: When you see something you love, something you know that needs to be defended, you do not simply run away and hide. You do not accept the attacks passively—you do not assume you have already lost.

No. You stand up and fight like hell to protect it.

## Coming to Consciousness

I wasn't always like this. Graduating from high school, I was every No Child Left Behind (NCLB) designer's dream product. I listened to what I was told, never questioned authority or any information I was told, and lacked the capability to critically think about hardly anything. Obey, obey, obey. . . . It did not matter if I knew the HSPA and the TerraNova—our state tests—were a waste of time and failed to measure my or any of my classmates' intelligence—this was just "the way things were," and there was nothing I could do about it.

Further, just two years ago, I believed that Teach for America was the route to solving educational inequities. I imagined myself as a TFA Corps Member after graduating college. The idea and vision made me all giddy inside. Similarly, after doing a Google search looking for ways to begin working on education issues, I came across Michelle Rhee's "StudentsFirst." Believe it or not, there was a time I was only a few clicks away from submitting an application to be a campus representative for that organization.

So, how did I eventually see through the manipulative neoliberal rhetoric? And even more important, how did I come to realize that what we do not agree with as students and future teachers is not to be accepted but rather must be challenged and can be changed? In 2011, I first discovered the inequities in our education system during my sophomore year of college. In my Introduction to Education course at Rutgers we read *Spectacular Things Happen Along the Way: Lessons from an Urban Classroom* by Brian Schultz. It was the first time I learned that there were youth right in our own country—hell, less than a hundred miles away from me—who were forced to endure some of the most oppressive education environments. The most extreme examples included stories from students about inadequate heat in the building, lunches eaten on the floors of the hallways, and classroom windows riddled with bullet holes.

Because of my experience in a suburban public school district in Egg Harbor Township, New Jersey, I assumed everyone approached school with a neutral lens as I did. I mean, my biggest concern about school growing up was wondering why we didn't have an escalator like another school had, or why our cafeteria was only one floor rather than two. I was unaware that there were students less than twenty to thirty miles away from me who were struggling to afford pencils and notebooks.

Minutes after reading our assigned portion of this book, I could feel my face flush red with anger and confusion. I was not only angry at the mere fact that such conditions existed but also that I was just finding out about these inequities. I vividly remember walking into class waiting to see my classmates in a similar distress. Sadly, I was disappointed. How was it possible that no one else was heated enough to start flipping desks? To march ourselves out of class and protest to our local government? At this point in my life, I didn't even know if protesting was an effective tactic; I just remember being pissed off and wanting to yell at whoever was responsible for such oppressive education environments. In the midst of my frustration, I was even considering changing my entire career path. I began contemplating the idea of becoming a politician, believing I'd have the opportunity to create direct change in our education system. Luckily, when I brought the idea of leaving the profession to my professor, she insisted that the most powerful work we can do regarding these inequities is right inside the classroom. She referred to the work that Schultz did with his students—incorporating civic education and social justice within his curriculum—and I realized that is what I would do, too.

After reaching this level of consciousness and awareness, there was no going back. Weeks after the semester ended, the book and what I had learned was still on my mind. That was how my blog *Teacher Under Construction* was born in January 2012. I figured if I could go through my entire K–12 education unaware of the existence of the blatant inequities in our education system, then there must be thousands of others out there in the same position. I came to this simple conclusion: nothing can be changed if no one even knows something has to be changed in the first place. I began writing as a hopeful means, as I phrased in my early blog postings, of "breaking bubbles of ignorance," doing something similar to what the book and class did for me.

Shortly after I started my blog, I began to challenge every aspect of the education system. In essence, I was evolving into the type of student that the NCLB era wasn't meant to produce. I began connecting, via *Teacher Under Construction*, with other like-minded individuals throughout the country with whom I shared a commonality: dissent against the education "reform" movement.

## From Reflection to Action

Before I could fully devote myself to the education justice movement, I had to examine where I fit in the system. Throughout middle and high school, rarely did I raise my hand in class, rarely did I have confidence to share my points of view if they conflicted with the dominant opinion of my classmates. Sure, I was able to adapt and assimilate to succeed in the system, but what does that mean in terms of the education that youth of color like myself deserve? What does it mean to have the skills to adapt to a system that is designed only to benefit a select few rather than be emancipatory for all youth? This laid the groundwork for the direction my activism would take and for my role as a future teacher. When there is something you believe is worth fighting for, you are stripped of all fear. Fear is petty in comparison to the larger goal at hand. I have a clearer sense of what I am fighting for. I have gained the courage to take actions that previously would have been unforeseeable.

For instance, until 2012, a student organization solely focused on future educators at my university was nonexistent—I, along with about seven other students, worked to change that. Within this space, we have had open dialogues about various issues regarding education and the teaching profession ranging from the problems of Teach for America to merit pay and how the increase in high-stakes testing will affect us as future teachers. My fellow future teachers and I have now taken on the challenge of making our program more democratic in regards to coursework. I believe that calling for a democratic university can result in an increase in democratic practices in the classroom.

Similarly, in November 2012, I, along with other activists from Madison, Wisconsin, helped launch Students United for Public Education (SUPE). We took aim at reactionary, neoliberal organizations such as Students for Education Reform that manipulate students into advocating for corporate education reform. With this national organization, college students across the country had a means of fighting for various issues surrounding public education on their campuses. Some of our chapters' most memorable actions included working with local Chicago youth and standing as allies at local protests, petitioning against the Parent Trigger Bill in Florida, and launching our first national campaign: Students Resisting Teach for America. Yet, some of the greatest "victories" and hints of progress do not only exist in relation to our actions and strengthening of organizations but in the very act of normalizing dissent against the corporate education reform movement. Simply raising questions in class such as "Aren't there more effective ways to assess student progress?" or "How does high-stakes testing affect students in higher poverty schools compared to students at wealthier schools?" has proven to spur my classmates to think critically about the status quo.

## What's Really at Stake?

The impact of high-stakes testing was not always as clear to me as it is today. Growing up, test weeks meant a whole week of half-days in school—what could be better than that?! For a lot of us, state tests were seen as a joke. Few of us took our state tests seriously because many of us knew we would pass with little to no effort. Yet I don't recognize the faults of high-stakes testing only through my own schooling experience; I am also seeing its faults and impact on students in the K–12 school system whom I mentor, tutor, and simply talk to today. As the focus of corporate education reformers' policies is strongly based on increasing test scores and making profits, the focus on the real issues that should be dealt with is almost nonexistent. When I tutored at a local youth correctional facility in Camden, New Jersey, two students stood out to me. While I tutored them in elementary mathematics and grammar, they often told stories of their experiences within the K–12 system. They discussed how they rarely had support from their schools, that living in the most dangerous city in the country consequently meant having teachers and administrators with low expectations. One said, "It's like they didn't even feel like trying because they thought we'd just become drug dealers or gang members anyway." The other said that he felt dropping out of school was the better choice. He said that he couldn't relate to school, that what he was learning was boring. He felt that dropping out and spending more time working would get him farther and was the better option, especially because he didn't see college as an affordable expense. Some would disregard them as "dropouts," but it is more accurate to describe them as being systematically forced out by corporate standards of education, what's also known as the school-to-prison pipeline. For them, what they were learning in school was pointless in comparison to the daily challenges they faced beyond the classroom. I came to realize that our system is designed to fail America's youth.

## The Left-Behind Children's Call to Arms

As a student currently in a teacher education program, it is frustrating to be taught how to adapt to the ever-changing, increasingly high-stakes testing school framework rather than have an open discussion on what this means, why it is happening, and, most crucial, what we can do about it. Recognizing this has illuminated the importance of finding ways and the courage to make that space where such a space was never meant to exist. When I am eventually in the classroom, I aim to provide a liberating education, not a standardized one. I hope to give my students an education that provides them the tools and opportunities to challenge the systems that oppress them rather than simply assimilate to them. Yet, I know this will be almost impossible if we do not continue challenging and resisting profit-based school reforms pushed for by neoliberals. In essence, I have to recognize that the most crucial challenges our students deal with will never be resolved in a multiple-choice bubble form. This leaves me, as an educator, unable to teach for liberation under the paradigm of high-stakes testing. If liberation is denied, resistance becomes necessary to education. Luckily for aspiring teachers, resistance has already begun.

The next generation of teachers—me included—are the students who were "schooled" in the NCLB era. It's obvious in working with and talking to other future teachers that we've been conditioned to see standardized testing as inseparable from school, education, and—well, teaching. Getting those scores to meet that "standard" are what we know and what we grew up believing was elemental to an "education." This becomes problematic because as "products" of NCLB, many future teachers won't push back against something that has been ingrained as the norm—unless they recognize not only how boycotts such as that against the MAP in Seattle can in fact be victorious but also why *they* should boycott high-stakes testing, and what type of education can emerge when our schools are freed of these standards.

But, unfortunately, many future teachers believe that an education system freed from high-stakes testing is impossible. And this is one of the driving reasons I'm still pursuing the profession, and why I find it critical that we collectively work to assure that other future educators are aware of this movement and fight against high-stakes testing. We need to encourage future teachers to continually ask themselves: Why are you becoming a teacher? Because 99.9 percent of the time, the response will include some desire to positively change young people's lives. We need to make sure we connect this desire to the movement against high-stakes testing.

As proven by the Chicago Teachers Union strike and the boycott in Seattle, changing lives and making an impact on students can't and shouldn't be limited to only what we do inside a classroom. Actions such as the victorious MAP boycott and various student protests play a critical and absolutely necessary role in this fight. These moments of pushback and challenging these tests are rarely—if ever—discussed in teacher prep programs. We're being taught to simply adapt to the new policies and standards rather than say what we all know each other to be actually thinking: these policies do nothing for student learning, and they are not what education should be.

To my fellow future teachers: Our fight begins now. If your college program fails to reveal and provide the space to discuss what is happening to our education system and to our profession—which we know deserves a hell of a lot more respect than it currently gets—then you need to make that space. If you know what you want for your future students, then you must fight against the policies and reformers who will do everything they can to prevent you from giving it to them.

It is our duty to not only create space now but later, too. We are going into this field because we believe we will have the ability to create an environment that fosters growth, creativity, and courage in our future students. Our space, our teaching, has the potential to build that space where students discover the volume of their voices, the power in their actions—that is our space, and we cannot stand by and let people who have no idea what this profession requires rip that away from us.

## 17.
# STUDENT REVOLUTION
## Nikhil Goyal

The first standardized test I ever took was the TerraNova. I was in Ms. Racovitch's third-grade class at Charles Campagne Elementary School in Bethpage, New York. It had been a handful of years since the No Child Left Behind (NCLB) Act had been put into effect by president George W. Bush. The law required states to implement tests in reading and mathematics from third to eighth grade. In order to prepare for these tests, we were forced to complete hours of reading comprehension worksheets every night for homework. We also learned countless test-taking strategies and how to correctly bubble in Scantron sheets. The process, which lasted many months, was miserable for the students. And the teachers were clearly bent out of shape.

A few months after the administration of the TerraNova, we received our scores in the mail. I remember that I did well on the mathematics section, but did fairly poorly on the reading section. I couldn't understand how such a beautiful and elegant language was being condensed into absurd multiple-choice questions. It felt very unnatural to me. I had been someone who was a voracious reader, consistently consuming roughly a hundred books every year.

Overall, my first brush with standardized testing made me begin to think that there was something obviously irrational with the school system. I was told that these tests were for "my own good" and that "I better get used to them" since these rituals would continue every year for at least another decade.

During my experience in school, I have been used as a guinea pig by various politicians and education officials to try out their neoliberal education reform experiments without my consent. The verdict is in: they have all horribly failed.

Consider standardized testing—the latest educational fad sweeping the nation. They are the make-or-break assessment that determines a school's status with the department of education. They are the numbers published in major newspapers across the country. They are the scores real-estate agents tout when verifying a neighborhood's value. Corporate education reformers believe that if you make children take more futile tests and attached higher stakes to them, that somehow leads to better outcomes.

Educator Marion Brady once wrote in the *Washington Post*, "Even if standardized tests didn't cost billions, even if they yielded something that teachers didn't already know, even if they hadn't narrowed the curriculum down to joke level, even if they weren't the main generators of educational drivel, even if they weren't driving the best teachers out of the profession, they should be abandoned because they measure the wrong thing."[1] No standardized, multiple-choice test can possibly assess creativity, problem-solving, imagination, critical thinking, and collaboration.

What are the ramifications for the obsession with high-stakes, standardized testing? One is the waste of nearly two billion dollars spent annually on testing that could have been better allotted to fighting poverty, for example. Another is that for the first time in decades, new research found that US creativity levels of young children have been on a sharp decline since the 1990s.[2] That is almost surely because of the increase of testing in school. Test scores are also internalized by children. They begin to think of themselves as failures or successes. When so many of the most brilliant and creative people on the planet have reportedly performed poorly on tests in school, why do we, as a society, continue to have a fetish for them? It was indeed Frederick Kelly, the inventor of the multiple-choice test, who later admitted that it was a "test of lower order thinking for the lower order." Tests in general are simply the worst way to measure learning.

And even when school days revolve entirely around testing, whether it be created by teachers or the state, students still perform poorly. In a talk, Cevin Soling, director of the remarkable documentary *The War on Kids*, put it succinctly:

Schools only test what they teach students and the remarkable thing is that despite this insanely dishonest approach, schools completely and utterly fail at what they spend all of their time doing, which is teaching children how to pass their test. To subject home schooled and unschooled children to these kinds of tests is quite absurd, because they have different objectives. Yet on the whole, they still greatly outperform compulsory schooled children. That is like beating the house in Vegas. Schools are like casinos run by imbeciles. They create the game, regulate the game, manage the game, and somehow they still lose. The incompetency of rigging a system that still fails to produce a desired outcome cannot be understated.[3]

Let's add ten years to my first testing incident and arrive at my senior year at Syosset High School in Syosset, New York. At the beginning of the school year—fall 2012—the school district approved a new teacher evaluation system. Earlier that year, New York governor Andrew Cuomo, after a lengthy feud with the state teachers union, came to an agreement over a comprehensive teacher evaluation system for the state. The arrangement was made so that New York State would be eligible to receive $700 million of Race to the Top funds, a national sweepstakes spearheaded by President Obama that allocated monies to states that adopted his education policies. Under the new system known as the Annual Professional Performance Review (APPR), 40 percent of a teacher's evaluation would be based on standardized test scores, while the remaining 60 percent would be based on subjective measurements, like classroom observations and student surveys. Then, teachers would be sorted into four categories: ineffective, developing, effective, or highly effective. However, there's one catch. In the bill, it states: "The new rating system would prohibit a teacher or principal who is rated ineffective in the objective measures of student growth from receiving a developing score overall." In other words, if a teacher is unable to raise their students' test scores for two consecutive years, even if he or she is deemed highly effective on the subjective measures, the teacher could be fired.

That fall, the Student Learning Objective (SLO) exams were unleashed on all the students in my school in every subject, including art, music, and physical education. Yes, in gym class, multiple-choice exams with colorful green Scantrons were doled out. I wish I were kidding. Teachers would administer the same exam at the beginning and at the end of the school year. By means of value-added measurements and an obtuse formula, the teachers' effectiveness would be determined. In a hilarious note, my teachers were telling students point-blank that it would be wise to fail the exam in October and then marginally improve in the exam in June. Moreover, in New York, general state aid for schools is now tied to teacher evaluations, which puts further strain on the most impoverished communities in our state. Naturally, I, with the reputation of being a rabble-rouser, opted out of every SLO exam.[4] Each time, I put my name on the test booklet and Scantron and then handed the blank items back to my teacher. There were no consequences.

All over the state, there has been an outpouring of indignation at the APPR system. I cannot begin to describe some of the conversations I've had with educators, many of whom are veterans with decades of experience in this profession, who are feeling humiliated, demoralized, and beaten down by this process. Many would subscribe to Bob Seger's lyrics, "I feel like a number. I'm not a number. I'm not a number. Dammit I'm a man. I said I'm a man."

Two principals, Sean Feeney of the Wheatley School and Carol Burris of South Side High School, took the lead and drafted a letter protesting the evaluation system. As of January 2013, 1,535 principals as well as 6,500 parents, educators, and students have signed onto the document. In addition, in one survey, an overwhelming majority of New York principals said that the test scores are "not a very accurate reflection of teacher ability." Some have said it would be easier to flip a coin. An analysis by the *New York Times* of some teacher evaluation systems in the United States discovered that almost all of the teachers were rated effective: "In Florida, 97 percent of teachers were deemed effective or highly effective in the most recent evaluations. In Tennessee, 98 percent of teachers were judged to be 'at expectations.' In Michigan, 98 percent of teachers were rated effective or better."[5] So much for spending millions on junk science.

If there's one thing that is absolutely clear to me, it's that Governor Cuomo has ignored the voices of students, teachers, principals, and parents who have grave concerns about the evaluations. He is frankly telling millions of students and teachers that their value is no more than a number in a spreadsheet. What he's forgotten is that evaluation is best done when the purpose is not to punish and reward teachers but to lend them support, foster collaboration, and encourage self-evaluation.

What are some alternatives to testing? Many schools have introduced portfolios as a form of assessment. Students collect their best work—projects, blog posts, essays, videos, and podcasts—and present it in a professional manner to their teachers, peers, and the community at large. When they aren't trying to constantly "prove that learning happened," it is done for its own sake via intrinsic motivation and curiosity. Much research has found that external rewards like grades and test scores are extremely deleterious to the learning process.

Fortunately, more companies are realizing that test scores and grades are fundamentally trivial in the assessment of potential employees. Google is one of the more famous ones. Laszlo Bock, senior vice president of people operations at Google, told the *New York Times*, "One of the things we've seen from all our data crunching is that G.P.A.'s are worthless as a criteria for hiring, and test scores are worthless."[6] When hiring people for technology positions, candidates are often asked to send a link to their GitHub account or portfolio. Pathbrite, a startup based in San Francisco, allows people to showcase their work, learning, and achievements through digital portfolios.

In early April 2013, representatives from student unions and groups from around the country gathered in the basement of the St. Stephen Church in Columbia Heights in the nation's capital at the strike of midnight. Sitting cross-legged in a circle on the cool linoleum floor, we discussed our successes and hashed out a plan moving forward. All of us in our own right were rebels with a cause, dreaming the impossible dream, and hungry to spur a movement led by young people.

My peers, from Portland, Seattle, and Providence to Chicago, Newark, and Philadelphia, have been walking out of school, protesting, and rallying against high-stakes testing, budget cuts, and the corporate assault on public education. Whether it is for gay rights, voting rights, civil rights, women's rights, in every successful social movement it is young people taking charge, leading the way, and sparking outrage within us all. No longer are we willing to stay on the sidelines while our society, schools, and communities are being wrecked.

As I said at a rally in Albany, New York, in June 2013: revolutions begin in the basements of churches, in the backs of bars, in the rooms of community centers, and on Facebook and Twitter. It's time for our stakeholders to rise up and revolt. We will walk out. We will opt out of testing. We will boycott. We will protest. And we won't stop until our demands are met.

Sarah Chambers addresses the Saucedo elementary school community during the boycott of the Illinois Standards Achievement Test (ISAT) in March 2014.

University of Massachusetts students rally to support Barbara Madeloni (wearing the "What would bell hooks do?" T-shirt) in the wake of her termination for supporting their stand against standardized testing. © 2012 by Rene Theberge

The Portland Student Union marches against high-stakes testing in winter 2013.

Quyen, five years old, Castle Bridge/Puente del Castillo student. Photo by Dao X. Tran.

The Garfield High School faculty gather on the front steps of the school on February 6, 2013, listening to Seattle NAACP president James Bible pledge his support as part of a national day of action in solidarity with the MAP test boycott. Photo courtesy of scrapthemap.wordpress.com.

Students and teachers at Ballard High School in Seattle rally in support of the MAP test boycott, winter 2013. Photo by Noam Gundle.

Teachers at Berkeley High School in Berkeley, California (above), and at Lafayette Elementary School in Washington, DC (below), join a 2013 national day of action in solidarity with MAP-boycotting teachers in Seattle. Photos courtesy of scrapthemap.wordpress.com.

Members of the Providence Student Union lead a zombie march, graphically portraying what high-stakes testing does to students' brains, in spring 2012. Photo by Aaron Regunberg.

Stephanie Rivera joins with parents, students, teachers, and activists in a three-day march touring the fifty-four Chicago public schools slated for closure in 2013. Photo courtesy of Stephanie Rivera.

Rally during the student walkout of the Prairie State exam in Chicago, April 2013. Top, opposite: Malcolm London joins in the Prairie State protest outside CPS headquarters. Photos by Sarah Jane Rhee, loveandstrugglephotos.com.

Educating the Gates Foundation rally in Seattle on June 26, 2014. Photos on pages 190–192 by Elliot Stoller.

# PARENTS

# 18.
# LONG ISLAND OPTS OUT
## MY STORY OF RESISTANCE
**Jeannette Deutermann**

*I would rather die than go to school.* These words of despair, uttered by my then third-grade son, changed the course of my life.

As a child I was always around educators. My father was a high school physics teacher. My sister became a special education teacher, my other sister a school psychologist. I myself taught for six years at an alternative high school, for kids who were in danger of dropping out or failing to graduate. It was there that I learned firsthand what teaching to the individual child could do to turn a student (on whom most had given up) into one who took pride in completing high school and graduating with a diploma. I feel that the biggest tragedy to come out of this mess is that we ignore the educational needs of every individual child. Too many education reformers have lost sight of how important it is to treat children as individuals, and to understand that success cannot be measured in any one single way.

My decision to act was in fact brought on by witnessing firsthand the changes in my then eight-year-old son. These changes began a few months before the third-grade tests and continued until the day he was informed he would not be taking the fourth-grade exam, a little over a year later. My son has never been an emotional child. In fact, I would generally have to pry any expression of feeling out of him. He became a child who cried at night over difficult homework, had frequent stomachaches (which his doctor believed to be caused by stress and anxiety), and begged not to go to school in the mornings. On more than a few occasions he stated, "I would rather die than go to school." This obviously caused me tremendous panic and worry. I was determined to get to the bottom of why he was feeling this way. I spoke with the school psychologist, the teacher, the principal, and the superintendent. All of them alluded to how there was a big change in curriculum, the tests were new as well, and that he may just be reacting to all of these changes. The final straw was hearing that my son was being offered "Academic Intervention Services" to prepare him for these new tests an hour before school, twice a week, for two months. I posed this offer to my son, and words cannot describe the anguish that came out of my unemotional, now nine-year-old child. It was at that moment that I decided I was finished with this testing madness. I did not even know I could opt him out at this point. I simply knew that my son would not be taking this test.

My research began. First, I spoke with every educator I knew. My sister was the first stop. I asked her, "What are these tests even for?" She responded, "They serve absolutely no purpose other than to evaluate teachers like me." I asked my friend who was a third-grade teacher; same response. I asked teacher after teacher and the responses were similarly frustrated with the overuse of standardized testing in our education system today. I began to get the sense that these teachers were not only relieved to be asked the question but also that these tests had made them angry, dejected, and sad.

My research continued. My sister and I had another conversation in which she told me about a Facebook group she had stumbled upon for upstate New York on which some members posted about having successfully opted out their children from the state assessments the previous year. We both agreed that if it were in fact true, we would follow suit. My next course of action was to speak with my principal and the school psychologist, as I had been working very closely with both of them on helping my son get his smile back. I informed them I discovered that in fact my son did not have to take this exam, and that I would be looking into the specific details on how we could successfully pull this off without harming my son, the teachers, or the school.

I expressed very plainly that I felt it was unethical to evaluate the teachers based on my son's test scores, and that I trusted our teachers to evaluate my son, not corporations, politicians, or testing companies. They fully supported my decision and pledged to honor my parental rights.

I was relieved by the support of the school, yet something still just didn't feel quite right. I had now ensured that my son would not have to participate in these tests, but as I heard my friends in the schoolyard discussing their fears over the looming April assessments, I knew it would not be right if I kept the information about how to opt out children from the test to myself. I began the careful process of talking to my close friends about what I learned and what I was planning to do. Some were not on board at first. Some thought I must have had some bad chili and was obviously delirious. No way could this be what is actually going on. I tried not to bombard or pressure them, but I showed them articles I had found. Articles like the one written by the Principal's Group on how APPR was affecting the classrooms. A letter written by the Wantagh principal to his district parents on the harmful effects of high-stakes testing. Articles written by Carol Burris, an award-winning Long Island principal. Slowly my friends got on board. If they hadn't, that may have been where this story ended. Instead, watching how fired up they became, I decided to go even further. My sister and I once again met to discuss my plan for making my own Facebook group, similar to the one we had seen from upstate New York. I needed a way to spread this information beyond just my own district, but I wanted the information to be specific to my community in Long Island.

And thus the Facebook page "Long Island Opt Out Info" was born. Now came the really hard work. My friends were added. Their friends were added. Then friends of friends were added. Within the first week we were up to a few hundred. By the end of the second week we were close to a thousand. All the while, we (me, my sister, and other educators and parents who knew the relevant information) were continuing to research how we could successfully pull off a large-scale boycott of the upcoming tests. Much was learned from the parents in upstate New York who had already been through this process. I would frequently contact Eric Mihelbergel and Chris Cerrone, who ran the New York State group, for advice on the details of opting out. I was very careful not to post any information on the site unless we knew for sure that it was accurate. My sister and I pored over State Education Department documents, NCLB waiver documents, RttT information, Title 1 information and guidelines, assessment administration guidelines; everything and anything we could get our hands on that would allow us to accurately inform parents what their options were for shielding their children from these abusive tests.

Around the time we hit about four thousand members, a few weeks before the test, some issues came up on the Facebook page. While most people were cordial, friendly, and respectful of opposing opinions, some were not. With that many people (strangers) involved, arguments can get out of hand. There was a clear divide between the people who believed that Common Core (CC) was the source of the problem, and those of us who believed excessive high-stakes testing tied to teacher evaluations was the source of the problem. Whenever someone would post something in reference to ending high-stakes testing, those in the CC camp would attack. I myself was verbally attacked for not putting CC at the top of my list of things I was fighting against. It was during this time that I considered throwing in the towel.

I had also been speaking at PTA meetings and forums around the island, and while I found that I have a natural ability for public speaking, in those early days the stress before speaking was almost unbearable. I lost about ten pounds just in that first month, and I was already on the thin side. Sleep was not my friend, and pretty soon I looked a bit zombielike. I had to dig up my fifteen-year-old makeup concealer to cover up the lovely new dark circles under my eyes. I would panic before posting something for fear that it would turn out to be incorrect or that I would be criticized. I was not used to being in the "public eye" and even started being recognized in public places. It happened very fast and I was not quite prepared for it. When it all started, I didn't have the slightest idea that it would get that big or go that far. Problems on the page continued even as we continued to grow. There was quite a bit of infighting, and I did not like the negative turn the page was taking. I had to make a decision whether or not I could handle all of this, whether I was willing to devote the required time to making it work, and whether I could make the page something I could be proud of.

I decided to regain control over everything. I restated our mission publicly on the page, changed the settings of the page so that I could approve each and every post, and explained to everyone that I would ban people from the page who could not show respect to others. Again, these same people attacked, called it censorship, and some jumped ship and created their own Facebook pages. Those who continued on our opt-out page had a clear understanding of where I stood and what the goals of the group were, and we were able to focus on the task at hand: opting out of the state tests. The week leading up to the tests was a blur. Eighty percent of my day was spent fielding questions, calling school administrators, and managing the page. My children had the fortunate experience of eating takeout food every night for a week!

By the first day of testing there were close to eight thousand members on the LI Opt-Out Facebook page. Hundreds of Long Island students refused to take the assessments that first day. The numbers for middle school students were much higher than the elementary school students, as seventh- and eighth-graders can easily speak up and refuse for themselves. After a successful first day of test refusal, word spread quickly. The second day saw a huge jump in the numbers of students opting out. When the ELA assessment was administered the following week, the numbers doubled. Although we had no way to confirm exactly how many opted out over those two weeks of testing, we did receive numbers for 12 out of our 122 Long Island districts. The number was well over 1,000 for those 12 districts alone. Reporters asked the state education department how many students opted out of the tests and they refused to comment for fear of revealing the mass resistance that was organized to the tests.

While we were proud of this new movement, our work was far from over. Field tests were coming. Half of our Long Island schools were chosen as field test districts. Again we pushed for a massive boycott of the field tests in which the testing company Pearson uses our children as unpaid test subjects to design upcoming exams that they will then sell to school districts. We were successful once again. We had the same students who opted out of the state assessments opt out of the field tests, plus many additional students.

This year's testing was finally over. Or was it? I was informed that my sons were both going to be administered the final round of their local assessments, the Measures of Academic Progress (MAP) assessments—also known as the NWEA, the organization that produces the test. I did not yet know about these "local assessments" and had to work quickly to learn as much as possible to make an educated decision. The first thing I learned was that these assessments were also tied to their teachers' evaluations. I asked the teachers if they felt that the MAP assessments were necessary to provide them with diagnostic information on my children and what they need. Although hesitant, to be completely honest, their response was clear. These assessments would be of little value to my children.

My husband and I then made the decision not to allow our children to take any local assessments that were used in a teacher's evaluation. However, my younger son Jack was mistakenly given the test! The principal called me on the phone very upset and concerned that I would be furious. She explained that they caught the mistake in time to delete his scores from the system. I simply laughed and said, "No problem! His scores were deleted, I'm good!" It has always been important to me to make it clear to my administrators and teachers of my children's school that I trust them and I am on their side. I believe that is why I have so many teachers participating on my Facebook site. They trust that I am 100 percent pro-teacher, and am fighting for them as much as I am fighting for my children and all the students they teach.

As the end of the year approached, we had one more major event; the NYSUT (state teachers union) rally in Albany. Fifteen thousand educators, parents, and students came to Albany by bus, car, and train. It was an amazing event and it felt good to be surrounded by all the people I was fighting with and for. The highlight of the day was when Kevin Glynn, founder of Lace to the Top, and a person I greatly admire, said to me, "I'm not sure any of this would have happened without you." I scanned the sea of educators and parents standing arm in arm. Although I'm not comfortable giving myself credit for what is occurring in New York, I couldn't help feeling a bit of pride in all that had been accomplished in such a short few months.

At this point I was feeling a bit tired. The spring had gone by so fast, and I was looking forward to spending some time with my family. It is very hard to justify spending so much time being distracted and physically away from them but I knew at the same time I was doing it for them as well. It was a difficult time for them also. My older son Tyler was struggling with the feelings that it was his "fault" that I was now so busy and stressed all of the time. At one point he said to me, "Mom, I'll just take the tests," after hearing me on the phone talking to someone about the tremendous pressure I was under.

I have had to frequently sit down and explain to each of them what I was doing and why I was doing it. At the same time that I am explaining things to them, I am also trying to shield them. Their picture was in the paper a couple of times and we were also interviewed on camera. Both times I had a tough time deciding whether or not to even show them. My older son does not like attention, and I am always concerned that he will not feel comfortable with the role that he has been thrown into without his consent.

Luckily, as we have moved through this process, they have been taking it all in stride. My younger son was recently asked in his second-grade class to write what he is thankful for. In it he wrote, "I am thankful that my Mom feeds me and opted me out of the first grade tests." My first reaction was, "Is that all they see me as now?" My second reaction was relief that they understand that I am doing this for them. I admit that there are times when I doubt myself and feel that I am neglecting the very thing I am trying to help: my children. But I try and remember that this gift I am trying to give them may shape their very development as the human beings. Being part of an education system that allows them to thrive and grow to their full potential has to be worth the evenings away from them, the hours I spend administrating my Facebook page, and the constant phone calls I have to make to organize the movement. My husband, who works long hours in Manhattan, has felt the same pangs of neglect. He tries to support what I am doing as best he can, but due to his work schedule, has not been able to attend the lectures, meetings, and events I am involved in. This has definitely caused a divide, and a detachment in our relationship. I give him a tremendous amount of credit for enduring the never-ending discussions and my focus on all of this. I think the spouses of the movement leaders should start a support group called Spouses Who Play Second Fiddle to High-Stakes Testing!

My parents have been an incredibly strong support system throughout. My father was concerned in the beginning about the opposition I would face, and worried about my safety given the people I was up against. The pride I see in their faces and the faces of the rest of my family is another driving force for me. Without all their support and patience I could not have taken on a task this consuming and massive. I would count this balance between my family and this movement as my greatest struggle.

At the beginning of the summer the movement activity was relatively quiet. The membership on the page continued to grow, but at a much slower pace. The page itself became easier to manage. The members who wanted to see a greater focus on the Common Core and the political aspects of the reform movement formed their own pages. I was finally feeling settled and more in control of my Facebook page. At the end of July, there was a meeting, which turned out to be the tipping point in the New York State fight. Eric Mihelbergel and Chris Cerrone, who in the beginning of this struggle taught me everything I needed to know about the logistics behind refusing or "opting out" of the state assessments, had come up with the idea to have all the various leaders of the opt-out movement from around New York meet in Syracuse to discuss planning and strategy. It was at this meeting that we decided to form a group whose sole purpose was to unite the various organizations throughout the state that were fighting the corporate education reformers. The website and organization New York State Allies for Public Education was launched in August 2013. This group includes the most amazing individuals I have ever had the pleasure of working with. We have our own closed Facebook page to discuss strategy, events, and press releases. As of November 2013, we had more than forty organizations that have signed on to be allies. This is a very important step in this fight. When a plan is formulated, it is now distributed to every organization under the "umbrella," and in turn to all of its members, which collectively number in the thousands. An added benefit to me as a member of this amazing group of leaders is that I am now part of a support system in which I know that these colleagues all have my back. I can share ideas with them and get a better understanding of the issues. Many have areas of expertise that they bring and share. We are in a fight to save public education, and it can get ugly. This group of individuals keeps above the fray and conducts itself of a manner in which we can all be proud and stand behind.

As we headed toward the 2013–14 school year and a renewed fight to protect our children from the abuses of standardized testing, I knew I needed to delegate responsibilities or I would drown in my to-do list. I decided to ask for volunteers to represent the 122 districts of Long Island, or, as I called them, "liaisons." I was able to enlist a group of about ninety volunteers to serve this purpose. These parents (some of whom are teachers in other districts) request information from their superintendents about the assessments used in a given district and what the refusal (opting-out) policies are. The liaisons attend board of education meetings and fight for resolutions against high-stakes testing, data sharing, and fair refusal policies, are responsible for spreading the word in their districts, and, most important, organize forums for me and others to come and speak to members of the community about education reform.

These forums and organizing meetings have taken place from one end of Long Island to the other, and have drawn crowds of between fifty and one hundred people. Local legislators have been participating in these as well. Some have scheduled the forums themselves, and some are invited to speak. Event halls have donated their spaces, or we have gathered in local libraries.

It is a marvel to watch as each week these educational forums are scheduled, come together, and advance the movement for authentic assessment in a truly grassroots effort.

Inexplicably, the New York Parent Teacher Association (NYPTA) has been deafeningly silent about our new movement against standardized testing, and its refusal to take a stand on the primary issue motivating parents to become active in their schools created a major obstacle when we first tried to organize parents across Long Island's districts. The NYPTA has missed out on playing a crucial role in this fight, and if they do not quickly shift to join our movement, they surely risk becoming irrelevant to parents on one of the most critical issues facing our education system today. Many local PTAs have now begun to step out in front of the statewide organization to take action and show support for their parents and teachers.

As a wholly volunteer effort without major institutional support, we knew we faced the challenge of gaining visibility for our efforts to attract new recruits to our opt-out movement. New parent recruits rose to this challenge and designed and ordered hundreds of lawn signs, similar to election signs, that read, "Parents, Refuse the NYS Assessments," complete with our Facebook name and our ally's website, www.nysape.org. They also created a magnetic bumper sticker. These publicity tools are very important components in spreading the word to people who may not be on Facebook or may live in a district that is less aware of the havoc that these reforms are causing in our schools.

I have learned a great deal about myself over the last six months. In March, the thought of public speaking sent me into a severe anxiety attack. I now stand up in front of a hundred parents and educators without much more than a few butterflies. Much of that is simply practice. But a lot has to do with the confidence I have gained in myself and the message I bring.

There hasn't been a single moment when I have had to ask myself, "Am I doing the right thing?" I know it is the right thing with every fiber of my body. Every single story I hear of a child who has lost her ability to believe in herself, or even worse has declined into mentally and physically self-abusive behaviors, I resolve to fight harder. Every time I hear of a teacher who has lost his love of teaching, I resolve to fight harder. It is important to fight hard, but how you choose to fight is just as important. The success of this movement in New York is based on the well-developed, multifaceted strategies we employ. Critical to our success has been our ability to work as a team, rejecting the political infighting and mudslinging that can be so destructive, instead respecting each other and the job each has done. We fight with intelligence and truth. This is our power. This is our weapon.

As of January 2014, there are over fourteen thousand members of the Long Island Opt Out page. I believe we will win this fight. I once asked Diane Ravitch, "The good guys always win, right?" She responded, "No, they don't. But we will."

# 19.

# PLAYING FOR THE SCHOOLS WE WANT

## Kirstin Roberts

On April 17, 2013, parents, children, and early childhood educators arrived at the Chicago Public Schools headquarters bright and early. Instead of the normal macabre theater on display at 125 S. Clark Street for board of education (BOE) meetings—in which people who attend, send their children to, or work at public schools are forced to line up hours ahead of time in order to testify for two minutes to an uninterested and unelected school board, begging for support for their schools that never materializes—we decided to sit down. Bored silly and demoralized by the over-testing and lack of play-based learning opportunities in our early childhood classrooms, we decided to bring our message to the BOE in a way that couldn't be ignored.

An advance team of several parents and children, arms loaded with blocks, picture books, bubbles, board games, and picnic blankets arrived at the drab BOE building in the Chicago Loop shortly before 9:00 a.m. We were joined by Julie Woestehoff, a veteran educational justice activist and leader in the movement against over-testing. We entered the main lobby and spread out a couple of our blankets on the linoleum tile floor. A couple of the kids set up a chessboard at an empty table nearby. Another child sat down on the blankets and began to draw. A parent and preschool-age child began to erect a block construction. So far, we were ignored by the folks behind the security desk. I propped up a few of the handmade picket signs designed by a preschool teacher who had to work and couldn't join us but who wanted her voice heard too: *We're more than a score! Play is how we learn, Play is every child's human right!* A few folks walked past, hurrying for the elevators, with looks of bemused curiosity. It's not often that children and parents make themselves at home at the headquarters of the Chicago Public Schools.

We were soon approached by a member of the security personnel, who inquired about what we were doing. "We're playing," was our reply. "Who told you could do this here?" he asked. At this point, more parents and children began to trickle in. As Julie kept the security guard occupied with questions ("Who should we talk to at CPS to get permission to play?"), the rest of us welcomed the arriving families with their armloads of art supplies, dress-up clothes, and toys, and we began to stake out more space. Eventually security guards were joined by the head of security for CPS and negotiations over the location of our sit-in (or, more accurately, *play-in*) began in earnest. Since we clearly weren't leaving, and as more and more arrived to join the play, the security team offered us a compromise: move your stuff to the hallway of the building, a few feet away. Since there was lots of foot traffic and good visibility there, we took this offer and spread out our materials.

An arts educator pulled out rolls of paper, glue, collage materials, and markers, and young children dug in. Boxes of dress-up clothes were spread out and children and adults changed into costume, donning fairy wings, rainbow clown wigs, and superhero costumes. Infants crawled on blankets and gnawed on board books while toddlers chased after bubbles that floated down the hallway. Soon a couple musicians arrived, with cello and guitar, and we sang along to "This Land Is Your Land" and other protest standards. The boisterous fun was supervised by a few junior high students and their parents, wearing taffeta tutu skirts from the dress-up box and fluorescent orange crossing guard vests labeled in marker, "Play Patrol."

For the first time in my many experiences at CPS headquarters, children felt welcomed, and adults were laughing and smiling. We were "playing in": Kind of like a sit-in, but with play-dough. And we weren't going to move until our children's laughter could be heard ringing through the halls.

Let me explain how this came about. On March 8, I posted this on my Facebook page:

> I have simply had enough of the inappropriate academic push down into early childhood education. . . . Are you with me? Then help me organize a

PLAY-IN! We'll go down to the Board of Education with our blocks, our play-dough, our finger-paints and our children, and we will assert the RIGHT of every young child to learn through play. No more standardized test drills, no more worksheets, no more expository essays in kindergarten. Please get in touch with me if you want to help and feel free to share.

This Facebook status struck a nerve with several of my coworkers (I'm a Chicago Public Schools preschool teacher) and friends with children in the public schools, and I received many e-mails and messages of support. As a member of the Chicago organization More Than a Score (MTAS), which is battling to save our schools from the nightmare of high-stakes standardized testing, I was already part of a network of dedicated parents and fellow Chicago Teachers Union members who were ready to help organize. MTAS had been founded earlier in the school year by parents and teachers frustrated by the sheer scale, expense, and consequences of the testing regime in CPS. We had worked together to petition and leaflet at more than thirty schools the previous February, spreading the news about over-testing and the alternatives, as part of a national day of solidarity with teachers in Seattle who had boycotted the MAP exams.

A few days before my Facebook post, I had toured my neighborhood school's kindergarten classrooms in preparation for registering my then five-year-old son for his first day of elementary school that coming fall. The classrooms were overcrowded with small tables and chairs—enough for the thirty or so students they're typically cramming into CPS kindergarten classrooms these days, although many, many kindergartens have far more. Brightly colored plastic tubs full of books lined the shelves. Walls were covered with teacher-made posters about colors, shapes, classroom rules.

All this was pretty typical, and, to an early childhood teacher such as myself, it looked pretty familiar. But something was amiss. Or I should say: something was missing. I scanned the rooms for any sign of building blocks. None. I looked around for signs of dramatic play areas or props, like puppets. Nope. Sand or water table? No. Hands-on science area, with opportunities for children to touch, examine, experiment? Uh-uh. Art materials or any sign that children were being encouraged to represent their ideas in creative or meaningful ways? Don't even ask. What passed for creativity were displays of Xeroxed snowmen, colored in crayon, each indistinguishable from the last, and each apparently only an excuse to practice words ending in "*-ow*," as their kindergarten scrawl clued me in on closer examination. No art for art's sake here.

I was informed by my tour guide that recess happened for twenty minutes a day, weather permitting—and this is better than many schools get, since this school has a good playground, with newer equipment and space to run. Many schools, particularly in low-income areas, don't even have that. I left feeling depressed, wondering how my five-year-old son would possibly adapt to a seven-hour school day that allowed for a measly twenty minutes of play. I imagined picking him up after school and coming home to face the large amounts of worksheet homework CPS kindergarten teachers are now assigning in order to ensure their students are capable of passing fourteen standardized tests administered over the course of the year. It seemed impossibly cruel.

I came home and took a look on Facebook. I read about a colleague in New York City, a kindergarten teacher, who had been written up by her administration. What was the bad practice she was being punished for? During a classroom observation, an administrator asked one of her students what they were doing during center time, and the child responded, "Playing."

## The Forgotten Principle of Play

The last seven years of teaching preschool has been a constant battle to defend what should be—and used to be—a given in the world of early childhood: Young children learn most naturally and most deeply through well-supported play. Play is how young children explore their worlds, build relationships, experiment with their environment, test theories, and construct knowledge. In short, play is how young children learn and grow.

It is both a joyful and serious endeavor, as anyone who has spent any amount of time watching young children build with blocks, play house, or attack the playground can attest to.

Yet for all the power of well-supported play to enrich children's spirits as well as their intellects, play in our early childhood classrooms is under threat in elementary schools around the country. The dramatic increase in testing of the very young over the last decade, in response to the No Child Left Behind and Race to the Top federal education mandates, has pushed out developmentally appropriate curriculum, including play-based learning, from early childhood classrooms. The preparation for the adoption of the hugely profitable Common Core State Standards has exacerbated this trend.

Teachers who value and use a play-based curriculum are forced to come up with creative ways to "hide" children's play from know-nothing administrators who accuse us of promoting play because it's "easy"—which shows how very little they know—or who belittle our classrooms for their lack of rigor and discipline. Worse is the pressure in the poorest neighborhood schools, where test scores—seen as the sole measure of the worth of our schools—are low. Teachers in these schools are told that play is a luxury that underprivileged kids cannot afford. In order to make up the achievement gap, time for play and experiential learning has got to go. The "drill and kill" of narrow academic skills isolated from context and meaning, scripted instruction, and test preparation have replaced the kind of rich educational experiences that support the intellectual and emotional capabilities of all young children.

According to play-in participant and Concordia University associate professor Isabel Nuñez:

> One of the most destructive consequences of having non-educators running our districts and schools is that we have forgotten the fundamental principles of human development. Any developmental psychologist will tell you that young children learn through play. There is no debate on this within the discipline. Maria Montessori, Johann Pestalozzi, Friedrich Froebel were scientists. Their vision for education is based on research, not a touchy-feely desire to let the children play just because they enjoy it. A play-based curriculum for early childhood classrooms is developmentally appropriate, because play is the way children learn.

As parents and teachers of young children, we know the harmful effect of high-stakes testing on schools and school systems. We have marched and protested as many of our schools in the poorest areas of the city are shuttered, punished for not winning in a game rigged from the start. We also know the harmful impact of high-stakes testing on individual children; children who we love who are being labeled failures at the age of five years old.

We're tired of our children being used and abused by corporations out to make money off their tests and their curricula matched to the tests. The politicians, recipients of financial kickbacks in the form of campaign contributions from these same corporations, are more than happy to throw our children's schools into disarray and misery, as their children's (private) schools continue to thrive with multiple opportunities for creativity, play, and experiential learning.

Despite the peaceful and joyful experience of direct democracy experienced by all during the play-in, CPS security eventually called the police on the toddlers chasing bubbles. We had been warned a few times by the head of CPS security that bubbles represented a safety hazard, which surprised one parent of a preschooler and veteran emergency room nurse, who remarked, "I've been working in the ER a long time and have never once treated a patient for a bubble-related injury." The six police officers deployed stood nearby, powerless to stop three-year-olds from pounding play-dough and giggling. After an hour and a half, and snack time, we packed up and went home for our naps, as planned.

We played in at CPS to demonstrate our vision of appropriate early childhood education and to demand that our schools start listening to the experts and return play to our classrooms, end standardized testing for our youngest learners, and allow the joy of teaching and learning back into our schools. We're already discussing where we're going to play next. Anyone want to set up a play date?

# 20.
# FORGET TEACHING TO THE TEST—CASTLE BRIDGE BOYCOTTS IT!

## Dao X. Tran

When I first heard from my then five-year-old daughter's principal, Julie Zuckerman, that our school's kindergartners, first graders, and second graders would be taking a multiple-choice ("bubble-in") standardized test in September 2013, I thought she couldn't be serious. But she was. And the children would be taking this test not once but *twice*—in the beginning weeks of school and again in the spring. I wondered who was requiring this and why. No letter had come from the New York State Department of Education (NYSED) or the city's department of education (DOE) informing us parents of the testing our children were about to be subjected to. And when I searched online for a reason, or even an acknowledgement of this uncharted practice, I found very little. There was a story in the *New York Times* from the previous summer about the possibility of tests for kindergartners being rolled out, but not much else.

Apparently the scores—specifically, the difference between how these kindergarteners through second graders fared in the spring compared to in the fall—were to be used for part of the evaluation scores of their teachers. In fact, this was the sole reason for the test.

## The Elusive Search for Play

In 2009 when my daughter's father (full disclosure: he is a public high school teacher and a social justice union activist) and I first started looking around for a school for our then two-year-old, we tried to envision the ideal school for her. There would be lots of hands-on, exploratory learning; nurturing teachers working with small groups of children; classrooms filled with bright natural light; lots of resources and space for art-making and imaginative play; and cozy corners for reading. But that was a short-lived delusion. After all, we live in New York City and the days of early childhood schooling characterized by play, recess, laughter, art, and singing were far past unless you were willing and able to go the private school route. As we would soon discover, we would be lucky to find a public school that even had recess.

We were also committed to public schools and even though we live in a severely under-resourced and historically neglected school district, we wanted Quyen to attend our local zoned school. I called for an appointment to tour the school and some warning bells went off when the parent coordinator there seemed taken aback by the request—it was rare for parents to tour before deciding to enroll a child in this neighborhood school. The classrooms were big and bright, but the décor was bland and unexciting. The children wore uniforms and the teachers seemed to have a fairly "traditional" (read industrial model) approach to schooling, replete with children in rows of desks, teachers chanting "One-two-three, all eyes on me," homework (for three- and four-year-olds!), and a behavioral shame/reward system, which in one of the classes consisted of happy and sad "bumbaloo" faces—you didn't want to get a bumbaloo face. We met with the assistant principal, who was warm and seemed to understand where we were coming from, so we decided to give it a shot. It was just pre-K, we reasoned, and we could switch her to another school if it really didn't work out.

Quyen did not take to school well. She wasn't overjoyed to be in school at all (and away from me) for so many hours, but I expected that and thought she just needed time to adjust to such a big change. She began the year speaking a fair amount of English and Spanish, but used Spanish less and less as time went on. I noticed that even though the majority of children at her school heard or spoke Spanish at home, it was not valued or encouraged at school. Although I only saw them at drop-off and dismissal for a few minutes each day, it seemed that the children were restless and joyless. I thought it might have something to do with their feeling cooped up all day, with most of the day spent in regimented, structured "learning." I started campaigning for the school to have more play in class and outdoor recess, and was surprised to discover that recess, preferably outdoors, is encouraged by the city DOE. Yet the teachers told me that the administration had gotten rid of recess years ago and parents did not miss it. The assistant principal in turn assured me the teachers didn't want recess and most parents were happy not to have the children go outside since there were "safety concerns." There was a methadone clinic nearby and school officials claimed that they didn't have enough staff to monitor the children in the concrete yard. And besides, I was told, no one wanted to be outside in the cold. But I insisted that they try, and recess was reinstated.

Sadly, several weeks and months into the school year, the reinstatement of recess notwithstanding, things were still not improving. Quyen began almost every morning in tears, complaining that she wasn't well and was too sad to go to school. This was a child who was normally effusive, hard to suppress, and full of curiosity and ingenuity. I, probably channeling some of my own strict and unforgiving childhood upbringing and not wanting to coddle her, forced her to go and adapt to her new environs. But I also wanted to spend some time at her school to try and get a handle on why exactly she was unhappy. It turns out that parents weren't welcome in the school. The teacher (who was untenured) was nervous about my being in the classroom and the Parents Association (PA) was barely functional. The several meetings we attended were run by the principal and consisted mainly of reading the minutes from the previous meeting and various announcements by the PA president and parent coordinator. I tried several times to meet with the principal to no avail. Unsurprisingly, even though I was one of two parents of Asian descent in the school and among the small handful of parents of any ethnic background who came to PA meetings, she also never bothered to learn my name or Quyen's for that matter. And the school was clearly committed to the model of schooling that insisted low-income children of color need vast amounts of rigor and discipline instead of joy, nurturing, and creativity. We finished out the difficult and depressing year there; we had given it a try, but it was time to look for something that hewed just a little closer to our ideal, which admittedly seemed utopian at the time.

## A Progressive, Dual-Language Option

During our original search for pre-K, the progressive public school Central Park East One (CPE1) was our first choice, but it's a small school that is highly sought after and we were not able to gain admission for Quyen. So when we learned that Principal Julie was leaving CPE1 to found another school in Washington Heights that would be dual language (English/Spanish) *and* progressive, we were thrilled. Quyen would be going to a school with a mission to provide a high-quality education that is project based and infused with art and music, promotes hands-on learning—and where staff, children, teachers, and families would work together to nourish and support the children's development.

So, getting news of an impending mandatory, standardized, multiple-choice test was like getting a brisk slap. We had managed to get Quyen into a nurturing and challenging school, where the principal and tightly knit staff knew every single child and most of their grownups by first name, and yet we still could not escape the distorted clang of the school "reform" bell. By this time Quyen had gone through a remarkable first year at Castle Bridge. She was learning by doing about a range of topics—life cycles through chicken egg incubation and caring for chicks, balance, math, physics, and problem solving in block work, expressing herself in drawing and writing, as well as having time each day to explore projects of her choosing. She was a "natural" at math, was learning to love music and singing in a choir, developing her socio-emotional self, had learned how to read and write in English, and was starting to do the same in Spanish.

## Bubbles Are for Blowing, Not Filling In

It turns out Castle Bridge (as a new school) was among the thirty-some schools in the city that were mandated to give these tests to the littlest students because we did not have students in third through eighth grades who would take the New York State exams. A few of us parents met with Jane Hirschmann from Time Out from Testing to discuss these mysterious tests. We then formed a committee to investigate further.

We put ourselves in our kids' shoes and imagined coming to school—a school we loved, with caring teachers and a supportive environment—and being suddenly thrust into the standardized testing environment: *We usually spend time playing and learning how to take care of ourselves and our friends. But one day, our teacher sits us down and puts a test booklet put in front of us. It has, say, twenty-seven multiple-choice, bubble-in math problems, from which she will read aloud and ask us to "fill in the bubble for the right answer."*

*Never mind that some of us haven't yet had much experience holding a pencil. Never mind that some of us haven't yet learned how to read. Never mind that we may not recognize numbers yet. To help us locate which question we are to answer, our teacher will prompt us to find the image of the cat, or the key, or the eye. But she can't help us if we are confused, and we can't work together as we are usually encouraged to do. How odd!*

*Oh, and if we don't speak or understand much English—too bad. If we have learning challenges or disabilities—too bad. We'll actually "get" more time to sit in front of the test and get more frustrated, more stressed, more upset. All this to do what? To help our teacher understand what we know and are able to do with math? No. To make sure we get needed services and support? No.*

If supporting our children's learning had been the actual purpose of the Measures of Student Learning (MOSL) tests and they were developed by educators, I and other parents might not have been so up in arms. As it turns out, these tests were not about our children's learning at all. They were in fact about ranking and sorting their teachers.

Our political "leaders," both Republicans and Democrats, from President Obama and Arne Duncan to Governor "1%" Cuomo and New York State education commissioner John King, have ignored what's important to parents and instead listened to powerful and wealthy education *de*formers. These officials don't even send their children to public schools. *They* are failing our children, yet they push for our children's teachers to be accountable based on children's test data. All while they opt for their own children to go to schools that don't take these tests, that have small class sizes and project-based, hands-on, arts-infused learning—that's what we want for our children!

## From Opting Out to Mass Refusal

By this point, a handful of us had decided that we would opt out our own children from these MOSLs since, as Diana Zavala, a parent activist and educator affiliated with Change the Stakes (CTS, a citywide parent group), put it, "They can't fire parents." But we worried about the rest of the children at our wonderful school and hundreds more at the other targeted schools. It was also clear that this test, if unchallenged, would be used to normalize testing kids in younger grades, something that had been off the table for years. We thought, Why not make this a collective stand? After all, we felt sure that other parents, if they knew about these tests and why they were being given, would want to refuse as well.

Elexis Loubriel-Pujols (PTA co-chair with me) and I knew it would be crucial to get the parent body and families informed and mobilized. We and other parents gathered what little info we could, revised an information sheet and sample opt-out letter that we grabbed from the CTS website, and presented at the next PTA meeting. We had a lively discussion about what we understood the test to look like and why it seemed wrong to grade our children's teachers based on our kids' test scores. One Spanish-language-dominant parent brought up his own negative and painful experiences with test anxiety, another talked about transferring his child to Castle Bridge especially to avoid the widespread focus on excessive high-stakes testing in public schools, and yet another of her decision to enroll at the school because of its focus on developing the whole child. There was a question about whether there was any possible benefit to the tests, and we could not see any.

At roughly the same time, a *Daily News* article about the wrongness of bubble testing kindergarteners came out, confirming some of what we knew.[1] Reporter Rachel Monahan had contacted me for that article and I told her that a handful of us had committed to refusing for our kids to take the tests—and that there was a potential larger boycott brewing. Our reasons? There was no educative reason for the tests. We checked with several of our school's teachers and found that they agreed the tests would be no help in their knowing more about our children's development and would potentially be harmful because of the lost class time and focus they would require.

We found overwhelming support among families and the more letters we collected, the more confident other parents became to join the refusal. Of course, it helped immensely that we had the principal's support from the beginning and we were building a community where parents, teachers, students, and staff work as a team for our kids' benefit. We really felt like our voices as parents were valued and thus were able to speak out strongly. We also did some very specific follow-up. Elexis and I pored over lists of who had submitted opt-out letters and went around to try to speak to everyone who hadn't. We emailed, called, and met face to face with people to find out if they planned to opt out, and did not hear from any parents who wanted their child to take the test.

Opposition to the test really took off once parents saw what the math assessment (the first of the tests to be administered) actually looked like. I mentioned earlier that the test implicitly acknowledged that the young test-takers might not yet recognize numerals by placing images next to questions to indicate where a child should look. The test is also given only in English regardless of whether a child has fluency or not. Now, I'm not opposed to assessments per se. I do want to know if my child can understand how numbers work or if she can read. But I've got a pretty solid, if perhaps old-fashioned, way of knowing that—by just asking her! Or asking her teachers, who, after all, spend the majority of the day with her, explaining, exploring, supporting, and observing. I don't think that Pearson Inc. or Discovery Education™ can have more insight into her learning than her teachers. Especially when their way of doing that entails asking four- and five-year-olds to, say, count the number of stars printed on a page (talk about abstraction!) and then fill in the bubble for the correct answer next to the word *seven*—remember that upon entering kindergarten few kids know how to count abstractly (without manipulating concrete objects) or read yet. Or when their way shows an image of an older brother marking the top of his younger brother's head on a wall, asking if children could determine what the older boy was measuring: his younger brother's weight, height, or age. Of course, it probably never crossed the minds of the test developers that measuring children against a wall is not a universal practice and could just seem absurd or naughty—*why is that big boy drawing on the little boy's head or the wall?* Getting kids to learn to count or read by making them take a high-stakes test is as effective as getting a baby to learn to walk by pushing her down the stairs.

We did the only thing we felt we could do to protect our kids and their teachers—we organized a schoolwide boycott of the MOSL test. A second *Daily News* article that focused on our actions appeared and was a key milestone.[2] Having our story presented positively in a mainstream newspaper did a lot to cohere our existing committee and galvanized our school community. We began hearing from other parents and teachers around the city so relieved to see a group take an uncompromising stand. In swift succession, we were featured in a video episode of the Real News Network, Julie wrote an op-ed that was published on WNYC's blog *Schoolbook*, Quyen's teacher Andrea Fonseca's piece "Should First Grade Take a Test?" (riffing off the title of Miriam Cohen's excellent picture book on testing young children) appeared both on the MORE (Movement of Rank and File Educators, the United Federation of Teachers' social justice caucus) blog and in *Labor Notes* magazine, a roundup piece on opting out including our story appeared at *Nation.com*, and an inside account was written up by one of our organizers, Don Lash.[3] We had already reached 80 percent refusal, yet the letters continued to come in as more parents wanted to make known their intention to refuse the test formally. I remember upon taking a tally of submitted forms Elexis and I did a little dance of joy. In the end, all but three or four families formally refused to have their kids take it. And, if you do *that* math, our resistance made the potential results "statistically invalid." We effectively "cancelled" the test and Julie announced it to the press. We forced the state government to back down on giving these destructive and developmentally inappropriate exams. It was a sweeping indictment of the wrongness of these assessments and ringing endorsement of our refusal to have our children subjected to pointless testing and to have their teachers evaluated this way.

In the weeks that followed, the state education department (already on the defensive because of the Common Core content, rollout, and implementation and Commissioner King's tone-deaf responses to parent outrage) came out definitively agreeing that multiple-choice tests for K–2 children were inappropriate. Sadly, we heard that most targeted schools administered the test anyway because families could not make an informed choice, administrators were confused about whether it was mandated, and we didn't manage to get in touch with them to join the boycott. The tests became a hot potato that neither the state nor the city wanted to be seen as responsible for requiring. It remains to be seen what officials will mandate be used in their place, but the biggest takeaway for me was that it showed the effectiveness of just one small school being loud together. Imagine what we could do with several schools and hundreds, if not thousands, speaking out against these kinds of tests and the very high stakes attached to them.

# 21.

# "OPTING OUT OF THE CORPORATE CONVERSATION"

## Interview with Peggy Robertson

*This interview was conducted on May 30, 2014, and has been edited and condensed.*

**Jesse Hagopian:** Peggy, can you tell me about how you came to education and also how you became politically conscious?

**Peggy Robertson:** Well, my mom was a music teacher and so I grew up around educators. My grandfather was a teacher as well and I actually tried my darnedest to avoid being a teacher. I changed my major five times. I finally just realized okay, this is it, so—

**JH:** That sounds similar to me in that my mom was sure I was going to be a teacher so that meant I was sure I wasn't going to be one.

**PR:** Exactly, I know, and I also saw how hard it was and I was like, oh my gosh, you don't make any money, it's so hard. My whole life I taught a little bit of piano. I taught swimming and I just always loved teaching, and so I finally had to quit denying. I was raised in Missouri so I started teaching in Missouri.

I eventually got my masters in English as a second language and made my way west across Kansas to Colorado where I am now, and I'm in my seventeenth year of teaching. So that's how I came to teaching, but the political piece of it is just something I'm kind of really coming to grips with now. What's interesting is my dad was a writer; he was a reporter and he mainly did political writing. I was around this my whole life but didn't really realize that I was political. Because I was surrounded by it I think it just was something that became a part of me.

I was teaching here in Colorado during No Child Left Behind and I was in a district that decided to adopt a basal, the open-court basal, which of course was one of the favorites of Bush and everyone during that time and I was the literacy coordinator for the entire district. So when it happened I came to work one day and they said, "You know, we've adopted this Basal, and I said, oh my God, I can't do this. I hate this Basal. It won't even work for our population of students. I can't do this. And they said, "Well, you can never say that again, ever."

**JH:** Describe the basal. It's a reading assessment?

**PG:** Yes. It was the McGraw-Hill basal. It's a horrific reading program and I was used to having a lot of autonomy. In all the elementary schools where I worked we had what I call a resource room, just tons of books of all different topics. You name it, you can pick and choose, and so teachers had a lot of autonomy to determine, based on student interests and challenges of a book—they could pull from these resource rooms.

So what this district did is they said, We're going to go to this basal, and I mean the "on the same page every day" kind of system that No Child Left Behind was notorious for. I had several jobs during this time, but I guess for about three years I worked with the Learning Network all over Colorado in different schools. You would have these schools that would be lockstep on the same page every grade level, every day, you know, it didn't matter what the kids needed. So, long story short, when they said we were going to purchase this basal I knew I was done because I couldn't work under those conditions—so I quit.

**JH:** Wow.

**PH:** I had my second son and stayed home for six years. I mean this is so funny to me now, Jesse, but I swore I would never go back to teaching and I was going to open a pizza restaurant, that was my goal.

**JH:** [Laughs] That's great. I bet you would have made a great pie, but I'm glad we have you in the opt-out movement.

**PR:** In my mind it really required little thinking. It was just open a restaurant, work hard, and let's forget all of this. . . . That was my goal when my son was older. I was going to do that because I had friends who had done it and had been very successful.

**JH:** So No Child Left Behind drove you out of the classroom with the scripted curriculum?

**PR:** Oh, completely, yes.

**JH:** Were you scared to leave teaching right when you were having kids, needing the income?

**PR:** No. . . . I had reached my limit because I felt like my hands were tied and at that point I hadn't done a lot of research on what was going on, so for me it was just like I was in this small world where there was no escape. I didn't realize at that point that I could be empowered by doing my research and being an activist and advocating for what was right. All I could think was I can't do this; these are my boundaries so I have to leave. I think it's interesting because I think a lot of teachers, this is just my opinion, who are leaving right now are leaving because they feel that those boundaries . . . they can't get past those boundaries.

**JH:** Right. These policies of corporate education reform have pushed out so many great teachers from the classroom over the years.

**PR:** So I left.

**JH:** How did you decide to come back and try it again?

**PR:** Well, what happened was I stayed home and of course being an educator and a learner I started researching. I couldn't keep away from it. You know I was doing my stay-at-home mom thing and having a great time, but during my son's naps and in the evenings I was reading, reading, reading and realized what was going on. And once I realized what was going on, there was no stopping me after that. I had this knowledge. I knew that there had to be ways to stop it and my brain was just going 24/7 thinking through this. And around that time I started writing again. I just saw a lot of interesting things around politicians and writing and how strategy worked and things like that. I've been a writer my whole life, but I had quit there for a while and I started writing more as an activist. I wrote a letter to President Obama, and I had been following Anthony Cody online, and I thought you know what—I'm just going to send this little piece to Anthony and see what happens. Anthony wrote me back and said, "Oh my God, this is amazing; I want to post it on *Living in Dialogue.*"

**JH:** All right!

**PR:** Well, you could imagine after being home for . . . well, at that time, about four years and just kind of being in this box, it was like there's a world out there and that's the power of social media. So Anthony posted it on his blog and it went viral and then he said, "You know Peg, you really should start a blog," and I was like, "Well of course, that's what I should do." So I started writing *Peg with Pen* and shortly after that began to think about strategy and how to take down corporate education reform. And so that's when I began to see these online pockets of [standardized testing] opt-outs here and there, but I could see by looking at all of them that there was no clear organized strategy to pull everyone together. So I began to think about how can I do this. I looked at Facebook and different organizing tools that were free to me because obviously I didn't have a lot of money and we were down to one income. So I looked at Facebook and I saw that if you did a group you could have all these files within that group and I thought, well, here you have it. Here is the perfect strategy. I could have a file for every state. We could plug in opt-out information per state and we would be organizing.

And at that time Morna [McDermott-]McNulty and I were in correspondence, and I just said, "Hey Morna, I've thinking of starting a Facebook page; do you want to help me?" She was like, "Oh sure, yeah, I'll help you." You know we were just thinking some small little thing and I said you know I think I'm going to call it—again I'm thinking strategically, how can I make it really sound big and powerful even though I'm really just a stay-at-home mom—so I called it United Opt Out National. I knew it should be national and that this name is going to pull people in because it's going to sound like something big is happening. I titled it that because I had looked at all the other opt-out pages and none of them were taking off the way I thought they should be.

Once we started the page we couldn't keep up with the requests for help [from people asking how to opt their children out of tests], so immediately I was in this work mode of emailing every department of education and then pulling in Tim Slekar, who had created a page. He was really funny because he goes, "Why are you creating your page when I've got my page?" and I explained to him why and so then he joined us.

**JH:** Oh, that's great.

**PR:** Yeah. I mean it was just funny how we got organized and then Shaun Johnson was trying to help me with names. I think we were just messaging online. I didn't even know any of these people and then I said, "Well, Shaun, why don't you help?" And then Celesta, whom I had interviewed for my blog, got on board and then Morna recommended Lorie Murphy, who is great at strategy and also was involved in Save Our Schools—so there were the six of us. And what was funny at the time—I had no idea that Shaun and Morna worked together and I had no idea that Shaun and Tim were doing the radio show. I didn't know there were any of these connections out there, so it was just kind of this crazy thing. It just kind of happened. It was meant to be.

**JH:** That's great—what a crew you pulled together around this initial effort! I'd also like to know about what you guys hoped originally you would get out of this and then what frustrations you had in terms of the difficulties and pulling more people into the group.

**PR:** Well, what we wanted out of it at the beginning was to get mass opt-out of high-stakes testing and just, you know, shut them down. Again that's still obviously one of our main strategies—so that was our goal. You know there were a lot of bumps along the way because this is new territory, and so we made some mistakes. We organized with some folks who tried to tear us apart and take us down.

**JH:** Really?

**PR:** So there were a lot of things like this that occurred along the way that were pretty painful but good learning experiences and we're all a lot wiser for it, I think.

**JH:** Were there real political debates or was it just personal infighting?

**PR:** One of the political debates was, and you still see this today, this idea of opting out versus home schooling—the whole Tea Party, and all these sort of different factions. We had a lot of people who would get on our page and say *We're homeschoolers; we want to opt out and we also want to end public schools. We want to dismantle them and get rid of them forever* kind of thing. And of course we could not agree to that. So when all these people started getting on our page we had to figure out how to handle it and it was pretty ugly, but in fact it helped us get our message very clear. Now it's really clear what we stand for, but all of that stuff made us say, "Yeah, we support opt-out, but hey, we support opt-out in improving and reclaiming public schools!"

**JH:** I'm really glad you shared that because I think it has strengthened your organization as you've said, but I also think it holds immense lessons for the current struggle right now against Common Core.

**PR:** Yes.

**JH:** And I think we have to be really careful, and I would guard against making alliances with the right wing because I think in the end that's a very fragile coalition that will end up doing more harm to public education by emboldening the voices of the Tea Party than anything we get from working in coalition with them against Common Core. And I think we have very different reasons for opposing Common Core that we shouldn't be shy about, you know, voicing.

**PR:** Right. I'm with you on that 100 percent and you're right; when the Tea Party situation came about and we realized, oh my God, here we go again. It's obviously another challenge. . . . We're getting our new campaign going and I'm trying to organize opt-out leaders to help me, but when I talk to people I have to send them a statement saying this is what we believe in, do you agree? Because there are so many Tea Party people out there opting out that you've just got to be careful, you don't know.

**JH:** That's right. Well, can you tell me about how United Opt Out grew and what some of your major accomplishments have been in the last few years?

**PR:** Sure. So we started with the Facebook page. We immediately started building the troops more or less through that page. We thought you know we need to again have an event that is very political, that's very loud, and Morna said one night, "Why don't we occupy the [federal] department of education?" And I'm like, "Oh yeah, we'll occupy the department of education, that's of course the natural next step in opposing the policy of high-stakes testing in education reform." So again we just kind of would jump into these things and take this leap, but it seemed like what else would you do at this point? How do you get louder? How do you get heard?

So we had our first occupation in DC—on our best day [we had] maybe fifty people. But the cool thing was we met all these amazing activists. People came from all over the country to that, so you might have only fifty people but those fifty people took that information and went back and spent a whole 'nother year organizing.

**JH:** That's great.

**PR:** What was so funny is I'll never forget that first day standing up and looking at that crowd, thinking, oh, dear God. We did all this advertising and promoting and pushing it and pushing it, but that day only fifty folks came out. So that was really difficult, but we also knew we had to have a base and start somewhere, so those people I met at that first occupation are people who now are doing amazing things and are leaders in their communities. So we did it again the second year. The second year we had on our best day a hundred, but we had three hundred for the march to the White House, so that was an improvement. What's interesting about the second occupation is that's how we got a lot of New York folks. The following year was that year of massive opt-outs in Long Island and those people will continue to say to me, Hey, it was that second occupation that got us going. It empowered them, it gave them confidence to take that back home.

**JH:** That's such a great lesson. You've got to start somewhere.

**PR:** It was and it was a good lesson to be okay with small numbers. People say to me again and again about the second occupation, "You guys are going to get slammed in the news," and I said, you know what, I don't even care. We're organizing. This is local, this is grassroots. People are going to take it back in small numbers. Even though it's hard to look at, those people were so empowered and such amazing activists we knew that they would go back and pull in more people.

**JH:** That's right. I wasn't able to get out to those demonstrations, but I was so glad to read about them on social media. They were inspiring to me and there were countless thousands other across the country who were with you in spirit. And we don't have the billions of dollars that the other side has to organize mass rallies, but those connections you made have proven invaluable, so I'm so glad you did that work. And that was in 2012. What are you doing now?

**PR:** This year in 2014 we decided to take on a new strategy and I'm really excited about what we did this year. We looked around the country and we said, okay, where are there hot pockets that are really intense, where people are ready to mobilize but they need support? My city [Denver] was one obvious answer. It's a hotbed and people are kind of organizing in different little areas, but they need to come together. And so we decided to create a conference that was really a democratic classroom, a three-day action in which we would pull together everybody from around Colorado who wanted to attend and asked them what they needed and then created an action plan to really map out goals for the next year.

It was a fascinating process and I think one of the strengths that people often don't recognize is teachers are organizers—we believe in democratic classrooms. That right now is such an amazing strength because we can use that to harness and empower people and so that's what we did. We set it up and I think we had thirty national activists who came in to support Denver.

We had about a hundred and twenty folks sign up for the event. On our best day we probably had eighty-five.

**JH:** Nice.

**PR:** But people stayed over those three days and worked so it wasn't sit and listen to lectures; it was, "What are you going to do?" And they were having conversations with experts: We had Lois Weiner; we had Sam Anderson. We had [Finnish education policy advisor] Pasi Sahlberg. We just had some amazing people who came in and sat down and helped us map out a plan of resistance.

**JH:** Now that's a map I support! You know last spring was dubbed the "Education Spring" by a lot of commentators. In my time being politically active around education I haven't seen anything like the last year and this year in terms of a revolt against standardized testing. I'm wondering what are the most inspiring struggles you've seen around the country.

**PR:** Oh, wow. Well, in terms of just the opt-out piece, watching New York with thirty-three thousand opt-outs is just amazing. I mean, my God, thirty-three thousand!

**JH:** I know!

**PR:** Also watching Barbara Madeloni get elected [as president of the Massachusetts Teachers Association] literally brought me to tears. You know, watching CTU come out against Common Core; we are gaining momentum. Those three things this year have just been mind-boggling—it's happening and we've just got to be really careful and keep it moving.

**JH:** Why do you think this movement has exploded in the last couple of years? I mean you've talked about small rallies and some frustrating early beginnings to the opt-out movement. But the people I've talked to around the country who are involved in this work, like Monty Neill at FairTest and people at Rethinking Schools like Wayne Au, have talked about the current moment as the biggest revolt against high-stakes standardized testing in US history. I wonder if you see that and why you think the movement has taken off in this moment.

**PR:** Sure. Well, I think it's the Race to the Top policies; what we always said was Race to the Top is No Child Left Behind on steroids, in terms of the explosion of standardized testing.

But I really think it took a few years for this truth to really sink in and hit home. It's the parents and the teachers—we've got these parents who are calling and saying, "I don't understand what's going on. Every time my child goes to school they are taking a test," or "My child is coming home crying," or "My child has a stomachache and won't go to school." And so you know I get these stories day in and day out, some absolutely horrific, and so the parents are just up in arms. It's in everybody's backyard now. It doesn't matter where you are, it's there.

I think the other piece of this is the teachers are beginning to put it together. They have been denied information. Honestly our unions and the mainstream media have been denying us information about what's going on.

It's fascinating because I've had teachers say to me, "I don't understand what's going on, Peggy, why is this happening?" And so it's kind of like they are waking up and the ones that have been kept from this information or are too exhausted to look, they are beginning to look—that's been my experience. Teachers will email me and say, "Oh my gosh, I just read your blog and it clicked and now I can't quit researching." It's this mass awakening because it's not so easy to hide [the destructive effects] of testing anymore. It's so blatant in the schools the teachers are going, "Yes it was bad, but now it's really, really bad—to the point where I'm ashamed to even be standing in this room doing what I'm been told to do," and I think that's another big piece of it.

**JH:** I totally agree. To have examples like United Opt Out or like the MAP test boycott or the CTU doing the work they're doing seems like it's created a situation not just of despair, but now of hope that we can build an actual civil rights movement to reclaim education, you know, not the corporate-style, billionaire-backed, "civil rights movement" that Duncan keeps prattling on about, but a real movement.

**PR:** Yeah. I sure do hope—I mean thinking about the MAP boycott, what's so funny for me is I watched that whole thing, Jesse, and I was amazed, but I thought, Colorado is so far from getting there. So I just hope that other cities are going to do that next year. I feel like next year is the year, you know?

**JH:** I actually got a phone call from a parent somewhere in Colorado who is working with teachers to try to organize a boycott.

**PR:** Oh, thank God.

**JH:** So I wouldn't be surprised if we saw one there soon. You know I got calls from teachers in Chicago and New York who are organizing a boycott, and I think one of the incredible opportunities we have in the next coming period is to unite parents and teachers in common struggles against these tests. You know, teachers refusing to give them and parents opting their kids out has proven to be a powerful model in Seattle and Chicago and New York and I hope that spreads.

But just in terms of where you see this movement going and for parents, students, and teachers who will be reading this book—how they can join with United Opt Out and what resources do you have to offer them to help strengthen their movement to defend their schools from reducing them to test scores?

**PR:** Right. Well, in terms of resources, our website with an opt-out guide for all fifty states—I'm sure you know it was hacked and destroyed, so I'm rebuilding that right now. We still don't know who did it, but literally I can't even tell you what a mess. I mean they really pulled the rug out from under us.

**JH:** I hadn't heard that! That's really horrible.

**PR:** Oh, I mean, Jesse, this. . . . So our website was hacked and destroyed on the last day of our conference here in Denver and the folks I had look into it said, "Peggy, this is not your normal hack job, this person has dismantled every . . . ." They called it a SQ3 something, I don't even know what it is, but I mean completely gone, like destroyed, very intentionally destroyed. So I reported that to the FBI. Of course I've heard nothing back because, you know, who am I? I doubt they'll even look at it, but that really pulled the rug out from under us right there in the midst of testing season, the last day of our conference here in Denver. I have been since that moment working on trying to rebuild that website. We had to raise money. What was cool was within forty-eight hours people donated enough money to rebuild it.

Cynthia Lu from K12 News Network helped us with the rebuild and now that it's summer we're trying to upload all the documents. I got a bit uploaded a couple of days ago and I'm going to keep working on it all month. Obviously our Facebook group is a resource. We are going to with this new website we have with Cynthia to K12; we are organizing our opt-out groups by region, and it's going to be very strategic this coming year because we're going to be able to really hone in on a particular region of the United States and see what people need and send them news items or opt-out information that would be specific to that area.

In terms of where we're headed from here, I know a lot of people think we opt out of a test and that's it. . . . But we want to opt out of the whole corporate conversation and so the next step for us is coming here to really push forward reclaiming education and owning the conversation. So if we can push forward this opting out of the test, we also need to push for opting out of their conversation and owning ours. The moment is ours, we've just got to grab it and we've got to educate the public to see, yes, you can have portfolio-based assessment. Yes, you can have your neighborhood public schools. . . .

I mean the charters are not equal. They do not provide choice. They are less choice actually, and that's another funny thing that I run into again and again. I have charter parents constantly e-mailing me, wanting to opt out of curriculum or wanting to opt out of tests. And what happens is by the end of our conversation, and this goes on sometimes a whole week, the parents will realize, "Oh, wow, I have less choice."

**JH:** That's incredible.

**PR:** "I could help you very easily," I tell them, "but you're at a charter school and you have less choice in a charter and the bottom line is that you could opt out—go ahead and do it, but you may get kicked out." So they are waking up to that.

**JH:** I hadn't thought of it like that, but that's a great way to highlight the fake narrative of choice that they push.

**PR:** I know. In my emails to parents in Chicago and New York I always say, Now, you understand charters are really less choice because they can't opt out, or they do opt out and they get kicked out. . . .

So we've got to really push that forward and educate people on how to take [education] back through legislation and various other tools, so that's where we as an organization see the movement is headed.

**JH:** I'm excited to see the work you do in the next year. I think there's never been more coordination of folks that want to have parents, students, and teachers driving the education conversation rather than billionaires who have never attended public schools.

**PR:** Exactly.

# 22.

# FROM "SHAMING AND BLAMING" TO THE "MORAL AGENDA FOR OUR TIME"

## Interview with Helen Gym

*This interview was conducted on June 7, 2014, and has been edited and condensed.*

**Jesse Hagopian:** It's been really exciting following the work you've been doing, especially over the last year; the movement of parents resisting corporate education reform has been an inspiration around the country. I wanted to start by asking you about how you got into education politics, and, more broadly, how you developed your political consciousness.

**Helen Gym:** Those are really great questions. Well, I grew up in an immigrant household in Columbus, Ohio, in Ronald Reagan's America, so I wouldn't say that I developed a strong sense of politics as a teenager. The most important value I learned in Columbus came from growing up in a community where public spaces were highly valued, and so I really felt strongly that everything I had, especially since my parents were working and this was a new country for them, came through these public spaces—whether it was learning to read at the public library, swimming at the public pool, playing sports at my local rec center, and of course, going to public school. Having those opportunities had an enormous influence on my life and they inculcated in me the value of public spaces. These public spaces opened up the world around me, gave me new opportunities, and exposed me to a diversity of people and ideas. These public spaces were where people from all backgrounds came together and understood—in a deeply personal way—what it means when a society provides opportunities to its citizens. That was the lasting thing that I came away with from Columbus, but not a whole lot of sense of anything more than that. [I thought] most places are probably like this . . . I just didn't know. I was seventeen years old and not very well informed in any kind of political way. I did not have any understanding of the inequities and deprivation that I later saw.

I really didn't have a political sensibility about injustice until I landed at Asian Americans United a few years after college graduation. AAU became my political home—it was where I could understand for the first time a more multiracial perspective on class inequities and other injustices. That was where I finally started to pull things together . . . where I met so many incredible activists who were informed by their experiences and histories as Asian Americans but also focused on bigger issues to build a broader multiracial justice-oriented coalition. It mattered when we talked about immigrant rights, or educational opportunity, or police abuse and language access. As we worked on campaigns, the relevance of an Asian American "voice" finally became clear to me.

I came into education politics when I started out as a teacher in the Olney neighborhood of Philadelphia. I was the only Asian American teacher at a school that had a plurality of Asians, a near equal mix of black and Latino students, and a smaller percentage of white families. So it was truly diverse, but it was also enormously overcrowded—I had thirty-eight students in my classes, and I think there were twelve hundred students in one of the largest elementary schools in the city. Despite the diversity, there was not a lot of understanding about English language learners or Asian Americans or recent refugees and immigrants from Southeast Asia in particular, who were a significant population in the neighborhood and school. I really spent a lot of time just trying to be a great teacher and being exposed to all these amazing educators all across the city. I also got involved with education justice groups like the National Coalition of Education Activists and met a number of people associated with *Rethinking Schools*. That's where I met Bill [Bigelow] and Bob [Peterson] and Stan [Karp] and Linda [Christensen] and plenty of others.

**JH:** Nice! I have also learned so much from those educators. . . . So what caused you to then leave teaching?

**HG:** Well, I left teaching in part because of this horrible experience that we had at our school around race. In 1994, a series of newspaper articles were written about our school—claiming Asian American kids were living in paradise while African American kids languished in overcrowded classrooms. But the writer didn't understand or didn't bother to find out or really care much about the fact that the Asian kids were all ELL [English language learner] students taking language classes—many of them in converted bathroom and closet spaces. Instead, he wrote that they got special access to extra language services, they got extra teachers, they had smaller classes and nobody explained that these were all immigrant youth . . . this was what they are legally entitled to and we had fought to enlighten the school around this. But it didn't matter because a major newspaper columnist wasn't really concerned about our kids. He was more interested in taking down our superintendent who was honoring our school principal. So the major newspaper this columnist worked for ran a series of stories on the front page for weeks and it culminated in a march and protest all around our school. And, you know, it just made me realize that even after all this work, people did not understand the racial politics that created this terrible situation—where you had this horribly overcrowded, underfunded school and parents worried and upset about this; where you had so much diversity and people so ignorant of children's needs within this diversity; where you had newspaper columnists exploiting these fears and stereotypes to get at political targets like our superintendent, who had infuriated certain powers because he called the state legislature "racist" for its underfunding of our schools. I could be a good teacher, but I, too, did not understand enough about race and community, inequity, and the general anger and fear that comes out of that.

**JH:** Yeah, it sounds like a horrible divide-and-conquer strategy was implemented in your school to pit communities of color against each other over scarce resources.

**HG:** Exactly. It was pretty devastating.

**JH:** So that experience led you to want to figure out what is going on with education policies and racism in your city?

**HG:** Yeah. I clearly was not understanding something. We were prohibited from even answering parents' questions. We weren't having important dialogue within the school about overcrowding; the lack of resources that impacted the entire school was really a huge source of frustration internally as well. The district silence about this fueled the community anger, most of which came from outside of our school, and didn't help us internally address our needs. I tried to organize some staff people to do outreach, but I felt so inexperienced and overwhelmed by the media outrage and dialogue that was spinning far out of any one individual's control to address it. The following year, many of the programs designed to improve services for the ELL students were dismantled.

It was a really humbling lesson for me that the impact of education went far beyond my classroom. I decided to leave teaching and spend more time doing community-based work. I worked at Asian Americans United on campaigns and helped start a community charter school based around folk arts and serving immigrant and multilingual families. I helped start an education newspaper, the *Philadelphia Public School Notebook*, and did ethnic studies curriculum writing and antiracist/multiracial professional development. I tried to do things that would help me better understand the intersection between schools and communities and to hear the voices of families, parents, and students that were being ignored by people creating all these so-called reform policies. Most of all, I tried to understand where the possibilities were for renewed engagement and real improvement.

**JH:** Can you talk about forming Parents United for Public Education and helping to coalesce a movement against a series of privatization efforts?

**HG:** Yeah, so as much time as I spent in education—I had been a teacher, I had helped start an education newspaper, I had helped found a school, I had served on different boards—nothing prepared me more for understanding education than becoming a public school parent myself and being on the other side of everything that I thought I knew. I always thought that if you do the right thing, then it turns out right, or something. But being a parent and being on the receiving end of all these different corporate education policies was truly the most troubling and eye-opening experience that I've had.

We started Parents United in 2006 when our school faced a particularly severe and non-reported budget crisis, and we realized that there was no city-wide vehicle through which parents' voices could be raised about critically important issues—having enough teachers and aides and support staff, addressing culture and race in curriculum and practices, talking about safety and the lack of it while trying to develop responsible disciplinary policies. Instead a lot of education coverage was on policy "reform" totally divorced from the experiences of children and families at the school level. A lot of us were active in our local schools, but without a citywide voice, there wasn't really much more you could do than just advocate for your own school, which could only go so far because ultimately it was really about what the district would do, what the district's situation was, and whether there were enough voices that were moving the district in the right direction. A group of us were coming together to these various board meetings—and there were very few parents at the time attending. The day the school district passed a budget that stripped out arts and music, eliminated hundreds of teachers from the schools—which feels quaint now because we just lost four thousand [educators] from our schools last year—

**JH:** Ugh, that's atrocious.

**HG:** —there were only five of us parents in the room to witness the passage of this budget that was just going to eviscerate schools. So we made a vow among ourselves that we weren't going to see that happen again and that we would try to engage parents to look at budgets—not really so much as an accounting document, but really make it a moral document that reflected the priorities of communities. The following year we had more than a hundred parents come together to demand resources in our schools, and we did win back arts and music, we won a lower class size mandate in the primary grades, and we developed a new voice of parents for our public schools that pushed back against the negative stereotypes of public school parenting—and that was the founding of Parents United for Public Education. And since then, we've grown because the stakes have grown so high. We came together to talk about schools, but there's also this real need to humanize the dialogue around how we talk about poverty, cities, and our children. Parents are uniquely poised to ensure that dialogue comes through a framework of human dignity, equity, justice, societal responsibility, and love for our children and those who care for them. And I think despite all the struggles we've seen over the years, we've held to those ideals.

**JH:** I'm wondering if you can talk more about what corporate reform has looked like in Philadelphia. You've had scores of schools closed across the city, and seen privatization efforts first ushered in I think under Paul Vallas. Talk about what the corporate reform agenda has done to the schools there.

**HG:** Philadelphia is a city that has the highest poverty rate of the ten largest metropolitan cities in the United States. It has always struggled around issues of poverty, but over the course of multiple recessions and declining investments it has worsened. Philadelphia has just really fallen way, way, way down in terms of the quality of life for a lot of residents in general and our schools reflect that.

So in 2001 the school district of Philadelphia got taken over by the State of Pennsylvania and at the time . . . the plan was to bring in Edison Schools—back then the largest for-profit manager of schools in the country—for a $100-million-a-year contract to manage and run the entire school district of Philadelphia. Philadelphia would be the largest privatized public school district in the entire country run by a for-profit entity. Fifteen years later [Edison Schools] doesn't even exist anymore. It's now Edison Learning, an online educational services company, whatever that means. That to me is the story of corporate reform. You know, completely unfounded, unproven experimental ideas that come with grand promises, and they disappear and people don't remember that we did that already.

This struggle against the privatization of Philly public schools was one of the most formative experiences of my life. It was really about this vision between communities of parents and families and students and people versus the nonsense of Wall Street corporate interests.

**JH:** That's right.

**HG:** And for the most part I think that the community won significantly. Edison Schools, as I said, no longer exists. They were reduced from privatizing the entire school district of Philadelphia to running twenty schools. We got the state to change their whole language and approach. It wasn't just about Edison; now it included universities and nonprofits running schools—and, again, not a single one of those education management organization [EMO] contracts exists today. At the same time, a community demand for public school investment helped lead to a huge capital effort under Paul Vallas to build new schools and renovate others. We saw a massive expansion of EMOs and charters, yes, but there was also investment in the public sector as well. The consequences of it were complicated, of course. We went bankrupt, for one thing, since inequities in state funding were never seriously tackled, and we undermined neighborhood high schools with a set of small, mostly admission-based select high schools. But at the same time, the community really led this amazing struggle against a singular corporate reform agenda and the contrast was undeniable.

**JH:** That's beautiful.

**HG:** Now we fast-forward and we've got a governor today who is just wedded to undermining public education not just in Philadelphia but all across the state of Pennsylvania. He cut nearly one billion dollars from the state education budget in his first year in office, saying his was a budget that separated the "must haves" from the "nice to haves." Obviously schools would no longer be in the "must have" category. At the same time, we've seen a massive explosion in charter schools, and in particular charter management organizations. We've got 35 percent of our kids in eighty-six different charter schools. Our charter school population alone is the second largest school district in the state of Pennsylvania. So we're running effectively two parallel systems with less money, and that has been, whether it was purposeful or not, in combination with the rise of the testing industry, what has created the elements for the disastrous situation we face today.

Effectively what's happened is that the massively underfunded public school system is being cannibalized by the charter system . . . families are forced to choose between a school district with almost no resources and capacity to deal with their needs and a charter "system" with eighty-six charter schools that run the gamut from outright criminal endeavors to some pretty extraordinary and unique institutions. Throughout all this, we've never seriously addressed funding inequity. So we have had to close thirty public schools in the last two years; that forced out thousands of children into schools, every single one of which is worse than the school they attended the prior year. We lost four thousand staff people [from] last year into this year. We've had two children die in schools that lacked nurses, seen children's needs go unmet by the lack of school counselors, we can only afford to staff fourteen libraries in a school system with two hundred–plus buildings. We're running schools that our own superintendent calls a "doomsday scenario" for children.

**JH:** That's shameful.

**HG:** As painful as this is, we've seen an extraordinary amount of community action, students' voice, parent activity, and a real re-coalescing of the original state takeover coalition that brought together community members, staff people, parents, students, and teachers from all across the city to really make a stand for public education. There is a leadership vacuum, yes, but I hope people understand that the vision is being led and called for and enacted by a real grassroots movement to reclaim our schools.

**JH:** That's what's been so incredible to watch, students saying we refuse to let you rob us of the last public institution guaranteed for all for free, and leading walkouts, and parents, students, and teachers uniting to take this stand against the decimation of public space has been just really inspiring for us here. What are some of the strategies you have used to combat the titans of corporate reform in Philly?

**HG:** I've always felt that the corporate ed reform movement is homogenized, but the tools we use to push back are very local and unique to each place. We have a lot of strengths in Philadelphia—not the least of which is incredible student organizing and a pretty vibrant immigrant organizing movement. One worthy highlight is that we have independent homegrown media here in Philadelphia that has been key to the organizing effort. The *Philadelphia Public School Notebook* evolved mostly as a voice and a vehicle for communities to challenge the hegemonic dominant narrative of ed reform, and has become a major information outlet to get out research and studies and ask questions about the ed reform initiative. We founded the *Notebook* in 1994 to be a voice of the people, and today it holds the right people accountable.

We've had success in unmasking a number of reform charlatans and revealing that many of them are simply for-hire lobbyists. We've been successful in using city ethics and lobbying laws to confront foundations and self-styled reformers around work they had been labeling as "philanthropy" but which we successfully challenged as lobbying. We've also had success, with no small part due to the hubris and arrogance of these groups themselves, in exposing newer ed reform organizations to be the astroturf groups they are.

If people hear a lot about the Philadelphia movement, it's partly because we're producing a lot of media through outlets like the Media Mobilizing Project. We've been able to push out videos and publications and really spend a lot of time humanizing the story of Philadelphia so it just doesn't become full of statistics: "seven thousand children," "thirty public schools to close," "four thousand staff gone," "$93 million debt." I mean, your eyes can just glaze over as these numbers get bigger and bigger, and it can feel paralyzing. And the counterbalance to that for us, and a lesson and a strategy that we employ, is the need to humanize every situation. So when thousands of teachers were laid off, a group called Teacher Action Group Philadelphia started a website called Faces of the Layoff and told the stories of all these staff people who had spent their lives within the Philadelphia schools who were being laid off.

**JH:** That's brilliant.

**HG:** Philly people have created a ton of independent videos so that the student walkouts [against budget cuts] could be documented and deepened not just for that action but as political history and storytelling that we continue to use. It is really important to find the space for people to be able to educate one another on the politics and history as we go through this so that even among ourselves we don't get too beaten down, or as we are being beaten down, at least we remember that this has been a long fight and why we continue on.

**JH:** That's a great point. If we don't know our history and if our movement is constantly having to reinvent itself at every attack, we don't stand a chance. That's also a really important lesson about independent media that I hadn't fully realized—that you have had such a focus on alternative media in building the movement. I think besides the alternative media something that has been effective in Philadelphia has been direct action in terms of the walkouts of students, but I think I also remember that you went inside the mayor's office and commandeered his podium? Is that right?

**HG:** Yeah. And you may see more of that, hopefully! During the state takeover one of the strongest actions we did was taking over the board of education building during a real showdown about whether the state would completely take over and wipe out local control entirely. We had a real impact—it ended up being a city-state hybrid-run school board. We've had a number of actions at the mayor's office and at City Hall and in Harrisburg where Philadelphians just finished a five-day sit-in at the state capitol.

Mass action is great, but probably the most important thing we've been able to do is convert mass action to political power. Our governor is a first-term governor and his election is right around the corner. He's double-digit points down in the polls, and for the first time ever, the reason is public education has become a top voter issue in the state and in our city. That's the key: to convert mass action to political power to see a change in not just our power structure but in a new societally driven moral agenda for our communities.

**JH:** That's great. Without that kind of fight our schools will be lost. Did you see comedian Louis C. K.'s interview on [the *Late Show with David*] *Letterman* the other day?

**HG:** I did not.

**JH:** You should check it out. They are talking about Louis's kids in school and Letterman asks Louis, "So what happens if your kids don't pass these standardized tests?" And Louis says, "Well, my understanding is they just burn the schools down."

**HG:** [Laughs]

**JH:** And he's hilarious, but he's actually not that far off.

**HG:** —And kind of hitting way too close to home.

**JH:** Can you talk now more specifically about how high-stakes testing has impacted the Philadelphia public schools?

**HG:** High-stakes testing in Philadelphia has charted probably the same trajectory [as the rest of the corporate education reform movement]. After the state took over the city of Philadelphia, they needed to prove that the state takeover was worth it. And so the only way they felt they could possibly define progress in Philadelphia was through more frequent use of and increasing test score data. After all, if test scores rose, the takeover must have been successful, right? So as the state takeover proceeded and as the struggle of families here increased . . . test scores became the vehicle through which to silence critics and to force through an agenda that justified all manner of experimentation and abuse within schools. There was enormous pressure within Philadelphia to have constantly increasing test scores. We were seeing double-digit gains among students all across the board at certain schools that ought to make even a layperson skeptical. Philadelphia, as most people know by now, was investigated for cheating. The pressure on teachers and on principals and the demand that test scores increase were extraordinary. The idea that test scores were the only measure by which progress could be defined in Philadelphia led to abusive situations happening in schools and to children.

During the school closings process, test score data was brought out to justify the closing of a number of schools. This was clearly a very serious issue in part because the school closings were initiated by a private for-profit company called the Boston Consulting Group that was contracted with and paid for by a local foundation that solicited individual donors for the contract—some of whom, for example, were real estate developers and charter school investors. In our opinion they used their access to the city and district officials to press their agenda, and to this day, that list of sixty school closings has never been made public. But the more sinister part was that when the school district did come into these various school communities they would bring up the issue of test scores as one of the number of reasons to close a public school.

But that was never part of [the original] explanation of why children were supposed to take these tests.

A normal person would think testing was about informing you to become a better teacher, a better student, a better school system. . . . But that was not the case. It's not like a school that did well on tests or schools that showed some measure of gain were rewarded; they were just subjected to more testing—and fewer resources. And then of course the schools that struggled the most, the ones that couldn't demonstrate "achievement," were then punished as resources continued to be stripped away . . .

**JH:** That's terrible. . . . What has the resistance to high-stakes testing looked like?

**HG:** This past spring the district targeted two schools that they defined as being failures based on these new school report cards—which were based primarily on test data. In April, the district came in and told these two school communities that they had two options: one, they could either choose to remain with the School District of Philadelphia but they would receive zero resources, or two, they could vote for their school to be converted to a charter school. And they gave the parents in the schools one month's notice before their vote.

**JH:** Wow.

**HG:** One of the things we found was that the district would assume costs of up to $4,000 a student because of the charter contract. But if a school voted to stay within the school district, they would get no additional resources.

**JH:** That's exactly how they use testing to push this charter privatization agenda.

**HG:** One of the schools they targeted was the last public school standing in a predominantly African American neighborhood that had a long-time, stable community. This school had had three principals in over thirty years. Their current principal had been there for eight years. You don't see that level of stability in the district anymore. They had a teacher there who had taught for over twenty-seven years in the lower grades, and they had a significant number of staff people who had seen children through a whole generation at this school. And the perspective from the community was extraordinary. They completely rejected the narrative of failure and shame, which was really what the test score narrative is all about. It's about blaming and shaming communities into silence and accepting anything, literally anything, as a better option.

**JH:** Right.

**HG:** We had a month-long process as communities got organized and educated around this issue. We talked about schools as community anchors. We talked about stability and shared values of respect and culture. On May 1, parents voted by a margin of greater than two to one to stay within the district—plus to demand more resources!

**JH:** That's an incredible story of resistance that holds a lot of lessons for parents around the nation about the need to demand more for our kids. I just have one last question. You have three kids in the public schools and I wonder what you hope their education would be, you know, if our movement was to grow large enough to defeat the corporate education reformers and put in place your vision for the public schools—what would that look like to you?

**HG:** Education is fundamentally about creating these child-centered institutions that embrace all aspects of children. And I think that in some ways the narrow focus on testing has made crystal clear to a lot of communities how much testing and the corporate reform agenda disregard the life of a child. It's all about the test scores. It's all about reductive remedial math and reading. It has nothing to do with the arts or music. It has nothing to do with the needs of students, including counseling services, wraparound services, nursing and health care and the understanding that our schools are bigger than even the education of the child, that they are really responsible for the whole growth of a young person in the most vulnerable years of their lives.

And if we were to "win this battle," it would be about teaching and learning institutions focused on the whole growth of a child and really strong community school institutions that affirm the culture, dignity, and value of our families and our neighborhoods. And this is just the opposite of what I think exists right now, where we have abdicated a collective societal obligation toward public education in favor of hyper-individualized, transactional approaches to learning, where children and families are thrown to market-based forces. My colleague Stan Karp says it so beautifully: we're treating parents like customers in search of services rather than citizens deserving of their rights. I don't believe in "going back" to some old-fashioned idea of schooling, though. I'm thinking about a new vision in this time, a community-centered, community-driven vision of schools. . . . I think this incredible power of a community-driven vision is the moral agenda for our society.

# ADMINISTRATORS AND ADVOCATES

# 23.
# THE WORD THAT MADE ME AN ACTIVIST
## John Kuhn

I will not name the state senator who addressed the assembled school administrators at a hotel conference room in Austin that cold February morning. Having been a teacher once upon a time, she was considered an education expert by her colleagues in the statehouse. She had spent her political career advancing numerous education policies; most had either grown the standardized-testing culture in Texas public schools or fortified a blatantly inequitable school funding system.

During the legislative session that was under way then—when I sat alongside several hundred other Texas administrators listening to the senator's address—she had been at the forefront of pushing bills that promised drastic cuts in education spending as well as bills that thrust a new testing regime upon Texas's schoolchildren. STAAR—the State of Texas Assessments of Academic Readiness—was the name of the newly proposed test, and her pride in its rigor and technocratic brilliance was evident. Students in high school would be required to pass no fewer than fifteen (*fifteen!*) standardized tests in order to graduate. STAAR would be much harder than any previous test; it would eat up more class time than any previous test; and, at $90 million per year to develop and deliver, it would cost the state far more than any other test, ever. If no one else was happy about it, Pearson certainly was.

As an educator, I am not opposed to testing students. I have written and administered many tests myself over the years, some of them better than others. But standardized, high-stakes testing has at least three foundational problems that my classroom tests never had. First of all, the cut scores for standardized tests are arbitrarily set by politically appointed officials, in secret. In my classes, kids knew from the first day of the school year that a correct-answer rate of 70 percent was passing, and anything less was failing. Not so with STAAR—the percentage of Texas kids who pass would be determined when the education commissioner discreetly set the cut score, which I have come to call the "God number" of school accountability. With that single private decision, some person in Austin could make all of our students into "successes" or deem them all "failures." This is the magic undergirding the supposed science of school accountability, and it has very little to do with what's best for kids. Such a perverse misapplication of testing is anathema to many educators, and it is ripe for malfeasance and manipulation. A cut score really only has one use: to engineer a desired political outcome. Second, I had prompt access to the results of my classroom tests. I could hone my instruction based on the student outcomes captured by them. STAAR exams would be taken at the very end of the school year, however; results would be available the following year, when the teachers working with the assessed students no longer had them on their rolls. The tests hold no formative value. Third, with my classroom tests, there was appropriate flexibility in determining the stakes attached. I could throw out a test altogether if I decided it was a bad test. With today's prescriptive accountability, adjustments can't readily be made if test items are inappropriate. In fact, major multinational corporations keep their tests so incredibly secure—so that they can juice their profit margins by reusing old test items—that it's virtually impossible for teachers, students, or parents to even identify problems with the tests so that flaws in test development can be discovered. The great Pineapple-gate controversy in New York a few years back—when the state's education commissioner threw out several ambiguous questions from a nonsensical passage about a "pineapple with sleeves"—only came to light because students ridiculed the passage on Facebook.

In short, the problem isn't the tests. It's the convoluted and wrong-headed policies that have been overlaid upon the tests by people who really don't know what they are doing but are nonetheless eager to do it. STAAR and tests like it could conceivably become wonderful tools if they were to be "jail-broken" and entrusted to educators for the bottom-up development of appropriate uses. The tests could perhaps be saved if they were forcibly converted into instructional tools rather than being used solely for political purposes. But they are currently entirely used for political purposes.

After empathizing about the devastating funding cuts facing local schools and explaining that it was all the economy's fault, the senator positively gushed about her new test. Because student learning was so important, the growing cries of administrators statewide that the STAAR test be deferred would have to be ignored. Our state was so broke that we would have to lay off twenty-five thousand school employees, but it wasn't broke enough to defer Pearson's nearly $500 million contract. The senator looked across the roomful of administrators and said that the new test was simply "non-negotiable."

*Non-negotiable.* One word. The word that turned me into an activist.

When the senator took questions after her address, I took the audience microphone and explained that my district was reducing its staff of sixty-something by at least nine employees.

"How many people is Pearson laying off?" I asked.

"I don't know," she replied.

"You're saving the test but not the teachers," I told her.

I couldn't hear her response over the applause of my colleagues.

After the state senator wrapped up her remarks I returned to my hotel room and pondered the plight of public school students, teachers, and administrators. Our needs were ignored. Our cries fell on deaf ears. The senator was exactly right in her choice of verbiage, I realized. There was truly no means of negotiating for public education supporters. Teachers, administrators, trustees, and public school students and parents at that time had no voice in the halls of power. The wants of the Texas business lobby would not step aside for the needs of learners and teachers.

So I decided I wouldn't negotiate. On a February night in Austin, Texas, I shifted from being a passive pushover to a fervent believer in the power of what a prominent education reformer would later derisively label "aggressive populism." Before that night I had been mostly worried about myself and my future. I had harbored deep professional and personal qualms about the way testing was used to paint schools as "good" or "bad" while funding inequities in my state were downplayed so that lawmakers' educational decisions were protected from public judgment, but I had held my tongue. I had been a principal at a school that was funded at several thousand dollars less per pupil than neighboring schools, and I had labored to match better-resourced schools' academic results. I had seethed privately at the injustice done to my students, my teachers, my community, and myself by these policies. But I hesitated to raise my voice. I had three kids to take care of. I had a house payment and a car payment. Someone else would have to speak up. Maybe someone in the legislature would take up the challenge.

But I knew they wouldn't. I was pretty sure they didn't even understand what their policies were doing at the local level. It was time for educators to step out on a limb and publicize what was being done to kids and communities in the name of accountability. In my angst that night, I sought a way to express myself. I looked to a letter as famous and as sacred as any ever written in the history of my state—the letter penned by Colonel William Barret Travis just before the fall of the Alamo. In it, he pleaded in vain for help from Texas's leaders as a grave threat surrounded him on all sides.

I wrote what has come to be known as "The Alamo Letter" and submitted it to my hometown newspaper and to *Washington Post* blogger Valerie Strauss. Addressed to the state senator and the four state representatives whose regions touched my school district, the letter was provocative and direct.

Gentlemen,
I am besieged by a hundred or more of the legislators under Rick Perry. I have sustained a continual bombardment of increased high-stakes testing and accountability-related bureaucracy and a cannonade of gross underfunding for 10 years at least and have lost several good men and women. The ruling party has demanded another round of pay cuts and furloughs, while the schoolhouse be put to the sword and our children's lunch money be taken in order to keep taxes low for big business. I am answering the demand with a (figurative) cannon shot, and the Texas flag still waves proudly from our flagpole. I shall never surrender the fight for the children of Perrin.

Then, I call on you my legislators in the name of liberty, of patriotism and everything dear to the American character, to come to our aid, with all dispatch. The enemy of public schools is declaring that spending on a shiny new high-stakes testing system is "non-negotiable"; that, in essence, we must save the test but not the teachers. The enemy of public schools is saying that Texas lawmakers won't raise 1 penny in taxes in order to save our schools.

If this call is neglected, I am determined to sustain myself as long as possible and fight for the kids in these classrooms like an educator who never forgets what is due to his own honor and that of his community. Make education a priority!

    With all due respect and urgency,

John Kuhn

The letter spread like wildfire across Texas and even nationally. I was invited to give a speech at a North Texas college alongside reformer principal Steve Perry. I was then asked to read my letter at the first-ever Save Texas Schools rally later that spring. When I accepted this invitation, I didn't know how many people would be there to listen. I expected a small crowd of five hundred or seven hundred and fifty people. I was nervous: I would be standing on the steps of the state capitol and criticizing the powerful men and women inside. But I had already cast my lot. There was no turning back.

When my family and I showed up at a shaded park in Austin where the Save Texas Schools march would begin, I realized that this was a bigger deal than I had appreciated. Someone had done a masterful job of organizing. It probably helped that Texas teachers and public school parents statewide were in a panic; the talk from politicians and think tanks had been decidedly grim and antagonistic toward the very concept of public education. A distant bullhorn announced that it was time to march to the capitol building, and we filled the street. When I say "filled the street," I mean that both sidewalks and a four-lane city street were completely packed with a crush of people, and the crush stretched for who-knew-how-many blocks. I couldn't see where the crowd began or ended; the surging throng snaked through the city and the voices of the multitude—strangely joyous—bounced off the buildings. I had never heard or seen anything like it. Teachers and parents pushed their strollers side by side. Dozens of groups wore matching shirts emblazoned with the names of their schools. Everyone who counted on public schools had a dog in this fight—Republicans, Democrats, Independents. The bipartisan chorus chanted together and held their signs aloft, pleading for support in any way they knew how.

On that beautiful spring day, public education was the greatest unifier in Texas. I thought about standing in front of them all, standing behind that microphone and speaking. The biggest crowd I had ever addressed before was a campus faculty meeting, and it wasn't even a big campus. My heart began to pound. I kissed my wife goodbye, wondering if I wasn't maybe kissing my career goodbye as well, and I scaled the capitol steps. My middle child, six at the time, went with me up onto the stage. We sat in the ardent sun and I looked out at a sea of people. More than thirteen thousand public education supporters would listen to me read the letter and also a barnburner of a speech that I would reprise in July at the Save Our Schools National March and Call to Action in Washington, DC. Since then, I have written dozens of commentaries for Texas newspapers, education blogs at *Education Week* and the *Washington Post*, and websites like CNN.com. I've spoken at three Save Texas Schools rallies now, and I've participated in events from Missouri to Washington, DC.

I got involved in the movement against over-testing and testing misuse because I felt that I had a moral obligation to oppose a seemingly relentless onslaught of underfunding and testing and punishing, an approach to education born in Texas some three decades before, that, until recently, showed no sign of letting up. This approach to education was built on a lie, a "Texas Miracle" built on fudged numbers that had been thoroughly debunked. Miraculously, though, even though everyone everywhere knew the "Texas Miracle" never really happened, the policy prescriptions touted as its causal agents had stuck and spread nationwide. We were addicted, nationally, to a cocktail with harsh side effects that had never actually cured any disease.

As I sat and listened to the state senator brazenly proclaim that the newer, harder, longer, more expensive test was coming whether the educators approved or not, I decided to do something rash. I still lose sleep over what I've done from time to time. After the "Alamo Letter" hit Facebook, a friend said, "That might not have been the best thing you could've done for your career." I nodded. "You may be right," I said. But maybe it was the best thing I could've done for my kids.

I was soon gratified to learn that I was not alone. A school board member had started a movement called "Make Education a Priority" months before I took my stand. A group of superintendents would unveil a resolution opposing over-testing, which would be adopted by almost nine hundred school districts in Texas and would spawn a similar national resolution. And a group of Lone Star moms would unite to form the organization Texans Advocating for Meaningful Student Assessment—better known as Mothers Against Drunk Testing—dedicated to the elimination of "over-testing and under-investing in Texas students."

We would have something of a victory in Texas. The fifteen STAAR tests required for graduation would be reduced to five during the next legislative session. The state's speaker of the House would begin the session by declaring "To parents and educators concerned about excessive testing, the Texas House has heard you." Pearson lobbyists would be prohibited by law from serving on the committees that designed accountability. Legislation would be passed to reduce elementary testing and to permit a group of school districts the freedom to use an educator-developed alternative accountability system, though the governor would veto it. During the process, some of the staunchest advocates for more and more testing would be forced to confront the truth—they had lost the support of the people.

When I said what I said, and when I wrote what I wrote—when I did what I thought was right regardless of the consequences—I wasn't sure how it would turn out for me. (To be honest, I'm still not sure.) Superintendents don't tend to last very long in their roles anyway—it's probably not smart for us to go around poking at hornets' nests. But for a moment, I let emotion and passion trump rational self-interest. And I'm glad I did. I discovered a whole army of people in my home state who, like me, had seen the corrosive effects of over-testing and our nation's now conventional hyper-punitive education policy, and who were already doing something about it. I wouldn't have known they were even there if I hadn't spoken up.

In the end, the senator whose casual dismissiveness sparked my fire was wrong. Standardized testing in Texas was negotiable; in fact, it was highly negotiable. Powerful people wanted to set the rules, but the rest of us suddenly stopped agreeing to play by those rules. In Texas between 2011 and 2013, the "little people"—parents, teachers, and students—marched, spoke, wrote, resolved, organized, tweeted, testified, advocated, agitated, and drafted model legislation. Most importantly of all, they—we—changed the game!

# 24.
# BUILDING THE MOVEMENT AGAINST HIGH-STAKES TESTING

## Monty Neill

In spring 2013, parents, students, educators, community activists, and local elected officials across the nation rose in opposition to the overuse and misuse of standardized tests. This public eruption shows every sign of growing in intensity and reach. My organization, the National Center for Fair & Open Testing (FairTest), has joined with other groups to launch a "Testing Resistance and Reform Spring" initiative to advance this movement.

FairTest has been fighting *against* high-stakes testing and *for* educationally beneficial assessments for nearly thirty years. While growing numbers of colleges have adopted test-score-optional admissions policies, standardized exams and test preparation have metastasized and taken over public school classrooms. In this environment, teachers increasingly say they can no longer provide students with a meaningful or engaging education. The growing resistance could produce a social movement to reverse this damage. It is still embryonic, however, with far to go before it can win the changes our children and our society need.

## The Testing Explosion

I started working with FairTest in 1987. Among my initial tasks was to collaborate on a report, *Fallout from the Testing Explosion: How 100 Million Standardized*

*Exams Undermine Equity and Excellence in America's Public Schools*, which explored the expansion of standardized testing. In particular, the federal Elementary and Secondary Education Act (ESEA) mandated testing children in Title I programs with norm-referenced tests (NRT) in reading and math, a practice many schools applied to all students. Back then, sixteen states, mostly those with large percentages of African American and Latino children, imposed high school graduation exams. IQ tests were misused to place students in classes for the "educable mentally retarded" and achievement tests were misused for tracking and occasionally for grade promotion (particularly in large cities with many students of color). *Fallout* examined a range of harmful consequences, including racial and class discrimination. It also looked at educational damage to curriculum and instruction when states, districts, and schools used tests to make important educational decisions. FairTest's goal was then—and remains today—to roll back the amount of testing and end high-stakes uses, as well as to promote fair, educationally beneficial student assessment.

By the mid-1990s, our goal seemed increasingly in sight. A 1994 federal revision of ESEA dropped the NRT requirement and instead required states to test children in reading and math just once in each of three grade spans. While schools were supposed to demonstrate progress, the law contained no specific targets or sanctions. After another group of states briefly adopted graduation exams early in the 1990s, that tide receded from a high of nearly twenty-five states back to sixteen. Perhaps most significantly, the public conversation and some classroom practice shifted to authentic assessments such as portfolios, performance tasks, projects, and observations. For a few years, reformers were ascendant, diminishing the extent and importance of standardized tests and advancing high-quality assessment that could enrich learning.

Sadly, that tide quickly turned under pressure from business leaders and politicians who wanted to appear "tough on accountability." By the late 1990s, the mantra of "assessments worth teaching to" became "this 'new,' high-stakes standardized exam is the test worth teaching to." States and districts began to use student scores to rate and then to punish or close schools. More states adopted high school exit exams, with tens of thousands additional students denied diplomas each year. Despite including a few open-ended questions, the exams still failed to assess most of the knowledge, skills, and traits students actually needed. Simultaneously, the nation was backing away from addressing poverty, segregation, and school underfunding, the primary causes of low test scores and graduation rates.

A joint Republican-Democrat initiative, modeled on George W. Bush's fraudulent "Texas miracle," brought high-stakes standardized testing to the national stage with a vengeance. The federal No Child Left Behind Act—the 2001 version of ESEA—mandated testing all children in grades three to eight and once in high school with state math and reading exams. The results were to be used to punish schools that failed to make "adequate yearly progress" toward the clearly impossible goal that all students would score "proficient" by 2014. The threat of severe sanctions produced fearful compliance among all levels of educators. As FairTest and many others have documented, the "fallout" from the most recent testing explosion has been profoundly damaging, including:

- narrowing curriculum and instruction by focusing teaching on educationally inadequate tests and emphasizing test preparation;
- massively expanding the use of "benchmark," "interim," and assorted mini-tests to tie teaching ever more closely to high-stakes exams;
- increasing the use of grade promotion and graduation tests, which are once again found in half the states, including those where nearly 80 percent of African American and Latino students live;
- reducing professional development and educator collaboration to a focus on how teachers can more effectively boost test scores; and
- creating "zero tolerance" disciplinary pretexts to remove low-scoring children from the testing pool, bringing push outs to record highs and feeding the "school-to-prison pipeline."

Although Barack Obama criticized over-testing in his first presidential campaign, he appointed former Chicago schools chief Arne Duncan, a proponent of test-based accountability, to head the department of education. Duncan installed a like-minded coterie from organizations such as the Gates Foundation to senior policy-making positions. Duncan acknowledged that NCLB was not working. But he did not abandon its test-and-punish approach. Instead, he used Race to the Top (RttT) economic stimulus funds and then NCLB waivers to increase testing, mainly by requiring states to use student scores to judge teachers. These policies also shifted the primary focus of sanctions from schools to teachers, except for the lowest scoring schools, which suffer both kinds of punishments.

The administration also allocated RttT funding to launch two Common Core State Standards (CCSS) testing consortia, in which most states participate. An alliance of states produced the English Language Arts and Mathematics standards with substantial federal funding plus foundation and corporate support. The federal government also bribed states to adopt Common Core standards by linking new standards to winning RttT grants and the NCLB waivers. The tests are intended to measure and, in effect, enforce the standards. This will further centralize testing's domination over curriculum and instruction. Meanwhile, use of interim tests to get students ready for high-stakes exams continues to explode. Some districts administer as many as thirty standardized tests annually in a single grade, a practice reaching down to kindergarten.

The law deemed the National Assessment of Educational Progress (NAEP) reading and math tests to be the primary indicator of NCLB's long-term, national success. Rather than accelerate toward 100 percent proficiency, the rate of improvement on NAEP has slowed and even stalled in all tested grades, in both reading and math, for almost all demographic groups. High-stakes testing has clearly failed by its primary measure, while causing massive collateral damage to genuine teaching and learning. Yet test proponents have used vast funding from major foundations and corporations along with extensive support from mainstream media to keep pushing for ever more testing, with ever stronger sanctions.

# The Resistance

In the spring of 2013, parent, student, and teacher resistance to the overuse and misuse of standardized tests erupted on the national stage. FairTest has worked to support, promote, and strengthen this emerging movement. The resistance to high-stakes testing is growing rapidly in 2014, reaching new locales, while groups active in 2013 continue to build their capacity to advance the struggle.

Protest actions have included boycotts and "opt-outs," demonstrations and public events, community forums, petitions, extensive use of social media, news conferences, meetings with officials, and a strong legislative push in a few states. Activists garnered community support and often sympathetic media coverage. As a result, they built a larger, stronger movement and won some significant victories.

Students walked out of schools in Seattle, Portland, Oregon, Denver, Chicago, and New York. Seattle teachers in several high schools boycotted one test, called the Measures of Academic Progress, or MAP. When district officials then tried to administer the tests at Garfield High, most students, backed by their parents and community and civil rights groups, refused to take it. In New York, an estimated twenty-five hundred students and their parents boycotted the annual, NCLB-required state exams on Long Island. So did students at forty schools in New York City and many more in upstate New York.

Activists' goals varied, from demands to roll back the amount of standardized testing and end high stakes, to stopping or reducing specific exams, such as graduation tests. The Providence Student Union (PSU) opposed a looming graduation requirement that would deny high school diplomas to as many as 40 percent of seniors. They staged a "zombie march," then organized a group of prominent adults to take the state graduation test, most of whom failed it. They also asked the commissioner of education to sign a symbolic check for $500,000, the average amount of an individual's lifetime loss of income due to not having a diploma. When the board of education would not reconsider the graduation test, students and their allies persuaded the legislature to pass a resolution calling on the board to do so. Because the board did not significantly alter the policy, the PSU, teachers unions, and other groups will seek a legislative victory in 2014. PSU also called for a very different assessment system, modeled on the New York Performance Standards Consortium.

Another partly effective action was a "play in" at Chicago Public Schools offices to protest the dozen or more standardized tests given to kindergarten, first- and second-grade students. It was organized by More Than a Score, a parent-union alliance. In response, CPS proposed a minor reduction in testing in the early grades. Meanwhile, student walkouts led by the emerging Chicago Students Union pushed CPS to drop one high school test. Both organizations are continuing their campaigns.

In New York, public rallies continued the momentum through the summer and fall of 2013. Fifteen hundred people rallied on Long Island in August, then twenty-five hundred in Buffalo in September. Parents, teachers, and students harshly denounced state education policies at public events organized by the New York education department itself. Some Long Island parents mailed their children's student test scores back to the state, writing "return to sender, invalid tests" on the envelopes. Parent leaders called for one hundred thousand boycotters for spring 2014. More than 90 percent of the parents at Castle Bridge School, a K–2 public school in Manhattan opted their children out of tests whose sole purpose is to judge teachers. The supportive principal scrapped the exam. Numerous local groups created an umbrella organization, New York State Allies for Public Education (NYSAPE), to build a stronger statewide campaign.

Legislative efforts took center stage in Texas in the 2013 session, where parents led a successful charge to reduce high school end-of-course graduation tests from fifteen to five. The lead parent group, Texans Advocating for Meaningful Student Assessment (TAMSA, often called "Mothers Against Drunk Testing") was backed by community organizations such as Save Texas Schools, Texas Parents Opt Out of State Tests, unions, administrators, school boards, and civil rights organizations. In Minnesota, teachers unions and civil rights groups, with support from the state superintendent, backed legislation that successfully repealed the state's graduation exams. Many bills to roll back testing mandates were introduced in other states as a first step in efforts to alter policy.

Public forums served to educate and involve parents, students, teachers, and community members. Groups such as the Denver students have described these conversations as essential for building a movement. Chicago parents took petitions to their schools to inform others and develop contacts, and organized public meetings in a variety of neighborhoods. Resolutions helped build the movement. More than 80 percent of Texas school boards approved a resolution in 2012 stating that high-stakes testing "is strangling our public schools" and undermining the chance for "broad learning experiences." FairTest joined with other groups to launch a National Resolution on High Stakes Testing, signed by six hundred organizations and more than eighteen thousand individuals as of early 2014. A series of Florida school boards passed similar versions, leading the state association of boards to approve a resolution, as did the Pennsylvania association. This effort continues. In December 2013, the New York City Council approved a statement against high-stakes testing.

In some cases, testing reform actions built on or complemented other efforts to defend and improve public schools. Chicago youth linked testing to discipline issues and school closings. Youth in Portland, Oregon, also had been working on issues such as school closings. Growing efforts to connect students nationally in turn fed into the testing resistance. Students in several cities started talking together regularly, and Denver and Portland students walked out in concert.

In the fall of 2013, the American Federation of Teachers, in alliance with the National Education Association, the Opportunity to Learn Campaign, and Communities for Public Education Reform, launched "Reclaiming the Promise of Public Schools." They used "town hall" meetings across the country to develop unifying principles. (FairTest helped develop the principle that addresses assessment.) Five hundred teachers, students, and community organizers launched the campaign at a Los Angeles conference in October. Spurred by this, groups organized actions across the nation on December 9, 2013, many of which addressed testing.

## What Next?

Strong, creative actions—such as boycotts, walkouts, zombie marches, and play-ins—energize participants. They have framed issues well and effectively attracted the media.

However, many supporters cannot boycott, or cannot attend a demonstration on a workday, but want to participate. Groups need to involve significant numbers of people in forceful and visible activities that bridge opting out on one end of the protest spectrum and signing petitions on the other. They need to use a wide range of activities and means of communication to inform, educate, and shape the debate, relying on both mainstream and social media. Community meetings are essential to build support for a range of actions as well as an opportunity for people to share experiences and educate one another, policy makers, and the media.

Threats of reprisal are a real danger to boycott organizing. For example, some New York City administrators tried to keep students who opted out of testing from advancing to the next grade due to the absence of mandated test scores. Denver officials threatened to suspend test boycotters and bar them from walking in graduation ceremonies. However, pushing back against punishments is frequently successful, as was the case in New York and Denver. Anticipating such attacks and planning how to resist them, or even turn them to our advantage, are important. Seattle teachers' refusal to administer tests, combined with wide community support, including students opting out, led officials to drop threats and eliminate some testing.

It is crucial to stress that assessment can be a valuable learning tool and that schools should be responsible to their communities. Students in Providence, Portland, and Denver demanded better assessments as well as an end to high-stakes testing, as have teachers in Seattle and parents in New York and Chicago. In Texas, a proposal by a network of districts to create a better assessment and accountability system passed the legislature only to be vetoed by governor Rick Perry. Successful reform strategies often demand that a state or district shift from harmful practices to educationally beneficial ones.

If the movement only rolls back the tests without winning better alternatives, proponents of testing will use the vacuum to reassert the primacy of standardized exams. NCLB destroyed many promising assessment initiatives, but there are US and international examples, such as the New York Performance Standards Consortium. Activists can use them to counter the false claim that standardized tests are the only way to let the public know about or improve school quality. As the movement gains in strength, opportunities to overhaul assessment will open up. The movement must be ready with well-developed options.

The race and class composition of the movement is another vital concern. Urban, activist student groups are often multiracial. However, in some locales, boycott and opt-out movements are seen as mainly "white" or privileged. In other communities, activists say, privileged groups are less likely to collaborate with those from other neighborhoods. Suburban parents or teachers may not know or have ties to urban groups. Some wealthier city parents may capitalize on their children's higher scores to gain admission to elite public schools, using tests to perpetuate inequality even as they protest them. Urban parents of color are far more likely to have serious concerns about educational quality that have led many to support testing as a way of judging schools. The absence of an agenda for strengthening schools that rural, suburban, and urban communities can all support could fatally undermine the movement. Thus, activists must take steps to address race and class inequalities in schooling and in the movement.

The fundamental question is how to develop the power to win major reforms. Groups across the nation are grappling creatively with the issue as they develop strategic plans for the coming years. Facing the wealth and power of government, big corporations, foundations, and media, only large numbers of organized people will be able to turn the testing tide. Sharing experiences, analyses, strategies, and tactics, as well as providing mutual support, will strengthen our emerging movement.

Moving from resistance to legislative and policy victories is not necessarily simple or quick. Nonetheless, local campaigns have won meaningful gains in Texas and Minnesota and made significant progress in winning public opinion. Assessment reform activists have started to change the positions of journalists and elected officials in some jurisdictions. The rapidly expanding movement now has momentum and the next few years will be critical in the struggle to save public education from the standardized testing wrecking ball.

# 25.

# "DEAR PRESIDENT OBAMA, WE NEED LITERATURE OVER TEST PREP"

## DISCOVERING A DEEPER MEANING IN LIFE

## Alma Flor Ada

On Tuesday, October 22, 2013, I read Valerie Strauss's invaluable education blog *The Answer Sheet*, at the *Washington Post*, and was thrilled to learn that the National Center for Fair & Open Testing, known as FairTest, had spearheaded the drafting of an open letter to President Obama. Signed by some 120 authors and illustrators of books for children, the letter expressed opposition to Obama's support for standardized testing policies that were destroying children's love of reading literature, stating, "Our public school students spend far too much time preparing for reading tests and too little time curling up with books that fire their imaginations."

I was even more exhilarated when I saw some of my favorite authors had contributed to the letter. The legendary poet, actor, and activist the late yet immortal Maya Angelou lent her name to the effort. As Valerie Strauss put it, "Angelou is noteworthy on this list not only because of her position in the literary world but because she has been a big public supporter of Obama." It made me think of Angelou's line from her celebrated poem "Still I Rise": "Does my sassiness upset you?" The cherished children's author Judy Blume also signed the letter. Blume's *Superfudge* is one of the earliest stories I can remember my mom reading aloud to me, so her signature was particularly gratifying. The name of the award-winning social justice children's author Alma Flor Ada jumped off the page at me as my two sons and I have enjoyed and been deeply moved by her stories and poems. I decided to contact Flor to find out more specifically what motivated her to sign this letter against the abuses of standardized testing. I also wanted to know what she thought of the Common Core State Standards' emphasis on the use of informational text over literature.

—Jesse Hagopian

Alma Flor Ada wrote this response:

# Why Literature?

There are important reasons why literature should be an essential aspect of education, and whenever we say literature we are referring to good literature, outstanding books written for children and young adults, in poetry, in historical and contemporary fiction, in biographies, in nonfiction books of literary and artistic quality, in drama.

Children and youth deserve the best, and when it comes to language nothing is superior to good poetry, to good literature. Yes, it is important that students are able to read and understand informational text, but informational text does exactly what it is intended to do: it provides information. Literature does far much more; what it provides cannot be underestimated nor dismissed or restricted without terrible detriment.

Literature is the product of the pondering and analysis of human experiences and emotions. It invites reflection, allowing readers to gain insight on human behavior, to better understand themselves and others.

Literature requires mastery in the crafting of words, in order to be engaging and compelling. It not only gives an example of the power of language but becomes a model of living consciously, of paying attention to what happens around us, of discovering a deeper meaning in life.

All cultures have created poetry and various forms of literature, even in the oldest periods of history, or the most remote corners, even when they did not have a written language. This tells us something about the human thirst for the aesthetic experience literature provides. And the literary creations have been preserved, transmitted orally from generation to generation, as proof of how valued and cherished they have been.

Of course we want students to have information, and to learn how to retrieve existing information, but this must not be done at the expense of giving them the possibility to know and reflect about the dilemmas that life presents, the need to make choices that is part of daily living, as literature does.

A mind used to reflecting and analyzing will be much better prepared to face information with a discerning mind. A child or a young person who enjoys reading because he or she was given the opportunity to read enjoyable, exciting, intriguing, thrilling, delightful books will face with joy, interest, and ease informational texts.

There is a claim, to support the supplanting of good literature by informational reading, that as adults students will have to read manuals of great complexity. The argument must be made that perhaps manuals could be written with greater clarity if those who write them would have a better background in expository writing. Let's fix the manuals, not deprive the students.

A final point of great importance. Literature can also be highly informative about a multiplicity of themes. It seems, though, that frequently the only recognition to the contribution of literature to the enrichment of knowledge is given to historical fiction. Teachers could benefit from being pointed in the direction of books that combine high literary quality and sound information about a multiplicity of topics, not only historical ones. This would be more beneficial than restricting the time and support given to the presence in the curriculum to one of the most valuable tools to educate: great books.

Here now is the FairTest letter that I and others signed urging Obama to rethink his commitment to high-stakes testing:

President Barack Obama
The White House
Washington, DC 20500

Dear President Obama,

We the undersigned children's book authors and illustrators write to express our concern for our readers, their parents and teachers. We are alarmed at the negative impact of excessive school testing mandates, including your Administration's own initiatives, on children's love of reading and literature. Recent policy changes by your Administration have not lowered the stakes. On the contrary, requirements to evaluate teachers based on student test scores impose more standardized exams and crowd out exploration.

We call on you to support authentic performance assessments, not simply computerized versions of multiple-choice exams. We also urge you to reverse the narrowing of curriculum that has resulted from a fixation on high-stakes testing.

Our public school students spend far too much time preparing for reading tests and too little time curling up with books that fire their imaginations. As Michael Morpurgo, author of the Tony Award Winner *War Horse*, put it, "It's not about testing and reading schemes, but about loving stories and passing on that passion to our children."

Teachers, parents and students agree with British author Philip Pullman, who said, "We are creating a generation that hates reading and feels nothing but hostility for literature." Students spend time on test practice instead of perusing books. Too many schools devote their library budgets to test-prep materials, depriving students of access to real literature. Without this access, children also lack exposure to our country's rich cultural range.

This year has seen a growing national wave of protest against testing overuse and abuse. As the authors and illustrators of books for children, we feel a special responsibility to advocate for change. We offer our full support for a national campaign to change the way we assess learning so that schools nurture creativity, exploration, and a love of literature from the first day of school through high school graduation.

| | | |
|---|---|---|
| Alma Flor Ada | Tracy Barrett | Shellie Braeuner |
| Alma Alexander | Chris Barton | Ethriam Brammer |
| Jane Ancona | Ari Berk | Louann Mattes Brown |
| Maya Angelou | Judy Blume | Anne Broyles |
| Jonathan Auxier | Alfred B. (Fred) Bortz | Michael Buckley |
| Kim Baker | Lynea Bowdish | Janet Buell |
| Molly Bang | Sandra Boynton | Dori Hillestad Butler |

Charito Calvachi-
Mateyko
Valerie Scho Carey
Rene Colato Lainez
Henry Cole
Ann Cook
Karen Coombs
Robert Cortez
Cynthia Cotten
Bruce Coville
Ann Crews
Donald Crews
Nina Crews
Rebecca Kai Dotlich
Laura Dower
Kathryn Erskine
Jules Feiffer
Jody Feldman
Mary Ann Fraser
Sharlee Glenn
Barbara Renaud Gonzalez
Laurie Gray
Trine M. Grillo
Claudia Harrington
Sue Heavenrich
Linda Oatman High
Anna Grossnickle Hines
Lee Bennett Hopkins
Phillip Hoose
Diane M. Hower
Michelle Houts
Mike Jung
Kathy Walden Kaplan
Amal Karzai
Jane Kelley

Elizabeth
Koehler-Pentacoff
Amy Goldman Koss
JoAnn Vergona Krapp
Nina Laden
Sarah Darer Littman
José Antonio López
Mariellen López
Jenny MacKay
Marianne Malone
Ann S. Manheimer
Sally Mavor
Diane Mayr
Marissa Moss
Yesenia Navarrete
Hunter
Sally Nemeth
Kim Norman
Geraldo Olivo
Alexis O'Neill
Anne Marie Pace
Amado Peña
Irene Peña
Lynn Plourde
Ellen Prager, PhD
David Rice
Armando Rendon
Joan Rocklin
Judith Robbins Rose
Sergio Ruzzier
Barb Rosenstock
Liz Garton Scanlon
Lisa Schroeder
Sara Shacter
Wendi Silvano

Janni Lee Simner
Sheri Sinykin
Jordan Sonnenblick
Ruth Spiro
Heidi E. Y. Stemple
Whitney Stewart
Shawn K. Stout
Steve Swinburne
Carmen Tafolla
Kim Tomsic
Duncan Tonatiuh
Patricia Thomas
Kristin O'Donnell Tubb
Deborah Underwood
Corina Vacco
Audrey Vernick
Debbie Vilardi
Judy Viorst
K. M. Walton
Wendy Wax
April Halprin Wayland
Carol Weis
Rosemary Wells
Lois Wickstrom
Suzanne Morgan
Williams
Kay Winters
Ashley Wolff
Lisa Yee
Karen Romano Young
Jane Yolen
Roxyanne Young
Paul O. Zelinsky
Jennifer Ziegler

# 26.
# "IT WAS THE RIGHT THING TO DO"
## Interview with Carol Burris

*This interview was conducted on January 15, 2014, and has been edited and condensed.*

**Jesse Hagopian:** Let's start with your own personal history with standard testing. Talk a little bit about what's been your experience with these tests, as a student, a middle school teacher, or now as a principal at South Side high school, that helped shape your views on standardized testing?

**Carol Burris:** One of my big passions as a principal has been the elimination of tracking and giving all kids the best curriculum that schools have to offer, and so part of the interest that I've always had in testing is the role that it plays in the sorting and selecting of kids and how inaccurate that process is. I became very concerned when I started to see the move toward sorting teachers by scores into categories, and sorting kids into one of four categories, and then having this label of "college-readiness" attached to it I felt that was part of a larger picture of the way American schools tend to look at kids, you know, almost in boxes, and make decisions on their lives based on test scores.

**JH:** That's right—unfortunately we see that test-and-track policy all over the country.

**CB:** Now, in our school, we don't believe tracking—that's not our philosophy, so for example, any kid who wants to take International Baccalaureate (IB), or any kid who wants to take science research, we let them take it.

We are not interested in sorting kids. At this point we have almost no sorting left; we have almost complete heterogeneous grouping. As of next year, there will only be levels left in twelfth-grade math and social students and even that will be by student choice. We have never been a test-score-driven school, that's not what we have been about. We do not give any standardized tests. We do have in the year course exams, the Regents exam, which is a curriculum-based test, and the International Baccalaureate exams, which are curriculum-based tests, but we don't have any of the standardized norm-reference tests that compare one student to another. In our district, although we've given the [grade] three to eight tests, we've never used them to sort children in any way. So the idea of sorting teachers into categories, in part by student test scores, was something that troubled me deeply. I do not believe it is valid or reliable in any way, and I just don't believe in the philosophy that a number on a test should be used to make big decisions for the lives of kids.

**JH:** Do you remember a time when you realized that these tests were being used to rank and sort rather than enrich education; was there something that happened in your own life?

**CB:** When it first started it appeared innocuous, with NCLB, and it was only in the fourth and eighth grades. It was not used for teacher evaluations, it was used for school accountability. In the very beginning, if you remember, it was pretty easy to make AYP [adequate yearly progress] and we used it primarily to identify kids who needed help and the tests were transparent. We could see the tests so that, for example, "Look at this, all of the kids got the poetry questions wrong, we need to put more poetry in our curriculum," and you know that wasn't a bad thing, Jesse, it was actually a good thing. So in the beginning when these tests first came out they were used to inform instruction, they were used to modify curriculum, and they were used to identify the kids who really needed help. But what's happened since then, because of Race to the Top, is everything has gotten far more intense. First the state started adding other grade levels from third to eighth grade.

Then all of a sudden what started to happen in 2011 is that the testing time zoomed up so that the fifth grade test, for example, was 227 percent longer than it had been prior. There were more testing days and they started adding more high-stakes consequences: high-stakes consequences for the teachers, evaluating them by the test scores; for principals, evaluating them by the kids' test scores. The Common Core tests became a lot more difficult, and they raised the cut score at the same time, which made them even more of a toxic mix.

**JH:** Well let me just ask you then about Common Core. I think teachers have widely criticized No Child Left Behind and Race to the Top as education policy that's just based on a test-and-punish model. Most educators are very displeased with those education policies. I think it's more mixed around Common Core. Some educators have held out hope that Common Core will help them improve education and I know your own thinking has evolved on this at well, and I was wondering if you could share your ideas about that.

**CB:** At first blush, the idea of making all kids college- and career-ready is one that I've embraced; we built a high school around the idea. We have all the kids in IB English—it took them a long time, we gave them a lot of support, but they do it. However, the more closely I looked at the Common Core, the more concerned I became. A lot of the concern that I had was when teachers started bringing in work that their kids in elementary school were doing. I started getting reports from my teachers—it is a young faculty and they have young kids. They told me about their kids crying, their kids becoming school-phobic, their kids saying they don't want to go to school anymore. They'd bring in this work from Common Core math, which supposedly is trying to get kids to develop a deeper understanding of mathematics. However, they're accelerating what it is kids should be able to do in younger grades. I'm not so sure they've really taken a whole lot out, even though they claim they did, and they're also teaching kids so many multiple methods that it's become very confusing for children. For example, they're learning that the number *fourteen* isn't the number fourteen anymore, it's *one-ten-four*. They're relying a lot on kids doing manipulations in their heads, which for a lot of kids, special ed kids and special needs kids, is very, very difficult. Rather than teaching them just the standard algorithm for multiplication, they're insisting that kids solve the problem in far more complicated ways. If kids are trying to learn all these different methods for solutions, what's happening is that they're going on overload. I think they're doing it too much, I think they're doing it too quickly, and I think that they're actually making math more confusing, not less confusing.

In English there is an overemphasis on informational text, with less literature. Literature matters. In literature you learn to dream. Readers identify with characters, their strengths and their flaws and their heroes. Perhaps you encounter a character who has a dysfunctional family, and your family is dysfunctional . . . all of a sudden you don't feel so alone anymore. Kids really learn so much from that. Yet the "modules" for ninth-grade ELA in New York suggest that rather than reading all of *Romeo and Juliet* students read excerpts of *Romeo and Juliet.* They then substitute informational such as readings on the life of Bernie Madoff, the swindler on Wall Street. You know what? I'm just not seeing the value in that.

I feel though what they're really trying to do by having all of these short bursts of reading instead of full texts is to prepare kids more for tests rather than for the kind of reading that they're actually going to do in college. You go into your college English class that first day and what do you hear? "Here are the six novels we're reading." Students are not reading excerpts in college. I just think that they're doing kids a disservice. In English at my high school we will not read excerpts—we are going to continue to read all of *Romeo and Juliet,* thank you very much—

**JH:** Resistance! I love it!

**CB:** —Math resistance is harder. Math is far more content-driven. I think in math we're going to have a lot of kids who are very confused. Our first round of Common Core testing was last year. It was very difficult. In ELA, the Common Core wants kids to read deeply, you know, to look for evidence. Yet there was too much to read on the test, kids had to race and they couldn't finish. And then on top of that, the State Education Department yanked up the cut scores . . . it was just a mess.

**JH:** Wow. Well, I want to ask you about how you moved from understanding into action, because your launching the petition campaign and the open letter against high-stakes testing provisions that were designed to have your state compete for Race to the Top funding really helped inspire people around the country, including teachers at Garfield who launched the MAP test boycott. When we saw that principals were standing up it was part of our inspiration.

**CB:** It started with the letter, the Annual Professional Performance Review—APPR—open letter against using test scores to evaluate teachers. First, the idea of even putting a number on a teacher we believe is professionally insulting and not productive. The union [officials] have their reasons why they think it is a good idea, but—you know, the principals who signed the letter (more than a third of all in the state), did not. I found the whole

APPR system, when I looked at it, and looked at it closely, to be appalling. Even though student achievement is only 40 percent of the model, the way they constructed it was bizarre. For example, if a teacher was found to be ineffective on test scores, they would have to be found ineffective overall. That, we felt, was just wrong. We kind of get why teachers want something objective in there. I understand why with a high-stakes evaluation teachers want a system that's more than just a principal's opinion, especially if you could lose your job. Frankly, I was just fine with the way everything was, I didn't feel like I had to run around this building firing teachers. Besides, teachers with issues, you work with them, work through the issues, or eventually they, with some push, decide most of the time to go.

When I looked at APPR, I recognized the problems. I said, "What are they doing? There are going to be so many unintended consequences of doing this!" We talked about it in the letter, where teachers would start to feel as though the kids in their class were almost a threat to their job if they didn't perform. I had no faith and still have no faith in value-added measures and we're delighted that Randi Weingarten in the AFT has just come out against them. We felt that the science behind that was terribly, terribly flawed. We were really worried that it would ruin the collegiality that we had built in our schools, where teachers might see themselves as rivals rather than working together for the benefit of kids. And we were just appalled at the whole APPR system, which by the way, principals had no voice in, no voice at all. When they created the APPR, that was the legislature, it was NYSUT, it was NYSED, and it was the governor's office. They never even said, "Gee, what do you guys say? Do principals think this is a good idea?"

Anyway, we wrote the letter—Sean [Feeney] and I drafted it. Basically we did that because the commissioner was coming to town and I wanted to organize a protest, and Sean wisely said, "Carol, let's try something more productive on this." We wrote the letter and we were amazed by how many principals on Long Island felt the same way that we did. I think in the end over 80 percent of the Long Island principals actually signed the letter. Then we started blasting it around the state and we had people all over New York sign on. We thought, "My goodness, people are going to listen to us! They're going to listen because we're principals, and a lot of us are good principals at excellent schools." I thought, "I'm sixty years old, what do I have to lose?" We thought that that would make our voice powerful. What we got, essentially, was the hand. The commissioner never responded to us, ever. The Board of Regents never responded to it. We sent it to the governor's office. The governor was furious with what we were doing, and he actually accelerated the APPR process. It was unbelievable. We got to a point where we had over a third of all the principals signing that particular letter. We would have had many more, except that an extremely large number of principals are in New York City and it was still the Bloomberg days. They were afraid.

**JH:** Were you worried about consequences?

**CB:** Did I feel any fear?

**JH:** Yeah, were you worried when you guys sat down to draft the letter that there might be consequences against you for launching this campaign?

**CB:** I think some were, but I didn't care. It was right—it was the right thing to do, and I felt at the time, even if something happened to me and I had to leave my job, I was prepared to do that.

**JH:** Wow.

**CB:** And I would have gone into early retirement. I figured out it would have cost me about $25,000 a year if I had to leave early on my pension, but it was worth it. There comes a point when you just have to stand up for what's right and I still feel that way. I have often said that if the law required that I tell what a teacher's score was to a parent, I would not do it. I would be brought up on charges first and let them take my license. As it turned out my district decided that it would be the district that would reveal the score, and interestingly enough—this is so interesting, Jesse—not one parent in our district has requested a teacher's score.

**JH:** I bet that's right . . . your resistance is making the hair stand up on the back of my neck because it sounds just like the place that the teachers at Garfield reached, where every threat that was leveled against us only emboldened us more because we knew what we were doing was right, and we weren't alone and others felt the same. Right on. That brings me to the fact that your protest was described by the *New York Times* as the first principal revolt in history and I wonder what you think the role of administrators should be in this growing national movement against high-stakes, standardized testing?

**CB:** I think that they need to be stronger. I think that the principals were admirable in the stand that they took. However, I think that there's a lot more that more people can do. I think that superintendents could stand taller. You find a lot of people who in private will tell you that all of these things are so wrong, so very wrong, but publicly they won't say it. I'm very proud of my superintendent, who has been terrific and who has been a real leader with this and who respects the parents' right to have their children refuse the test. He doesn't encourage it, but if a parent makes that decision, he respects that right, as opposed to some of his colleagues who are very punitive. We have superintendents in New York, for example, who are not allowing children who refuse the test to be on the honor roll.

**JH:** Wow. I wonder, from the superintendent on up to Arne Duncan, to Bill Gates, why are they attacking us so much in public education? What's your view on why all this test-and-punish legislation is coming down on us?

**CB:** I think that a lot of what motivates Arne Duncan is that there is a group of people, the Democrats for Educational Reform, who were very generous to Barack Obama during the election. He was part of that group and I think that philosophically he believes this is the right thing to do. They think that kids are for the most part victims of poor teaching. They will not acknowledge the role that poverty plays, nor do they acknowledge the role that student motivation plays. We don't talk about this anymore, right? The kid who just says, "I'm not doing it." That kid is out there—he is in every school. I believe reformer see students as the victims of their teachers, and they believe that if they punish schools enough and they punish teachers enough, that that will change. I think they're wrong and I think that thinking is foolish and destructive. I don't think that Mr. Duncan has an adequate background and understanding in education to really have the right perspective, nor do I believe he should even be in the position he is. I don't think that he's qualified for that position. I don't think running the Chicago Public Schools for a couple of years as CEO (and not a particularly effective one) qualifies you for that position. He does not have a teaching license. He doesn't even have a masters degree. I think that he views this more from a political perspective. The statement that he made that white suburban moms oppose the Common Core because they think that their children are geniuses was outrageous, outrageous.

**JH:** It shows a clear lack of understanding of the educational process.

**CB:** I think Bill Gates may be well-meaning, but he does not understand all of the issues in education, even though he believes that he does. He wants to have his will, his research, and his vision transform education in the United States. He has all the money, and I really wish he would focus his reform on something else, maybe a more effective traffic light system. You don't want him messing in health care because that can have dire consequences. I don't think his support for these reforms is helpful at all. It is one thing to give the research community money to answer questions. It is quite another to push an agenda. That is ego.

**JH:** I wanted to get at the bigger question of what you think the role of education should be in our society and what type of assessments do you think would help us meet that vision for the purpose of education.

**CB:** Well, I think that, for one thing, we need to put our focus not on worrying about the test outcomes, what we commonly refer to as the "achievement gap," and start to focus on the "opportunity gap." There was a wonderful book that was edited by my friend Kevin Welner and his colleague Prudence Carter; you can find it online at the National Education Policy Center. If we worry about closing those opportunity gaps, I think the scores are going to follow.

We have to understand, this is slow and difficult work. Education doesn't get transformed over night. The transformations that we've made in my high school, which is a far better place than it was twenty years ago, took time. It's been a slow, deliberate process of working hard, of getting kids support, of looking at what it is that we do to maintain progress, and then moving forward. We managed to de-track our high school—if you know anything about tracking and de-tracking, you know de-tracking is one of the hardest reforms you can do. There has to be an acknowledgment that what we do, it's not going to be a miracle overnight, which is what they're hoping to do.

The kinds of assessments that we need for kids are child-centered assessments: assessments that inform curriculum, that identify places where kids still need to learn and grow, and that also give an accurate reading of what it is that the child is able to do. When we start to move away from those child-centered purposes of assessment and instead start to focus on the other purposes—closing schools, evaluating teachers—we lose our focus. Those grades four and eight tests, when they first came out, teachers could see the test. (Up until about 2010 in New York we could see the tests.) That was so helpful. We could really understand what kids were not understanding. Now that everything is hidden and closed and you can't see the tests, those assessments have lost their instructional power. We have to get back to the idea of why we assess kids to begin with and that that purpose is to help the child grow and to make us better teachers. This is not doing it. It's not.

I love the assessments of the International Baccalaureate. We use them. They exist not to figure out what a kid doesn't know but to let a kid show what they do know. Many of them are scored by the teachers. The IB has good checks to make sure that they're being assessed fairly and with validity. They are interspersed throughout the curriculum. They're a natural part of the teaching and learning process. For example, there are papers that kids write over the course of two years. There are oral presentations that are part of it. There's a portfolio in art, with kids reflecting on their work. They really are model assessments, and if we had assessments like that and we did not use them for high-stakes purposes, we would just be in such a better place.

**JH:** That's wonderful. What is your definition of the opportunity gap and what do you think we could do to close that?

**CB:** I look at it through the prism of the book entitled *Closing the Opportunity Gap*. There are a lot of different facets—per-pupil spending [is one]. The gap includes opportunity to have support services like guidance counselors, social workers, and to make sure that those support services match the needs of the community. I often say, 16 percent of our kids are eligible for free and reduced-price lunch, and I have three social workers. If I have three social workers with a population of 16 percent on free and reduced-price lunch, how many social workers should there be in a school where 97 percent of the kids are on free and reduced lunch? That's a part of the opportunity gap. Certainly tracking is part of the opportunity gap. Our movement has to be about making sure that all kids have access to the very best curriculum that a school has to offer.

# 27.
## "WHAT COULD BE"
## INQUIRY AND THE PERFORMANCE
## ASSESSMENT ALTERNATIVE
## An interview with Phyllis Tashlik

*This interview was conducted on July 26, 2014, and has been edited and condensed.*

**Jesse Hagopian:** I first heard of the New York Performance Standards Consortium Schools when I met Avram Barlowe in Washington, DC, during the spring of 2013 at an education conference put on by the Advancement Project. It was a really powerful moment because I was relating the story of the MAP test boycott in Seattle and saying we need to move away from high-stakes testing, and then Avram's was next, presenting with a colleague of his and a student he had taught at a consortium school, explaining how perform-ance-based assessment is so superior to standardized testing. It was a power-ful coming together of both how we resist the current testing regime and then what we put in its place. Did you follow the MAP test boycott while it was going on, and what was your initial reaction was to it?

**Phyllis Tashlik:** Oh, yeah. Sure, we heard about it. Well, you know, we're always interested in knowing other people across the country who've come to the conclusions that we've come to because you don't want to feel all alone in this. We saw that you were objecting to a very specific test, and it looked like lots of very good reasons to oppose that very specific test. We were interested in seeing what would happen next and definitely wanted to let you know about what we were doing in New York.

**JH:** I'm so glad that you and Avram and the folks with the consortium schools built on that relationship. I have to thank you for flying Garfield teachers out to see your schools because their experience learning about performance assessment at your schools has really deepened their understanding. And their presentations at Garfield have been really impressive, and I think our whole staff has gone beyond opposing the MAP test to collectively developing better assessments in our schools. So I thank you for that.

**PT:** That was great to see Rachel [Eells] and Heather [Robison] most recently. We had an afternoon group that day with people from New Mexico, New Hampshire, Maine, Kentucky. It was clear you were at a beginning stage and it it's great that Rachel and Heather can bring the skills they learned at the Moderation Study back to other people at Garfield.

**JH:** It's changing the culture of our schools. You know, I think a lot of us who are interested in developing critical thinking in the classroom have spent a lot of our time defending the public schools from the corporate education reform attack. And at the same time that we want to defend the schools from this attack, we also have to think about how we need to reorganize our schools, rethink what the purpose of school is, and develop better forms of assessment. So I wonder if you could tell me about how you came into the field of education and how you decided that a new approach to public education was needed.

**PT:** It was very long time ago. [Laughter] And it actually for me started with more political activism and gradually I just got more involved in the whole issue of the public schools as a sort of political issue—I mean, this was during the Vietnam War and there were social movements going on in those days—but I just started to get really interested in education, in how schools run, and how kids learn and how teachers teach.

And in those days, they needed people desperately in the schools, so I didn't really have much teacher preparation. It was pretty much an on-the-job kind of preparation. So, you know, when you're a new teacher, you've got tons of energy and ideas, the school was just filled with new teachers. There weren't many mentors in those days or models or good examples, I'd say, of really good teaching just because everyone was so young and inexperienced.

I got involved with the consortium because I knew Ann Cook and Herb Mack, who are legendary in New York City public education circles. (They founded Urban Academy more than thirty years ago. Herb just retired this year after being involved with public schools for over forty years. Ann Cook, also cofounder of Urban and an activist in New York City public education, is the executive director of the consortium.) I met them when I started to work at Urban Academy. It was the late 1990s when Tom Sobol was the commissioner for New York and his whole philosophy was top-down support for bottom-up reform. Tom Sobol gave us the go-ahead. Also in New York, there had been an alternative school division, which I was involved in. I was interested in looking at those kids who were dropping out and trying to find other ways to reach them. And I recognized that the status quo is not the way to reach these kids. You really had to come up with interesting approaches to teaching and learning. So there were lots of ways that different schools were doing that, and Sobol was very interested in building on that and supporting it. Sobol gave us a waiver that allowed us to opt out of the state standardized tests. I think that first waiver was for five years.

**JH:** And so that waiver provided the basis for the founding of the New York Performance Standards Consortium.

**PT:** Yes, that was the legal basis of it. But what happened after Tom left is the next commissioner, Richard Mills, had a whole different approach and his whole idea was that everybody in the state should be doing the same thing, and the same thing would be five high-stakes exit exams. It was going to be a requirement that every single kid in the state was going to do these five exams, regardless of what kind of program they were in or what their goals were. Mills gave us a just a one-year waiver. And some people saw that as a defeat, but we saw it as another year to work at getting another extension. And so, in all these years, we've gone from waiver to waiver: five years, one year, four years, five years.

**JH:** So yours is really a story of, year by year, having to build resistance to standardized testing both in a political struggle with the state and also in the classroom by showing the alternative.

**PT:** Right. What happened is the very first waiver gave us a certain number of spots under what they call a "variance." And so in 2007 we were able to bring in seven more schools, and we've just brought in two groups of schools. It's given us the opportunity over the years to really develop what we're doing, to refine it as a system. We've always said the consortium is not just an assessment; it's a whole system that we're engaged in.

**JH:** My question to you then is why are the consortium schools public schools rather than charter schools? Because we always hear that you have to be a charter school in order to be innovative and take a different approach.

**PT:** Yeah, it's funny. When we describe our schools, people say, "Oh, I know, so you're a charter school." No. We take all kids. If you look at the data report, we have more kids on free and reduced[-price] lunch than the general school population. We have a higher number of Latino students. So we take all [the] students [we can]. The charter school movement has so much funding that comes from private sources. We don't do that. We're public schools. We accept the same amount of money as every other public school does and we accept all children. We have a high number of kids with special needs. I mean, I think the average in New York City is about 14 percent. Some of our schools have over 30 percent of kids with high needs.

**JH:** Wow.

**PT:** So you don't find that in the charter schools.

**JH:** Right, in too many instances they want to push out the kids with high needs from charter schools so they don't drag the test scores down.

**PT:** Yes, and in fact many of our schools wind up with the kids who get asked to leave the charter schools.

**JH:** Can you talk about the principles that the consortium is founded on?

**PT:** It started technically as an assessment issue, but it's always been about creating a more inquiry-based classroom. Having an element of choice for students and teachers, respecting students' voice. The way we define ourselves now is a teacher-designed, student-focused system with external evaluation.

**JH:** Yes!

**PT:** So we worked with psychometricians to develop a moderation study, which is what some of your teachers participated in. And we used a lot of the ideas about planning backwards. So if you're going to prepare students for the performance assessments, which involve extensive writing and an oral presentation of their work, what does that mean about the earlier grades? How do you prepare kids for that kind of opportunity to show what they've learned?

**JH:** I want to get into looking more specifically at what the performance-based assessments look like in a minute. But before we do that, I really liked what you said about how the school may have started around looking at alternative assessments but has really a bigger picture of what the purpose of education is and what skills we need to cultivate. And I was reading your book *Talk, Talk, Talk* and I was wondering if you could explain a little bit about what a discussion-based classroom is and how the inquiry method works.

**PT:** What happens in a discussion-based classroom is you're asking kids to take more responsibility for their own learning by participating in class, by expressing what they're thinking, what their ideas are, how they're responding to texts, how they respond to each other's responses to text. For a teacher, learning how to facilitate that kind of discussion. You know, it's interesting, I have a lot of opportunities now to observe other classes in other schools, including non-consortium schools, and I'm always struck—you know, now I sit in the back of the classroom—and I'm always struck by conversations that kids have among themselves that to a teacher who's in front of the room just looks like they're not paying attention. But so often, the kids are asking each other questions or they're commenting on something, and it never gets to be voiced to the class as a whole because it's not a classroom that values [that]. . . .

And, you know, it happens in all kinds of schools. It's been really interesting for me to see that and value even more the importance of a discussion-based classroom where kids know that what they have to say is valued.

**JH:** So instead of being chastised for asking those questions in the back of the room, they're invited to share them.

**PT:** Exactly. And instead of the teacher's questions becoming a question that the kid has to figure out what's the right answer that the teacher already knows, you ask these more open-ended questions so that there's not necessarily a right or wrong answer. There's an interpretation that can be supported with evidence from text or firsthand experience or building on what other kids have said in the classroom. And that's a very different kind of questioning. As teachers, we often make the mistake of asking empty questions when we already know the answer because you just feel more secure as a teacher. You feel like your role isn't being threatened. But to have the kind of open-ended questions where things could come up that you might not know, and you say, "That's a really good question. Maybe we'll have time to get to that," or "Let's put that on our list of questions for research later on in the semester."

**JH:** Right. And is this a model of inquiry-based and discussion-based classroom that you have in the consortium schools across the curriculum for all the different subjects?

**PT:** Well, you know, it's funny you ask that because I was just talking to some people and I said, "You know, I think we should have a theme for the year," which we hadn't done before, "and I think the theme should be discussion-based classrooms."

**JH:** Nice.

**PT:** Because it's not the way teachers have been trained, so it's something that you have to retrain yourself for. And at Urban, it's so pervasive that if a substitute comes in to teach, the class can run itself basically because the kids know how. And if a new teacher starts at the school, the kids will say, "Oh, yeah, you're not an Urban teacher. You have to learn how to be an Urban teacher." What we do, and what we encourage other schools to do is to have a whole mentoring system for new teachers. It's not always possible, and especially now. I know what's happening this year is budgets are being cut severely. So that means there's less time for more experienced teachers to help the newer teachers. The apprenticeship of new teachers is a whole other issue that we've tried to tackle.

**JH:** From what you're saying, it sounds like the method is to have the teacher really scaffold the discussion and point students in different directions and elicit questions from them and present material that challenges them to ask each other questions rather than present to them one fact after another to be learned. It sounds very Freireian to me and a way to engage the class in a lot deeper discussion.

**PT:** Right. And you know, it takes years to get good at it . . . you're a history teacher, right?

**JH:** That's right.

**PT:** It takes years to have enough materials at different reading levels to make this model work well. Avram's been teaching for a long time, so he can move the class in the direction where they seem to be going—what's catching their interest and how to really develop that and how to bring in enough good materials that are accessible to kids at different levels. We do a lot of what we call packets, where you have one topic, but you have reading selections at different levels related to that topic. For example, I was teaching a class on language, and we were talking about whether languages should be saved from dying.

**JH:** Interesting.

**PT:** There are languages dying all the time, just like different species. And so I had to find articles about some of the endangered languages that were very accessible to kids and then others that were even more challenging—because I had a completely mixed group of kids—so that we could all engage in the discussion. You know kids whose reading skills may not be as advanced as some other kids', but they can still think. And they can still discuss. You know, they still have the sharp intelligence.

**JH:** That's right.

**PT:** So you had to bring in enough materials at different levels so that as a group we can still have good discussions and we can still form more questions out of those discussions.

**JH:** That makes me think that real education reform would be about giving teachers time to collaborate so they can share the materials they have to develop those rich inquiry lessons.

I'd like to ask you now about the connection between your inquiry-based approach to education and then the performance-based assessments you use to evaluate and what advantages you feel performance-based assessment has over standardized bubble testing.

**PT:** The general public gleans what the media throw at them and the tendency is for people to think, "Oh, if you're against standardized testing, then you're against assessments," which is not the case at all. What we're against is an assessment that has the consequence of narrowing curriculum and teaching and learning. It's important to realize that as soon as you institute these standardized tests, you're also affecting curriculum, and you're affecting how teachers teach, and you're affecting how time is used. And it's that connection between assessment, curriculum, and instruction that just doesn't get explained enough in the public conversation about testing.  Performance assessments offer such a greater opportunity to develop interesting curriculum and structure more opportunities for the teacher to relate to the kids in front of them. So out of that relationship and out of what is occurring in your classroom, you can help develop the kinds of assessments that grow organically from the material that you've actually been teaching. Whereas when you impose a standardized exam, you wind up imposing a standardized curriculum.

**JH:** That's right.

**PT:** Which may or may not be relevant to what the class thinks is important, which will definitely narrow what's possible in a classroom, which will have an effect on the kind of teaching that goes on, and it just goes downhill from there. And those are the vital connections that just don't become part of the national conversation about assessment.

**JH:** Yes, thank you for making those connections. Can you walk me through the process of how performance-based assessment works in the consortium schools? What does it look like when a student reaches the end of a semester?

**PT:** Well, it grows out of the classroom. We have these four PBATs—performance-based assessment tasks—so in literature, it's a literary analysis that the Common Core is trying to marginalize. We maintain a literary analysis.

**JH:** Resistance through reading literature!

**PT:** Right. Social Studies, it's a research paper. Science, it's really working like a scientist. Kids are developing experiments that grow out of what they've been studying or coming up with a whole new idea about an experiment. And in math, it's an application of higher mathematics to problem solving. So those are the four main performance-based assessment tasks.

Now, that doesn't limit the content of it. I'll just give examples from my teaching. I taught a Latin American literature course, so the PBATs that were developed out of that would be based on Latin American literature. In Latin American fiction, one student might focus on the politics of Latin American fiction, and another might focus on the magical realism in Latin American fiction. So that varies. But the idea of a literary analysis task stays. And that goes across all the curricula.

**JH:** That's wonderful. So instead of a student at the end of a semester sitting down with a pencil, paper, test, and eliminating wrong-answer choices, they have to do a literary analysis. And what does that look like in the classroom?

**PT:** We have teacher-designed rubrics, and I think if you look at the rubrics, you'll understand what kind of standards we're trying to hold the students to. They are writing papers all semester long. It's not like all of a sudden they do a PBAT at the end of the semester. In every English class they're taking, they're doing maybe three literary analyses or taking in-class essay exams. There are lots of assessments going on during the year. I might say to a student, "This paper is a strong analysis and you came up with some really good ideas. I think you need to revise it , and it has a possibility of being a PBAT paper." Whereas I might say to another student, "We need to work on a lot of revision. You still need to get your writing to a better level, and maybe next semester you'll be able to do a PBAT paper."

Then the way the PBAT paper works is not only I but another teacher has to approve it using the rubric and saying this paper has reached at least a competent level on the rubric. And then the student conducts a presentation for someone other than the classroom teacher. Two other people evaluate a student's work. We're in the middle of Manhattan, so we've always been able to get a lot of people very interested in meeting with a student and talking to them about their work. They get the papers in advance. Or sometimes the student reads a completely new book and an external evaluator sits down with them and evaluates. We have lawyers and writers and journalists and other teachers participating. We're located very near Rockefeller University, which has graduate-level science and research, so for our science classes we've always had people come in and question the students on their work. And what's interesting is you can have a kid whose paper is at the competent level, it's not beyond that. It's not outstanding but shows a level competency. And then you listen to her defend her paper, and you can see that this is a kid who knows so much more than she's been able to express through her writing. Orally some students can sometimes express much more about what they've learned than might be evident in their paper. And the external evaluators are very impressed by what they see a student knows.

At Urban, we also have a studio art PBAT and an art criticism PBAT— each school in the consortium adds on supplementary PBATs. And we have artists come in and critique the students' work. I mean, I can't imagine being sixteen or seventeen and having had an adult come in and spend so much time looking at my work. It must be so flattering for the student to have that kind of critique and someone to take your work so seriously. That must be an incredible experience when you're young. So we have a number of people who are all too happy to sit down and have a really interesting discussion and ask the students questions.

**JH:** That's wonderful. So you draw on the community around you to come in and bring in their expertise.

**PT:** Yes and we've learned that the oral examination can be very much a learning experience, not just an assessment experience, and that's what we really want. We hope we can reach that level with every kid, where a kid at the end can say about our assessments, "That was really interesting."

**JH:** That seems like a big difference to the standardized test that is wasted pedagogical time. So the assessment is inspiring rather than mind-numbing and anxiety-producing.

**PT:** Yes.

**JH:** That's great. I want to ask you a follow-up question on this because

I was reading a book by Daniel Koretz called *Measuring Up*.

**PT:** Sure.

**JH:** And he has some critiques of norm-referenced standardized tests and some important things we need to look at in terms of pitfalls that the tests can create. But he also has critiques of performance assessments and I'm wondering how you would respond to his charges that performance assessments are difficult to score reliably. And he also charges that they're hard to compare the scores year to year and that this makes them invalid.

**PT:** On our Web site [www.performanceassessment.org], we publish exemplar papers. And those were papers that went through quite a number of levels of moderation within the consortium and then were sent out to educators who had nothing to do with the consortium. So those are models of competent, good, and outstanding papers. And we always refer people to look at those. Plus we do the moderation study every year. We're developing a new Web site. We're going to post more of those papers so that you can get an idea of what "competence" in science looks like, what "outstanding" in math looks like, for example.

One of the psychometricians we worked with a lot was Dr. Robert Stake, and he used to say to me, "So what if a paper gets judged outstanding by one person and just competent by another person? Really? How much does it matter?" The important thing for him—and I think for most psychometricians—was to determine if the work was passing or not passing.

But more than that, we want to find out what are the outcomes for our students in their lives. For years when we were doing this, all anybody cared about was test results. And from the very beginning we were talking about what happens to the kids when they graduate? Can they go on to college? Can they succeed? Can they sustain themselves in college? For years we said, you know, you need the big picture here. And that's kind of been our—what do they call it?—"predictive reliability." That's really what we've always thought was the important part.

I'm not saying that every student should be in college. Unfortunately, there aren't many vocational options available at this point. But you know, our goal has always been, we want to present every student with the option of college. We want to know that we've gotten every kid to the level where they can survive in college. And then looking at how many are doing that. Our very first study of outcomes from our program was done by Dr. Martha

Foote, who looked at transcripts of the students in their second year of college to see if they were maintaining their GPA, and had they even returned for a second year—there is often a big drop-off between freshman and sophomore year.

**JH:** Right.

**PT:** And we did very well. Then we did the more recent data report, with information from the National Student Clearinghouse, and it shows our students are surviving into eighteen months, into the second year of college. So for us, that's much more important than getting the statistical reliability on a standardized test.

**JH:** So, real-world application. From what I've seen on the data report, the consortium schools have higher graduation rates than the comparable New York Public Schools, and higher college attendance rates. And then what you pointed out, the students are actually staying in college—probably because they have the critical thinking skills that are more valued at that level. That's a really good reframing of how to look at the outcomes of schools rather than just the test score.

**PT:** See, it all depends on what question you're asking.

**JH:** Right, and I think it's important to point out in terms of reliability of scoring, that after our schooling is over, we stop filling in bubbles and the work we do is judged subjectively by human beings all the time.

We're at a really important crossroads moment in public education right now. I wonder how you would advise [secretary of education] Arne Duncan, and what you hope for the future of public education in the United States.

**PT:** One of the problems with the resistance movement is there's not enough being offered about what could be instead of standardized testing. So I just wish that there were more discussions about how education itself can benefit from a change in this kind of attitude of standardization, and there's not enough discussion about the amount of money that is going into wasteful practices. Can you imagine the billions that have been spent on the worst kinds of testing and activities and all the groups that have gotten rich from all of this? The amount of money that's being spent on so-called gurus and specialists and people who talk to each other but are so distant from the classroom and from the kids. It's just incredible. It's a topsy-turvy world.

But resistance is growing. The NEA [National Education Association] just asked Arne Duncan to resign. You know federal policies, like evaluating teachers using kids' standardized test scores, are the source of a lot of problems. It's important to note that most private schools, particularly the elite ones, are not subjected to an excessive standardized testing regime. I would say: what's good enough for the elite of the country is good enough for every public school child, too.

# AFTERWORD
## Wayne Au

There is an educational crisis upon us, but it isn't the one that the politicians, businessmen, pundits, and philanthropists would have you believe. Yes, there are significant and persistent problems with public education in this country. On the whole, working-class students and students of color and their communities have not been served well by our system of public education. Indeed, my language here is not strong enough. Historically speaking, public schools have done damage to working-class kids and kids of color. Historically, public education has been used as a tool for forcing cultural assimilation, first of poor European immigrants and then for all children in public schools. For decades we've had systems of tracking and funneling poor kids into low-level classes in preparation for low-skill jobs. By every available indicator (graduation rates, dropout rates, discipline rates, college entrance rates, even test scores) low-income black and brown kids are not getting access to equitable educational experiences and resources. The United States has one of the most stratified and inequitable school funding structures in the world, one that makes sure poor neighborhoods and communities also receive fewer resources for public education. Bilingual education is illegal in some states, and students of color are disproportionately losing recess, social studies, the sciences, and art, all in favor of increasing test scores.

This kind of disparity and educational inequality has been the result of one of the fundamentally defining functions of public schooling in the United States: to effectively reproduce social, economic, and cultural relations that exist "outside" of school (I put "outside" in quotations marks here because we cannot really separate what is outside of school from what is inside schools). No matter how we look at it, this function of schooling has been an empirical fact for at least a hundred years, and standardized testing has played a critical role in legitimizing the reproduction of this ongoing inequality in education. Going back to their origins in IQ testing, with strong connections to the eugenics movement, these tests have been continuously promoted by psychologists, psychometricians (the formal term for test-making professionals and experts), politicians, business leaders, and even the general public as providing efficient and objective measures of the learning and intelligence of human populations.

Based on that presumed objectivity, students have been categorized and placed into different levels with different expectations for achievement, higher education, and future vocation. The advent of formal high-stakes testing (attaching stakes to standardized tests) in recent decades has meant that these tests are now being used to do the same kinds of categorization of teachers, administrators, schools, districts, states, and countries. And all along this kind of categorization has been used to categorize and stigmatize entire populations—immigrants, the working class, and people of color, among others.

Given the historical and contemporary realities of educational inequality in the United States, it is no wonder that communities of color have a historical distrust of public education. It is also no wonder that the current crop of corporate education reformers have seized on public education's penchant for reproducing inequality as an opening for advancing their own solutions for fixing education in their preferred image: as a business model that sees humans as products, teaching and learning as data points, and education as a marketplace ripe for profiteering—all in the name of increasing educational equality, no less.

The chapters of *More Than a Score* are important in this political and historical moment. They highlight the hypocrisy of a corporate education reform movement—one backed by both major political parties, both major teachers unions, business leaders, and philanthropists—that claims to promote equality through policies built around high-stakes standardized testing. As the essays here illustrate, high-stakes testing is doing the exact opposite: It is ruining curriculum and pedagogy, hurting children and communities of color, and creating a substandard education for the masses of people, all while alienating parents, teachers, students, and administrators from public education in the process. Put differently, high-stakes testing is alienating the public from public education and filling the space with corporate interests instead of human ones.

*More Than a Score* is important here for another reason as well. It highlights one of the central contradictions posed by public education. In spite of its critical role in re-creating social, economic, and cultural inequality, public schools have also always carried within them a radically democratic impulse. In the rawest sense, this impulse is carried in the fact that learning always contains within it a potential for helping us understand things in new and different ways and thus spurring us to action. In just the same way that education can be used to suppress different kinds of teaching and maintain hegemony, education also can be used to help people better understand the conditions of their existence and take individual and collective action to change those very same conditions. Further, public education in this country is one of the last remaining public institutions: public schools are open to everyone and *can be* a meeting ground for all of our communities (unfortunately this is less true given the sharp increase in school segregation). In this sense, public education is a part of the "commons" for all of us, and they thus hold the possibility for community dialogue and collective action based on the needs of our children and society.

So *More Than a Score* is an important book because the chapters included here illustrate the radically democratic impulse of public education in action. Corporate education reformers are ruining public education and the parents, students, teachers, administrators, and activists included here are fighting back by saying *no!* and doing so on grounds that are principled, ethical, humanistic, and educationally sound. The authors and activists included here also point us to the real crisis in educational inequality: massive disinvestment in state and social services and massive socioeconomic inequality in our nation.

Test scores correlate most strongly with family wealth and education. We have known this for decades, and politicians, pundits, and, I'm sorry to say, some educational researchers, have either purposefully ignored this fact or obfuscated it behind the idea that we cannot even consider equalizing these things. Lack of adequate housing, food insecurity, inadequate access to health care—all things connected directly to poverty—are the real culprits here. But the neoliberal corporate education reformers do not want us to look for solutions in massive social and economic change. They do not want to admit that public education is part of a larger web of social services that are impacted by poverty. When poverty rises, for instance, we will see the effects in educational achievement in any way it is measured. Instead they play games with high-stakes test scores, blaming teachers for everything through the sham of VAM (value-added models), and they talk about "grit" and how any individual can succeed if she or he just works hard enough (of course never admitting that the privileged have to work less hard, thereby increasing their chances of success to begin with). They keep chanting the corporate reformer mantra of "the market will provide," closing their eyes to the increasing inequality associated with their schemes, and all the while making obscene profits. As neoliberalism and the logics of private industry continue their creep into mainstream politics, *More Than a Score* reminds us of the importance of defending public education from these corporate raiders and rebuilding our schools in radically democratic, humanistic, and equitable ways.

# ACKNOWLEDGMENTS

The primary belief of the testocracy is in the supremacy of individual achievement at the expense of collaboration. Consider this book a repudiation of that crackpot theory: the development of the ideas within these pages about why and how to resist high-stakes testing has been a profoundly social and collaborative project. I happened to be swept up in events that gave me the opportunity to help create this book; however, it was the collective protest of countless students, parents, teachers, administrators, writers, and activists that made this book possible. I am grateful to all the wonderful authors and activists who told their stories of resistance to high-stakes testing in this book. Special thanks are owed to Aaron Dixon, Alexia Garcia, Brian Jones, Karen Lewis, Marilena Marchetti, Monty Neill, Adam Sanchez, Lee Sustar, Dan Troccoli, and Dave Zirin, whose counsel has been invaluable to building this movement. A special appreciation is due to the members of the Social Equality Educators, who have devoted their lives to education and assessment justice.

I want to express my gratitude to the Bulldogs—the parents, students, and educators at Garfield High School. My colleagues at Garfield refused to administer the MAP test and in so doing changed the world. I am in awe of your bravery, talent, and commitment to the highest level of pedagogy. All of you were crucial to this collective effort, but I would be remiss if I didn't acknowledge those of you that I have worked so closely with in organizing the MAP test boycott and ongoing efforts to defend and transform public education: Mallory Clarke, Kris McBride, Kit McCormick, Jessica Griffin, Rachel Eells, Heather Robison, Adam Gish, and Jerry Neufeld-Kaiser. Many thanks as well to the Garfield Black Student Union and faculty co-advisor, Kristina Clark.

The folks at Haymarket Books are a treasure to many social movement activists, especially those involved in the fight to stop high-stakes testing. Anthony Arnove's and Julie Fain's vision, consultation, and belief in this book made it possible. I couldn't have been more fortunate than to have as my editor Dao X. Tran, an activist in the education justice movement and a contributing author—she was my teacher about what it takes to actually publish a book and provided invaluable feedback and revisions. Rachel Cohen's great talent and generosity with her time helped achieve the cover art and layout of the book, a beautiful frame to hang our stories on. Rory Fanning, Jim Plank, and Jason Farbman all believe deeply in this project and their many skills have facilitated its production. Thanks to Robin Horne and Meredith Reese for transcribing some of the interviews in this collection.

Garfield alum and *Rethinking Schools* editor Wayne Au has taught me an immeasurable amount about testing, education, and friendship. His consultations were crucial to this project. I would also like to thank the entire *Rethinking Schools* team for their support and for teaching me how to be a social justice education editor.

Without the mentorship of the great activist educators Michele Bollinger, Jeff Bale, Ben Dalbey, and Sarah Knopp, I wouldn't have had the theoretical tools or courage needed to fight for our schools. I am thankful that my greatest teachers—Paulette Thompson, Clay Steinman, Leola Johnson—knew I was more than my test scores and showed me the power of pedagogy to transform lives.

Without the support of my parents, this book would have never happened. Amy, Gerald, Dean, and Steve provided me with an upbringing that stressed the importance of education and activism. Amy and Dean were my first editors, taught me how to write, and gave me invaluable edits and feedback on this book. My mother-in-law Martha was extraordinarily generous with her support, encouragement, and care for my children, without which I wouldn't have finished this project.

Finally, the love of my family generated the energy to create this book. My sons, Miles and Satchel, have taught me so much about learning, human development, and myself—and their smiles powered the completion of this project. My wife, Sarah, my greatest collaborator, believed that I could be a success even when my test scores had me convinced I wasn't intelligent. Sarah's talents, insights, and support have made it possible for me to be an author and an activist.

# ABOUT
# THE CONTRIBUTORS

**Alma Flor Ada,** Professor Emerita at the University of San Francisco, has devoted her life to advocacy for peace by promoting a pedagogy oriented to personal realization and social justice. A former Radcliffe Scholar at Harvard University and Fulbright Research Scholar, she is an internationally renowned speaker. Flor's numerous children's books of poetry, narrative, folklore, and nonfiction have received prestigious awards; among them the Christopher Medal (*The Gold Coin*), Pura Belpré Medal (*Under the Royal Palms*), Once Upon a World (*Gathering the Sun*), Parents' Choice Honor (*Dear Peter Rabbit*), NCSS and CBC Notable Book (*My Name Is María Isabel*), Marta Salotti Gold Medal (*Encaje de piedra*).

**Wayne Au,** a former public high school social studies and language arts teacher, is an assistant professor in the School of Education Studies at the University of Washington, Bothell Campus. He is editor of *Rethinking Multicultural Education: Teaching for Racial and Cultural Justice*, coeditor of *Rethinking Our Classrooms*, volume 1, and writes regularly for *Rethinking Schools*. Wayne is also author and editor of many academic articles and books, the most recent book of which is *Critical Curriculum Studies: Curriculum, Consciousness, and the Politics of Knowing* (Routledge, 2011).

**Carol Burris** has served as principal of South Side High School in the Rockville Centre School District in New York since 2000. Carol received her doctorate from Teachers College, Columbia University. In 2010, the National Association of Secondary Schools Principals recognized her as their Outstanding Educator of the Year, and in 2013 she was again recognized by NASSP as the New York State High School Principal of the Year. Carol has coauthored two books on educational equity, and her third book is *On the Same Track: How Schools can Join the 21st Century* (Beacon Press). Articles that she has authored or coauthored have appeared in *Educational Leadership*, the *Kappan, American Educational Research Journal, Theory into Practice, School Administrator*, and *EdWeek*. Carol frequently blogs for the *Washington Post.*

**Nancy Carlsson-Paige** is an educator, author, and activist. She is Professor Emerita at Lesley University, where she taught teachers for more than thirty years and cofounded Lesley's Center for Peaceable Schools. Nancy has written five books and numerous articles on media and technology, conflict resolution, peaceable classrooms, and education reform. She advocates for education policies and practices that promote social justice and equity for all children.

**Sarah Chambers** is a special education teacher, union leader, and rabble-rouser for the Chicago Teachers Union (CTU) and within CORE, the Caucus of Rank and File Educators. She has taught at Maria Saucedo Scholastic Academy in Chicago Public Schools for five years. As a proud member of the CTU Executive Board, bargaining team, and House of Delegates, Sarah is a firm supporter of social justice for all workers and students.

**Mallory Clarke** is a reading specialist at Garfield High in Seattle. Her roles have included high school teacher, political activist, wildlife tracker, college professor, ABE teacher, and parent. In her classroom, students have advanced as much as nine grade levels in reading in only two semesters. She is coauthor with Melody Schneider of *Dimensions of Change: An Authentic Assessment Guidebook* (Peppercorn Press).

**Jeanette Deutermann** is a parent advocate, education activist, and mother of two boys, ages seven and ten. She is the cofounder of New York State Allies for Public Education (www.nysape.org) and the founder and administrator of the Facebook group "Long Island Opt Out Info," which currently has more than fourteen thousand members.

**Rosie Frascella** is an activist with the Movement of Rank and File Educators (MORE) and the New York Collective of Radical Educators (NYCoRE). She teaches English at the International High School at Prospect Heights.

**Alexia Garcia** graduated from Lincoln High School in Portland, Oregon, in 2013 and matriculated at Vassar College in fall 2014. Alexia served as the 2012–2013 student representative on the Portland Public School's Board of Education. Throughout high school Alexia organized with the Portland Public Schools Student Union and the Portland Student Union. Alexia currently interns with the Portland Association of Teachers.

**Emily Giles** has been a teacher and union activist since 2002. Since moving to New York City in 2006, she has been active in the education justice movement. She currently teaches at a public high school in Brooklyn, New York. As a founding member of MORE (Movement of Rank and File Educators), she fights for the rights of teachers and students and for a different vision of rank-and-file unionism in the UFT.

**Nikhil Goyal** is an activist and author of a forthcoming book on learning. He lives in New York. He has appeared as a commentator on MSNBC and FOX and has written for the *New York Times*, MSNBC, NPR, and *Forbes*. An international speaker, Goyal has spoken at Google, The Atlantic, Fast Company, NBC, MIT, Stanford University, Barnard College, SXSW, and others.

**Helen Gym** is a community and education leader whose work supports the right to a quality public education for all children. She is a cofounder of Parents United for Public Education, a citywide parent group focused on equitable school budgets. Helen also leads the board of Asian Americans United, focused on youth leadership, community development, and advocacy for Philadelphia's Asian American and immigrant communities.

Truman Buffett

**Jesse Hagopian** teaches history and is the co-adviser of the Black Student Union at Garfield High School, the site of the historic boycott of the MAP test in 2013. He is an associate editor of *Rethinking Schools,* a founding member of Social Equality Educators, and winner of the national 2013 "Secondary School Teacher of Year" award from the Academy of Education Arts and Sciences. He is a contributing author to *Education and Capitalism: Struggles for Learning and Liberation* and *101 Changemakers: Rebels and Radicals Who Changed US History,* and writes regularly for *Truthout, Common Dreams, Socialist Worker, Black Agenda Report,* and the *Seattle Times* op-ed page.

**Brian Jones** taught elementary grades in New York City's public schools for nine years and is currently pursuing a doctorate in urban education at the CUNY Graduate Center. He contributed to the book *Education and Capitalism: Struggles for Learning and Liberation* and co-narrated the film *The Inconvenient Truth Behind "Waiting for Superman."* He is also a member of the Movement of Rank and File Educators (MORE), the social justice caucus of the United Federation of Teachers. In 2014, he ran for lieutenant governor of New York with the Green Party.

**Alfie Kohn** writes and speaks widely on human behavior, education, and parenting. His thirteenth book is *The Myth of the Spoiled Child: Challenging the Conventional Wisdom about Children and Parenting* (2014). Kohn has been described in *TIME* magazine as "perhaps the country's most outspoken critic of education's fixation on grades [and] test scores." The father of two children, he lives (actually) in the Boston area and (virtually) at www.alfiekohn.org.

**Amber Kudla** is currently a student at the Rochester Institute of Technology, where she majors in chemistry.

**John Kuhn** is the superintendent of schools in the little Perrin-Whitt District in Texas and a vocal advocate for public education. His "Alamo Letter" and speeches at a Save Texas Schools rally and the Save Our Schools March in Washington, DC, went viral, as did his essay "The Exhaustion of the American Teacher." His books include *Test-and-Punish* (Park Place Publications) and *Fear and Learning in America* (Teachers College Press).

**Jia Lee** teaches fourth and fifth grades at the Earth School in New York City, which her son also attended. She is a leading member of two organizations working to oppose high-stakes testing, Change the Stakes and Teachers of Conscience, and an activist with MORE.

**Karen Lewis** is the president of the Chicago Teachers Union. A member of CTU since 1988, Lewis taught high school chemistry in the Chicago Public Schools for twenty-two years. She believes that students, parents, teachers, and community members are educators' natural allies. Her goal is to truly improve Chicago Public Schools and stand firmly against the privatization of public education. Lewis comes from a family of educators—her father, mother, and husband, John Lewis, all were CPS teachers.

**Malcolm London,** called the Gil-Scott Heron of this generation by Cornel West, is a young Chicago poet, performer, activist, and educator. Malcolm has shared stages with actors Matt Damon, John Krasinski, Emily Blunt, and artist Lupe Fiasco as a part of the *The People Speak, Live!* cast. Malcolm is a passionate teaching artist on staff at Young Chicago Authors. He visits schools, introducing their work to hundreds of students through writing workshops and performances.

**Barbara Madeloni** is a teacher educator and activist at the University of Massachusetts Amherst and president of the Massachusetts Teachers Association. Through activist groups Can't Be Neutral and Re-Claiming the Conversation on Education, she develops conferences and workshops to educate and organize resistance to the neoliberal assault on education. She blogs at *@The Chalkface.*

**Cauldierre McKay** was a senior at Classical High School and executive board member of the Providence Student Union during the time of writing. When not organizing his peers for better schools or speaking truth to power, he likes to debate, learn various crafts at New Urban Arts, and sightsee around Providence in the early morning. Cauldierre is currently a student at the Rochester Institute of Technology.

**Mark Naison** is a professor of African American Studies and History at Fordham University, author most recently of *Badass Teachers Unite! Reflections on Education, History, and Youth Activism* (Haymarket, 2014), coauthor with Melissa Castillo-Garsow of *Pure Bronx* (Augustus Publishing, 2013), and a cofounder of the Badass Teachers Association.

**Monty Neill, EdD,** executive director of the National Center for Fair & Open Testing (FairTest), has led FairTest's work on testing in the public schools since 1987. He has initiated national and state coalitions of education, civil rights, religious, disability, and parent organizations to work toward fundamental change in the assessment of students and in accountability. He chairs the national Forum on Educational Accountability. Under his leadership, FairTest has collaborated on testing reform efforts with organizations in many states. Among dozens of publications, he is lead author of *Failing Our Children, Implementing Performance Assessments: A Guide to Classroom School and System Reform,* and *Testing Our Children: A Report Card on State Assessment Systems.* He has taught and been an administrator in preschool, high school, and college, and he is a grandfather of three children in the public schools.

Jack Miller

**Diane Ravitch** is a historian of education and previously served as the US assistant secretary of education. She is research professor of education at New York University and a senior fellow at the Brookings Institution. Her most recent book is *Reign of Error: The Hoax of the Privatization Movement and the Danger to America's Public Schools* (Knopf, 2013). She is the author of numerous books and articles, including *The Death and Life of the Great American School System: How Testing and Choice Are Undermining Education.* She also blogs on educational issues at dianeravitch.net.

**Aaron Regunberg** is the executive director of the Providence Student Union, a youth-led student organizing program in Providence, Rhode Island. A graduate of Brown University, Aaron is a community organizer with experience organizing a range of direct action, legislative, and electoral campaigns.

**Mary Cathryn Ricker** is the president of the St. Paul Federation of Teachers and the executive vice president of the American Federation of Teachers. She grew up in a family of teachers on Minnesota's Iron Range and recognizes the power of labor unions to improve peoples' lives as well as the power of good teaching and strong public schools.

**Stephanie Rivera** is a student at Rutgers Graduate School of Education in New Brunswick, New Jersey. She is an educational justice activist and future social studies teacher. She blogs at *Teacher Under Construction.*

**Kirstin Roberts** is a preschool teacher and parent of a young child in the Chicago Public Schools. She is a proud member of the Chicago Teachers Union and the Caucus of Rank and File Educators (CORE).

**Peggy Robertson** serves as president of United Opt Out. She has taught various grades from kindergarten through sixth, beginning her career in Missouri and continuing in Kansas, for a total of ten years. She earned her master's degree in English as a Second Language at Southeast Missouri State University. She currently is an instructional coach at an elementary school and devotes the rest of her time to her work at United Opt Out National. Her blog can be found at www.pegwithpen.com.

**Falmata Seid** was a Black Student Union Senator at Garfield High School and a student leader in the MAP test boycott. He wrote the poem "Modern-Day Slavery" during the MAP test boycott and has performed it at press conferences, college campuses, and conferences around the Northwest. Falmata is currently attending Washington State University.

**Tim Shea** was a seventeen-year-old senior at Classical High School during the time of writing. After realizing how many hours of his education he had wasted taking standardized tests, he joined the Providence Student Union and was a member of its Citywide Leadership Team. When not fighting for student rights, he enjoyed either catching or receiving on Classical's varsity baseball and football teams. Tim is currently a student at Harvard University.

**Phyllis Tashlik** was an English teacher for more than thirty years in the New York City public schools. As part of her work for the New York Performance Standards Consortium, she has served as director of the Center for Inquiry for Teaching and Learning, the consortium's professional development center. She has authored a number of books, including *Hispanic, Female and Young, Active Voices II,* and *Back to the Books,* with Ann Cook.

**Dao X. Tran,** a product of the Philadelphia public school system from kindergarten through twelfth grade, is an editor based in New York City, where she lives with her daughter. Dao coedited *101 Changemakers: Rebels and Radicals Who Changed US History* (Haymarket, 2012) with Michele Bollinger and is working on the Teacher Oral History Project. She served as co-chair of the Castle Bridge School PTA in 2013–14.

# NOTES

## Preface

1. Rebecca Klein, "Joey Furlong, Fourth Grade Student, Asked to Take State Test While in the Hospital," *Huffington Post*, May 1, 2013, www.huffingtonpost.com /2013/05/01/joey-furlong-state-test-hospital-new-york_n_3193933.html.

2. Howard Nelson, *Testing More, Teaching Less: What America's Obsession with Student Testing Costs in Money and Lost Instructional Time* (Washington, DC: American Federation of Teachers, 2013), http://www.aft.org/pdfs/teachers/testingmore2013.pdf.

3. As of this writing, Rhee has stepped down from the active leadership of Students-First, though she remains on the board of directors. Many critics view Rhee's move away from the organization she founded as a retreat on the part of the corporate education reform forces that she represents.

4. Dean Paton, "The Myth Behind Public School Failure," *Yes!*, February 21, 2014, http://www.yesmagazine.org/issues/education-uprising/the-myth-behind-public -school-failure.

5. "Infographic: Why Corporations Want Our Public Schools," *Yes!*, February 21, 2014, accessed July 28, 2014, http://www.yesmagazine.org/issues/education -uprising/why-corporations-want-our-public-schools.

6. Walter F. Roche Jr., "Bush's Family Profits from 'No Child' Act," *Los Angeles Times*, October 22, 2006, http://articles.latimes.com/2006/oct/22/nation/na-ignite22.

7. Alfie Kohn, *The Case Against Standardized Testing: Raising the Scores, Ruining the Schools* (Portsmouth, NH: Heinemann, 2000), 63.

8. Chicago Teachers Union, "Resolution to Oppose the Common Core State Standards," May 7, 2014, http://www.ctunet.com/blog/chicago-teachers-union

-joins-opposition-to-common-core.

9.  Lydia Ann Stern, "More Area Parents Are Taking Children Out of Standardized Tests," *York Daily Record*, April 14, 2014, http://www.ydr.com/local/ci _25558877/more-area-parents-are-taking-children-out-standardized; Lisa Guisbond, "Testing Reform Victories: The First Wave," a report for the National Center for Fair & Open Testing, September 2014, http://www.fairtest.org/sites/default/ files/TestingReformVictoriesReport.pdf; PDK/Gallup Poll, "Public's Attitudes Toward the Public Schools," October 2014, http://pdkpoll.pdkintl.org/october.

10.  Kohn, *Case Against Standardized Testing*, 14.

11.  Lisa Gartner and Cara Fitzpatrick, "Confused by Florida's Teacher Scoring? So Are Top Teachers," *Tampa Bay Times*, March 1, 2014, http://www.tampabay .com/news/education/k12/confused-by-floridas-teacher-performance-scores-so -are-award-winning/2168062.

12.  American Statistical Association, "ASA Statement on Using Value-Added Models in Educational Assessment," April 8, 2014, http://www.scribd.com/doc/217916454 /ASA-VAM-Statement-1.

13.  "What Parents Should Know," Common Core State Standards Initiative website, http://www.corestandards.org/what-parents-should-know/.

14.  Lyndsey Layton, "How Bill Gates Pulled Off the Swift Common Core Revolution," June 7, 2014, http://www.washingtonpost.com/politics/how-bill-gates-pulled -off-the-swift-common-core-revolution/2014/06/07/a830e32e-ec34-11e3-9f5c -9075d5508f0a_story.html.

15.  "The Trouble with Common Core," *Rethinking Schools*, Summer 2013, http: //www.rethinkingschools.org/archive/27_04/edit274.shtml.

16.  Diane E. Levin and Dr. Nancy Carlsson-Paige, "One Size Doesn't Fit All," *Boston Globe*, April 18, 2010, http://www.boston.com/bostonglobe/editorial_opinion /oped/articles/2010/04/18/one_size_doesnt_fit_all/.

17.  Bill Gates, "Speech to National Conference of State Legislatures," Gates Foundation website, July 21, 2009, http://www.gatesfoundation.org/media-center /speeches/2009/07/bill-gates-national-conference-of-state-legislatures-ncsl.

18.  Alyssa Figueroa, "8 Things You Should Know about Corporations Like Pearson That Make Huge Profits from Standardized Tests," *Alternet*, August 6, 2013, http://www.alternet.org/education/corporations-profit-standardized-tests ?page=0%2C0.

19.  "Statements of Support," Common Core State Standards Initiative website, http://www.corestandards.org/other-resources/statements-of-support/.

20.  "Key Shifts in Language Arts," Common Core State Standards Initiative website, http://www.corestandards.org/other-resources/key-shifts-in-english-language -arts/.

21.  David Coleman, "Bringing the Common Core to Life," YouTube, posted by Tim Furman, March 2, 2012, https://www.youtube.com/watch?v=Pu6lin88YXU.

22. Daniel E. Ferguson, "Martin Luther King Jr. and the Common Core: A Critical Reading of 'Close Reading,'" *Rethinking Schools* 28 (Winter 2013/2014), http://www.rethinkingschools.org/archive/28_02/28_02_ferguson.shtml.

23. Javier C. Hernandez and Robert Gebeloff, "Test Scores Sink as New York Adopts Tougher Benchmarks," *New York Times*, August 7, 2013, http://www.nytimes.com /2013/08/08/nyregion/under-new-standards-students-see-sharp-decline-in -test-scores.html.

24. Ibid.

25. "The Gathering Resistance to Standardized Tests," editorial, *Rethinking Schools* 28, no. 3 (Spring 2014).

26. Wayne Au, *Unequal by Design: High-Stakes Testing and the Standardization of Inequality* (New York, NY: Routledge, 2009), 47–48.

27. Alan Stoskopf, "The Forgotten History of Eugenics," in *Rethinking Multicultural Education: Teaching for Racial and Cultural Justice*, ed. Wayne Au (Milwaukee, WI: Rethinking Schools, 2009), 49.

28. Au, *Unequal by Design*, 38.

29. Stoskopf, "The Forgotten History of Eugenics," 49.

30. Megan Behrent, "Literacy and Revolution," in *Education and Capitalism: Struggles for Learning and Liberation*, ed. Jeff Bale and Sarah Knopp (Chicago: Haymarket Books, 2012), 227.

31. Glenda Kwek, "Brains and Bracelets: Gates Funds Wrist Sensors for Students," *Sydney Morning Herald*, June 14, 2012, http://www.smh.com.au/technology /technology-news/brains-and-bracelets-gates-funds-wrist-sensors-for-students -20120614-20bqa.html.

32. Ibid.

33. Michelle Castillo, "Should Computer-Led Instruction Be the Teachers of the Future?," *TIME*, January 18, 2011, http://techland.time.com/2011/01/18/should -computer-led-instruction-be-the-teachers-of-the-future/.

34. The "Hare and the Pineapple" standardized reading test question was given to eighth-grade students in New York and sparked outrage for its incomprehensibility. Read more about it at: Valerie Strauss, "'Talking Pineapple' Question on Standardized Test Baffles Students," *Answer Sheet Blog*, April 20, 2012, http:// www.washingtonpost.com/blogs/answer-sheet/post/talking-pineapple-question -on-standardized-test-baffles-students/2012/04/20/gIQA8i01VT_blog.html.

35. Richard Shaull, "Foreword," in *Pedagogy of the Oppressed*, Paulo Freire (New York: Continuum International Publishing Group, Inc., 2009), 34.

# 1. Our Destination Is Not on the MAP

1. Sue Peters, "15 Reasons Why the Seattle School District Should Shelve the MAP® Test—ASAP," Seattle Education blog, March 15, 2011, http://

seattleducation2010.wordpress.com/2011/03/15/15-reasons-why-the-seattle
-school-district-should-shelve-the-map%C2%AE-test%E2%80%94asap.

## 3. "Well, How Did I Get Here?"

1.   Michael Winerip, "Move to Outsource Teacher Licensure Draws Protest," *New York Times*, May 6, 2012.

## 12. Testing Assumptions

1.   Kids Count Data Center, "Children in Poverty (100% Poverty): Rhode Island," 2012, http://datacenter.kidscount.org.

## 14. Walk Out!

1.   This Senate bill, as interpreted by the Oregon Department of Education, would require teachers to be evaluated based on test scores, while it is widely known that test scores really only correlate to students' socioeconomic status, not a teacher's ability to teach.
2.   These demographics included: All students, economically disadvantaged students, students with disabilities, limited English proficient students, American Indian/Alaska Native students, Asian students, Pacific Islander students, Hispanic students, Black/African American students, White students, and Multi-racial/Multi-ethnic students.
3.   Linda Shaw, "Garfield Teachers Refuse to Give District-Required Test," *Seattle Times*, January 10, 2013, http://blogs.seattletimes.com/today/2013/01 /garfieldteachersrefusetogivedistrictrequiredtest/.

## 17. Student Revolution

1.   Marion Brady, "Standardized Snake Oil," *Washington Post*, December 15, 2010.
2.   Po Bronson and Ashley Merryman, "The Creativity Crisis," *Newsweek*, July 10, 2010.
3.   Cevin Soling, Conference on Alternatives to Education, Harvard Graduate School of Education, April 27, 2013.
4.   Nikhil Goyal, "Why I Opted Out of APPR," StudentNation blog, May 21, 2013, http://www.thenation.com/blog/174468/why-i-opted-out-appr.
5.   Jenny Anderson, "Curious Grade for Teachers: Nearly All Pass," *New York Times*, March 30, 2013.

6.   Adam Bryant, "In Head-Hunting, Big Data May Not Be Such a Big Deal," *New York Times*, June 19, 2013.

## 20. Forget Teaching to the Test

1.   Rachel Monahan, "Kindergarten Gets Tough as Kids Are Forced to Bubble In Multiple Choice Tests," *Daily News*, October 11, 2013.
2.   Rachel Monahan, "Forget Teaching to the Test—at This Washington Heights Elementary School, Parents Canceled It!," *Daily News*, October 22, 2013.
3.   Andrea Fonseca, "Should First Graders Take a Test? Teachers Say No," *Labor Notes*, November 26, 2013; Owen Davis, "Turn On, Tune In, Opt Out," *Nation.com*, *StudentNation*, November 5, 2013, www.thenation.com/blogs/studentnation?page=0%2C9; Don Lash, "Our Kids Aren't Taking Your Test," *SocialistWorker.org*, November 11, 2013, http://socialistworker.org/print/2013/11/11/our-kids-arent-taking-your-test.

# INDEX